ALCIDE DE GASPERI: THE LONG APPRENTICESHIP

STUDIES IN
CHRISTIAN DEMOCRACY

Alcide

De Gasperi

The Long Apprenticeship

by ELISA A. CARRILLO

UNIVERSITY OF NOTRE DAME PRESS

Copyright © 1965
University of Notre Dame Press
Notre Dame, Indiana
Library of Congress Catalog Card Number 65-23517
Manufactured in the United States of America

To My Mother

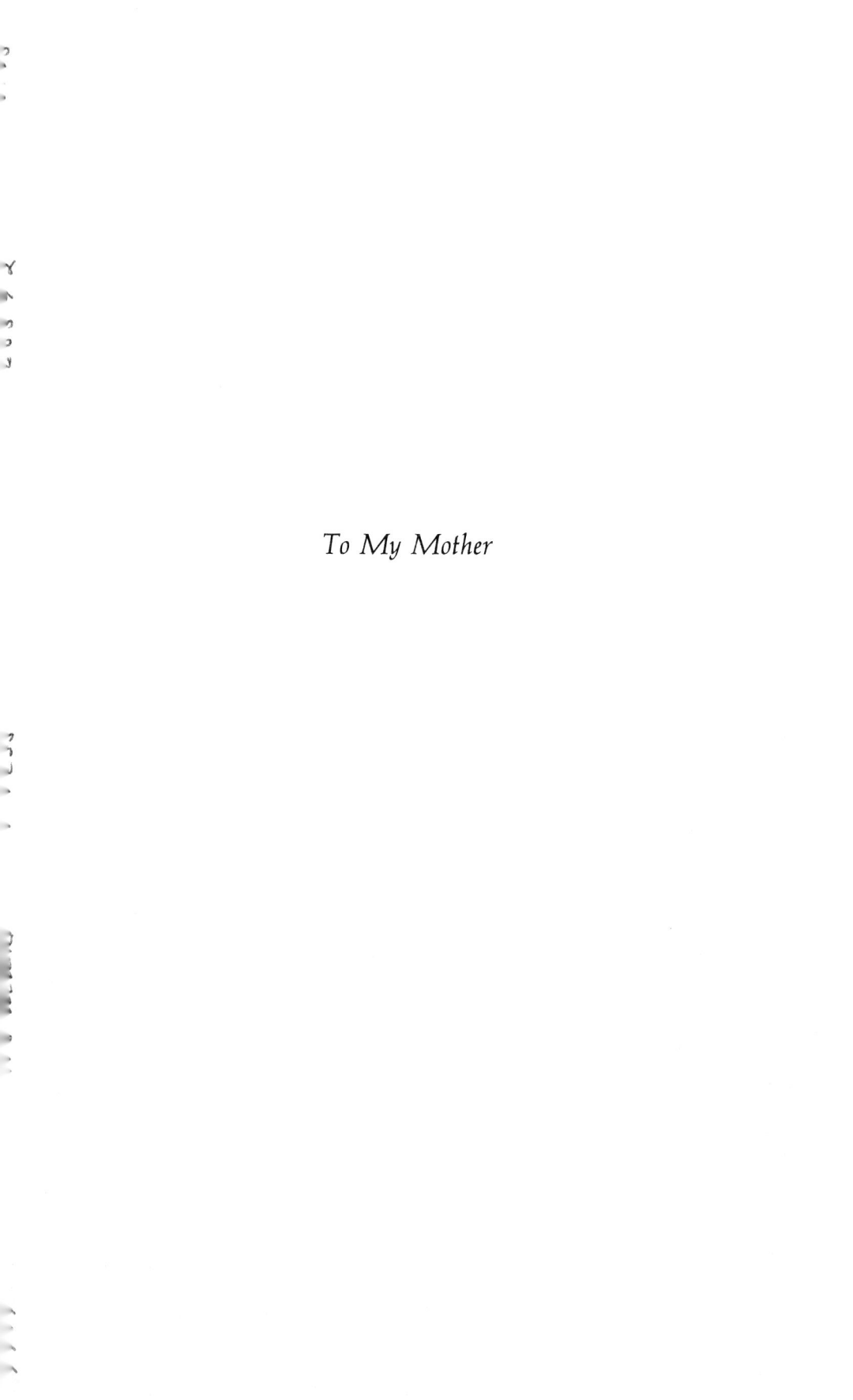

PREFACE

ALCIDE DE GASPERI WAS ALMOST SIXTY-FIVE YEARS OF AGE when he became president of the Council of Ministers (i. e., premier) of Italy on December 10, 1945. Few expected him to retain for very long the highest political office in the Italian government. His immediate predecessors had held short terms: Parri had served for five months, Bonomi and Badoglio each about a year. De Gasperi was to preside over eight consecutive ministries, lasting eight and a half years. His policies as premier earned for him the title of *Il Ricostruttore,* and the period of his premiership may be considered a fitting climax to the "Second Risorgimento."

If De Gasperi was so successful, it was at least partly because of his long apprenticeship in politics. The purpose of this volume is to provide an introduction to his life and thought from his years as an Austrian subject to his entry into the Viminale as premier. A subsequent volume will be devoted to his policies as premier. The chief characteristics of his political life will be seen to have been centrism and *possibilismo.*

In translating De Gasperi's words into English, I have endeavored to render a literal translation as much as possible; when such a translation would have resulted in ambiguity, I have abandoned it in an effort to convey his real meaning. I have changed capitalization and punctuation to conform to English usage.

A biography written only eleven years after the death of its subject could never be definitive, and this study makes no such pretense. I have utilized the major printed sources bearing on De Gasperi's life up to

1945, and I have also had access to some manuscript, including archival, sources. I realize, however, that I have not exhausted all or perhaps even most of the manuscript sources, but these are in private hands and are not presently available for consultation. In the absence of fuller documentation, judgments expressed in this book must be considered tentative and subject to revision.

For special assistance or encouragement in writing this book, I am grateful to the following: Professor Fausto Fonzi of the University of Rome and formerly also of the Archivio Centrale dello Stato (Rome); Monsignor Giulio Delugan, editor of *Vita Trentina;* Dr. Antonio Zieger, historian of Trent; Dr. Paolo Canali, Consul General of Italy in Montreal, Canada; Professor A. William Salomone of the University of Rochester, with whom I first discussed my plans for a biography of De Gasperi and who very generously agreed to read the manuscript; and Signora Francesca De Gasperi. For all errors, whether of fact or interpretation, I alone bear full responsibility.

I should also like to express my appreciation to the librarians of the following libraries: Biblioteca Apostolica Vaticana, Biblioteca della Camera dei Deputati (Rome), Biblioteca Comunale di Trento, and Marymount College.

For the typing of the manuscript, I am indebted to Catherine Palmer.

Tarrytown, New York
May 11, 1965

Elisa A. Carrillo

CONTENTS

	Preface	vii
I	*Cultural Formation*	1
II	*De Gasperi in Austrian Politics*	15
III	*De Gasperi during the First World War*	31
IV	*De Gasperi in Italian Politics, 1919-1922*	45
V	*De Gasperi and the Fascist Regime, 1922-1929*	67
VI	*The Years of Obscurity*	99
VII	*The Clandestine Period*	115
VIII	*Return to Political Life*	131
	Notes	153
	Bibliography	173
	Index	179

CHAPTER I

CULTURAL FORMATION

FEW REGIONS IN ITALY EXCEL IN GEOGRAPHIC AND HISTORIC interest that of Alcide De Gasperi's native land, Trentino-Alto Adige. Acquired by Italy under the terms of the Treaty of St. Germain (1919), this area occupies the northeastern corner of the peninsula. Under Hapsburg sovereignty, the territory was known as South Tirol (*Süd-Tirol*) and formed part of the Princely County of Tirol and Vorarlberg. Though largely mountainous in terrain, the area presents a highly variegated appearance: towering snow-covered peaks, barren grey rocks of quasi-lunar configuration, dark green pine forests, orange and yellow citrus groves, and innumerable crisscrossing valleys filled with the purple vine and golden maize. The richness of the landscape is enhanced by picturesque castles, churches, and monasteries, many of which date back to medieval times.[1]

The Trentino (the province of Trent), comprising an area of about 6,200 square kilometers, is the southern part of the mountainous basin of the Adige River and is ethnically Italian. Alto Adige (the province of Bolzano), embracing an area of about 7,400 square kilometers, constitutes the northern part of the Adige basin and is ethnically German. The linguistic division has not changed substantially since the Italian annexation of the area. The Austrian census of 1910 gave the Trentino a total of 360,847 Italians (the census did not distinguish between Italians and Ladins), 13,450 Germans, and 2,620 of other nationalities. The same census gave Alto Adige a total of 215,798 Germans, 22,500 Italians, and 1,643 of other nationalities. Administered by the Imperial Lieutenancy of Tirol, the area had a provincial diet at Innsbruck.

1

Like Alto Adige, the Trentino was almost entirely agricultural in the period prior to the First World War, with barely 13 per cent of the people living in towns. For a mountain region it was remarkably fertile and well developed, with 87 per cent of the territory productive to some degree.[2] From a commercial point of view, wine was the most important product, with vineyards found chiefly in the Adige valley, the Val di Non, and the Valsugana. Other important industries were the breeding of silkworms and cattle raising. Cereals and fruits were cultivated by small landholders, whose plots averaged about five acres. Although Trent, the principal city of the Trentino, boasted of considerable industrial activity, which included furniture making, weaving, and marble quarrying, the Trentino as a whole was in a state of industrial stagnation, if not decline, in the decades preceding the First World War. With the growth of an intense nationalism among the Italians, the imperial government was increasingly reluctant to develop the area's industrial potentiality. It regarded the Trentino not so much as an economic asset as a vast impregnable fortress, a formidable bastion, which was to be protected by all the resources of military science. Nevertheless, Italian language rights in the schools, courts, and administration were recognized, and a separate section of the Tirolian Board of Education was concerned with Italian school affairs.

In the small village of Sardagna, nestled in the Dolomite Alps and overlooking the city of Trent, the name of Degasperi was common in the second half of the nineteenth century.[3] The people bearing this name were for the most part farmers or artisans. One Degasperi, Amedeo, migrated to Predazzo, where he met the woman who became his wife, Maria Morandini. Four children were born to Amedeo and Maria: Alcide (1881), Mario (1882), Marcella (1889), and Augusto (1893).

Alcide was born on April 3, 1881, in Pieve Tesino, a village in the Valsugana, to which his parents had moved a short time previously and where his father commanded the local *gendarmerie*.[4] From Pieve Tesino Amedeo was transferred first to Grigno and then, in 1884, to Civezzano, where Alcide received his earliest education, secular and religious, from a priest, Vittorio Merler. At the age of ten, Alcide entered the episcopal college at Trent, a private secondary school whose fees were low enough to permit lower middle-class parents to send their sons to it. So much corn pudding (*polenta*) was served to the students that they were commonly known as *i polentoni*. In the episcopal college, as in the two seminaries of Trent, youths were educated in the knowledge and appreciation of the Italian language and culture.

Alcide was an average student, respectful, diligent, but not particularly brilliant, though excelling in Italian composition. He appears to have had a lively temperament, for a school report dated July 25, 1897, characterized his discipline as merely "satisfactory," while his moral conduct was designated "praiseworthy," and his command of the Italian language "eminent." Other evaluations were "satisfactory" for general diligence, Greek, mathematics, and natural history, and "praiseworthy" for religion, German, history, and geography.[5]

After completing the fifth year of the eight-year program, he left the episcopal college, and when he resumed his studies he did so as a day student at the Imperial and Royal Gymnasium of Trent, from which he graduated in 1900. His family had settled in Trent by this time, his father having become eligible for a pension. Amedeo's pension was supplemented by a small salary which he received as a minor functionary of the *Federazione dei consorzi cooperativi* (Federation of Cooperative Associations).

During his years at the *gymnasium* Alcide De Gasperi had become an Italian nationalist in the sense that he wished to safeguard the Italian character of the Trentino; he did not, however, think in terms of an underground struggle against Austria for the purpose of incorporating the Trentino into the Kingdom of Italy. He was not an "irredentist" according to the usual interpretation of the term. During these years he also became deeply interested in the religious and socio-economic problems of the day. He had his first contact with the Christian apostolate in 1896, when he attended an international antimasonic conference which was held in Trent. Here he met, for the first time, some of the exponents of the European Christian Democratic movement.[6]

At the turn of the century the Trentino was becoming a battleground for Germanizing Austrians, anticlerical Italians, and socially-minded Italian Catholics. While Germanizing Austrians disputed the Italian character of the Trentino, Italian Liberals and Socialists accused the Church of allying itself with the Germans. The Liberal Party of the Trentino was numerically small, but because it recruited its membership from among the wealthy bourgeoisie, its influence was greater than its numbers indicated. The same is true of the Socialist Party; though not large it commanded the allegiance of the workers of Trent, the only city in the Trentino to possess any marked degree of industrialization. These years also witnessed the growth of Christian Democracy. The Trentine

Christian Democrats were able, thanks to their intermediate geographical and cultural position, to fuse the teachings of the German social Catholic thinkers, such as Bishop William von Ketteler and Karl Vogelsang, with the Latin tradition as represented by Frederick Ozanam, Giuseppe Toniolo, and Romolo Murri.

The Catholic youth of the Trentino adopted the name of *i cristiano-sociali* (the Social Christians) to indicate the positive character of their struggle against Liberalism and Socialism. At first they were allied with the Christian Socialists of Vienna, but the campaign for Trentine autonomy and the influence of the Italian Christian Democrats led the two groups to separate from each other. By 1905 the *cristiano-sociali* were known as the *Popolari*.

The Social Christians had to contend not only against Liberals and Socialists but also against conservative Catholics. The latter opposed change simply because it was change, and they opposed a closer union, even cultural, with Italy, fearing the anticlericalism and masonry of its government. The Italian clergy, meanwhile, was becoming increasingly sympathetic to political and social reform. A new generation was growing up, educated in the school of Don Giuseppe Graziolo (the priest responsible for the Dante Monument in Trent) and Don Celestino Endrici (priest of the parish of S. Maria Maggiore and later Bishop of Trent), both of whom wished to preserve the *italianità* of the Trentino.

Newspapers were the chief vehicles for the polemics of the day, especially in Trent. *L'Alto Adige,* edited by Mario Scotoni, was the organ of the Liberal Party; *Il Popolo,* directed by Cesare Battisti, was the mouthpiece of the Socialist Party. Clergymen defended themselves against the attacks of the Liberals and Socialists through the pages of *La Voce Cattolica,* a paper which appeared two or three times a week. Directed by Don Guido De Gentili, it had a circulation which was considerably below that of either of its rivals. Although very loyal to the Hapsburg monarchy, it supported the movement for regional autonomy and for a reconstruction of the social order according to the principles of *Rerum Novarum*.

Don Celestino Endrici, who had recently received his doctorate in philosophy and theology from the German College in Rome, became the friend and mentor of De Gasperi. Together they were to sponsor a series of workers' conferences and to lend encouragement to the *Società operaia cattolica di Trento* (Society of the Catholic Workers of Trent). Under the auspices of the latter, a newspaper, *Fede e Lavoro,* was published for the purpose of diffusing Christian social doctrine. The organization was also responsible for the establishment of a credit union for workers and for the construction of some low-cost housing for the most needy workers. But the *Società operaia* was to be only one of many similar organizations that dotted the communes of the Trentino in the decade preceding the outbreak of the First World War. By 1914 there were numerous Christian cooperatives, savings institutions, and unions, both industrial and agricultural.[7]

Don Celestino and his youthful collaborator attached special importance to the organization of students, and in August 1898 both attended a meeting of students and workers held at Cles. After assisting at a Mass celebrated by Don Celestino, the students decided on the formation of an association of Trentine Catholic university students.[8] On February 2, 1899, the statute of the *Associazione universitaria cattolica trentina* (Association of Trentine Catholic University Students), soon to be known as the *AUCT*, was approved by Bishop Eugenio Carlo Valussi of Trent and, a short time later, by the Viceroy of Tirol. The *AUCT* was to meet annually thereafter during the summer vacation period.

The official birth of the organization took place on August 8, 1899, when the students convened in Pergine, in the parish recreation hall, whose entrance had been decorated with garlands, banners, and balloons for the occasion.[9] In attendance were also the student representatives of the growing Christian Democratic movement of Italy. Members of the Circles of Pavia, Milan, Parma, and Padua, they wore the berets distinctive of their organizations, and they were greeted with immense applause as they entered the hall. The name of Don Davide Albertorio, the Italian Catholic leader who had just recently been released from his imprisonment at the hands of the Pelloux ministry, was greeted with a powerful *Viva*.

The Pergine congress made a very vivid impression on De Gasperi. Although he had come with the intention of being only a spectator, he found himself jumping to his feet and applauding heartily when the Italian Christian Democrat, Paolo Arcari of Milan, asked: "And who are we? We are spring, not only in the gayness of our twenty years but also in the greatness of our Faith, which gives to the old man of the Vatican not the sadness of December but the perfume and strength of May...."[10]

There already existed an organization of Trentine students in Vienna, the *Società studenti trentini*, but having been founded by Cesare Battisti, the Socialist, it was openly anticlerical. The Trentine Catholic students felt a need for an organization of their own; even at Vienna the practice of Catholicism was a cause for derision. Of the two hundred and fifty Trentine university students in Vienna, only a dozen, including some priests, were members of any Catholic society.[11]

As the *AUCT* was being established, De Gasperi was nearing the end of his studies at the *gymnasium*. In 1900, with a teaching career in mind, he enrolled at the University of Vienna (German section), with the intention of specializing in German, Latin, and Greek. He left Trent on a rainy evening, with the church bell tolling almost mournfully. He had an inadequate knowledge of German, and he was apprehensive about life in the great metropolis.

Vienna was the center of the empire, the *Kaiserstadt*. With tall hills and an arm of the Danube forming a magnificent natural backdrop, the city drew its strength and inspiration from the past, which was perpetuated in its streets and buildings. At the turn of the century, Vienna suffered from the advancing blight of tenement housing as fields gave way to slums. But the center of the city remained intact, and its Gothic cathedral of St. Stephen's looked down on one of the most impressive streets in Europe. The *Ringstrasse*, two miles long and one hundred and fifty feet in width, was planted with multiple rows of limes and plane trees. Southwest of the cathedral and close to the Ring was the Hofburg, an enormous complex of buildings, differing in styles and periods, the oldest dating from the thirteenth century. As the home of the emperors, it included magnificent private and state apartments, as well as spacious parks and courtyards.

Beyond the Ring were a number of other imposing buildings and parks. Two domed Renaissance buildings, the museums of art and history, faced the Hofburg. Adjoining the museums to the west were the Palace of Justice, built in 1881, and the houses of parliament, built in 1883, in classical Grecian style. Beyond these was the *Rathaus*, a large structure in Gothic style, sharply contrasting with the classical and Renaissance structures that dominated the architectural visage of the city. To the north of the *Rathaus* was the University of Vienna, in Renaissance style. To the university came students of all nationalities.

As De Gasperi had anticipated, life in Vienna presented many difficulties, both material and psychological. Because his financial resources were extremely limited, he lived either in the *Casa dello Studente*, where it was possible to obtain a dormitory bed for a few cents, or in a furnished room. From 1901 to 1904 he rented a furnished room from Herr Hemala, whose daughter was later to become the wife of Leopold Figl, the Austrian statesman of the post-Second World War era.[12]

During his university years De Gasperi knew what it was to be cold and hungry; at times he satisfied his hunger by obtaining a bowl of soup at the door of a Franciscan church. Occasionally poverty, loneliness (he was not a gregarious person by nature), and sickness combined to produce in him a "cursed melancholy," but he refused to inform his parents of his wretched existence. His own family was in modest circumstances, and furthermore his mother could send him money only by concealing the fact from her husband. De Gasperi would not lend himself to such subterfuge, all the more so because his father apparently did not think him worthy of more financial assistance.[13] For Amedeo De Gasperi, stern and taciturn, Alcide probably nourished more respect and fear than spontaneous affection.

Repeated humiliations and material want made De Gasperi more reserved and sensitive than he might normally have been. His Catholic Faith was—and remained throughout his life—his greatest consolation; it was as strong and as unshakeable as the mountains amid which he had grown up. Profoundly spiritual by instinct rather than by training, he willingly went to Mass and recited the rosary daily. He did not, however, consider his obligations to God discharged by mere attendance at services or by mechanical acts of piety, for his was an integral Catholicism, the "spirit and heart of all things." Catholicism was something to be applied first to one's own life, then to society and all public activities. During the early years of the twentieth century, he had not yet arrived at the concept of the autonomy of political parties, or at least the idea had not yet become clearly formulated in his mind. On the other hand, he had an exalted conception—perhaps too advanced for his times—of the role of the layman, seeing him as the partner rather than the subordinate of the priest. As for clergymen, he did not think that they should limit themselves to preaching resignation and obedience to superiors but should also labor to improve the material conditions of the masses.[14]

With a keen sense of social responsibility, De Gasperi was impatient with the gay life of Vienna, and he preferred to devote his free time to the improvement of the masses. He soon familiarized himself with the program and activities of the Christian Socialists of Vienna, and he developed a great admiration for Karl Lueger, Vienna's famous burgomaster. Among De Gasperi's classmates in a course in sociology was Ignaz Seipel, the future Christian Socialist premier of Austria. At the same time De Gasperi was in correspondence with study groups established in Italy by Romolo Murri, Giuseppe Toniolo, and other representatives of the Christian Democratic movement. Of the two Christian Democratic movements, the Austrian and the Italian, it was the Italian which was to exercise the more pervasive influence upon De Gasperi's thinking.

Putting theory into practice, De Gasperi spent the time he could spare from his studies in organizing conferences for workers from the Trentino who were employed in the cosmopolitan capital of the Austrian empire. He also found time to organize the knife-grinders of the Val Rendena into a union, and to support labor unions that went out on strike. It was among the disinherited that he seemed to feel most at home. Reminiscing about these years in 1910, he wrote:

> Outside, on the street, no one greeted me. The powerful despised me because I was poor. The intellectuals pitied me, because I dressed like a peasant. Even many good people turned their heads and pretended not to see me. . . .
> Oh, how I looked forward to the holidays! It was then that I entered the small homes of the laborers, the humble dwellings of the peasants, and talked to audiences that were attentive and full of wonder. I used to preach that it was necessary to bestir oneself, to get together and to organize for a better civil life and for economic progress.[15]

The "prudent" were scandalized by his contacts with the proletariat, but these were dictated by his social conscience. They had the incidental effect of bringing him out of his shell, of helping to break down some of his reserve. His periodic talks to student groups had a similar motivation and effect.

When De Gasperi returned to Trent in 1901 for the summer vacation, one of his tasks was to prepare for the annual congress of the *AUCT*, which was to take place at Mezzocorona on September 17. He and his thirty-four companions felt that they had accomplished a great deal, at least from the point of view of diffusing Christian social doctrine. Elected secretary of the association, De Gasperi gave a talk entitled "The Present Culture and Christian Recovery." After describing the decadence of modern culture in science, art, and letters, he examined the signs of a Christian renaissance. Paraphrasing Cardinal Mermillod of Geneva, he said: "It is not the twilight of the evening that we witness but a splendid dawn announcing a triumphal day." He urged his listeners to become a part of modern culture, to infuse it with Christianity. It was necessary to utilize newspapers and reviews, and above all it was necessary to study: "I wish, colleagues, that each of us would feel the obligation of studying, both for its own intrinsic value and for its contribution to this Christian recovery."[16] A half century later he would use similar words in addressing the young Christian Democrats of Italy.

At the University of Vienna De Gasperi earned the esteem and affection of Ernst Commer, professor of theology, who introduced him to intellectual circles. Among those he met through Professor Commer were Count Franz Kufstein, the sociologist and parliamentarian, and Friedrich Fünder, the editor of the *Reichspost,* the largest Catholic journal of the empire. Fünder invited De Gasperi to contribute articles to the *Reichspost,* and thus he was able to supplement his income.

In the spring of 1902 De Gasperi made his first trip to Rome, where he wandered through narrow alleys and broad *corsi,* marveling at the Pantheon as well as at the great basilicas, especially St. Peter's. On Holy Thursday, March 27, he and Professor Commer were received by Pope Leo XIII, to whom they presented two addresses, one in the name of the Catholic students of Vienna and the other in the name of the *AUCT.* They also had an interview with Cardinal Rampolla, the papal secretary of state, who shared their interest in social problems. During this Roman sojourn they met two prominent Christian Democrats, Romolo Murri and Antonio Fogazzaro.[17]

On August 30, 1902, a meeting of the *AUCT* was held in Trent. As secretary of the organization, De Gasperi delivered the main report, in which he delineated the lines of the future program. He asserted: "The association has written on its banner *Pro Fide, Scientia, et Patria.* Allow me, gentlemen, to be absolutely practical today. I shall leave the realm of the abstract, and shall express our ideas more concretely: these are *Catholic, Italian,* and *democratic.*" While denying that Catholics were lacking in patriotism and in the love of their country, he urged his listeners to be Catholic first and then Italian. He deplored idolization of the nation and talk of the "religione della patria."[18] De Gasperi, the European, was already in the making.

At this same meeting De Gasperi was elected president of the association. The polemics aroused by his discourse, which in a sense constituted his initiation into politics, were sharp. *Il Popolo* criticized his motto, "Catholic, Italian, and democratic," and *L'Alto Adige,* commenting with equal acidity, began a debate with De Gasperi which lasted until the First World War.

The meeting of the *AUCT* had been held in conjunction with the first Catholic Congress, a gathering of the representatives of all the Catholic labor organizations of the Trentino. Problems concerning agrarian and professional societies were discussed, and it was resolved to bring the various organizations together in a *Consiglio trentino del lavoro* (Trentine Council of Labor). It was also decided to form a political union in order to bring Catholic strength to bear on the political scene.[19]

As a politically alert subject of Francis Joseph and as an occasional contributor to *La Voce Cattolica,* De Gasperi followed with avid interest the 1902 elections to the *Reichsrat*. The campaign gave him an opportunity to deepen his contacts with the Austrian Christian Socialists, and when the election returns were in, he rejoiced with them in the fall of Vienna as the citadel of anticlerical Liberalism.[20]

De Gasperi was also active in the *Unione accademica cattolica italiana* (Italian Catholic Academic Union) in Vienna, a student organization founded in 1897 upon the suggestion of Edoardo De Carli, a Trentine student at Vienna. Each week the members gathered together to discuss some topic of current interest, after which followed spiritual reading, especially from the works of St. Augustine.[21] Though an academic organization, it sought to establish closer ties between Italian students and emigrant Italian workers. Every two weeks, conferences were held for workers, and the papers read by De Gasperi were on such topics as "The Ideal of Perpetual Peace" and "The Principles and Methods of Conservatives and Democrats in the Christian Social Movement."[22] The topics may have been too theoretical for the workers, and at times De Gasperi's seriousness irritated even his fellow students. Exasperated by his insistence upon the adoption of his own point of view, his colleagues once bodily threw him out of a meeting. The experience helped to educate him in the virtues of moderation and tolerance.

De Gasperi did not confine his activities to academic gatherings. Late in September 1903 De Gasperi went to Vorarlberg to speak to numerous Trentine workers in that region (2,250 in Bludenz, 1,500 in Feldkirch, 1,850 in Bregenz). At meetings attended by from two hundred to five hundred workers, he explained the principles and goals of Christian Democracy, and he urged them to form organizations which would promote their moral and material welfare. His speaking engagements were not always pleasant experiences; at Wolfurt, for example, in October 1903, his talk was frequently interrupted by shouts and whistles from the Socialists.[23] De Gasperi was undaunted, convinced as he was of the need for organizing the Italians. While the German workers had admirable Christian organizations, the Italians had no one to instruct them in their social rights and duties; they lived segregated from civil and social life. As a result of De Gasperi's propaganda efforts, committees were formed to organize unions of Italian Catholic workers.[24]

De Gasperi did not, however, believe that unions based upon nationality should remain isolated from each other. In the summer of 1903, while attending a congress in Vienna sponsored by a union of German Catholic workers, he asserted that only a strong organization of workers, to which all nationalities could belong, would best serve the interests of the workers.[25] Again he was demonstrating a desire and ability to rise above narrow nationalism. In the early 1920's, he was to propose once again a Christian International.

On September 10, 1903, at 3:30 P.M., the *AUCT* convened in Caldonazzo for its annual meeting. It was held in the spacious headquarters of the Catholic Circle, in a hall decked with white and yellow garlands and containing the portraits of Leo XIII and the newly elected Pius X. Within the hall were six hundred persons, and an equal number stood in the adjoining courtyard. As president, De Gasperi gave a report in which he reaffirmed the loyalties of the Italian Catholics of the Trentino: "All of us, young and old, have in common two loves: love of the Catholic Church and love of the complexus and sentiment that I would call 'Trentism,' the love of this our fatherland, which we wish to defend as much from the external enemies as from the internal."[26] This meeting was especially noteworthy for the development of stronger ties between the university element and the workers.

To his associates in the *Unione accademica,* he urged self-evaluation. In a talk delivered January 1904, entitled "Reforming Ourselves," he said: "Friends, as long as our vigil lasts . . . seek clarity and sharpen your ideas on the questions with which life confronts us, because the Christian, as Rosmini points out, must never walk in darkness but always in the light. This light, as a matter of fact, is nothing more than the clear comprehension of the task of our life, above all of our integral progress."[27]

With Don Celestino Endrici, De Gasperi's ties remained close. In 1904 Endrici arrived in Vienna to enter into negotiations with the Austrian government concerning his appointment by Pius X as Bishop of Trent, succeeding Bishop Valussi who had died in October 1903. De Gasperi became his unofficial secretary in the negotiations, which were complicated by the fact that Endrici was noted for his strong attachment to Italian culture. Nevertheless, the political difficulties were surmounted, and the consecration ceremonies, attended by De Gasperi, were held in Rome on March 13, 1904, in the chapel of the German College. On the following day, Pius X received the Trentine pilgrims, and when informed of the apostolate of De Gasperi among students, he said to De Gasperi, "Bravo, Bravo! May you fill these youths with fervor, and may their goodness be preserved."[28]

In the autumn of 1904 De Gasperi participated in a meeting of the officers of the *Unione politica popolare,* a new party formed for the purpose of unifying politically the various Catholic organizations of the

Trentino. De Gasperi was elected counselor of the new group, and in this capacity he seconded energetically an order of the day protesting against the restrictions placed by the Hapsburg government on the rights of minorities and reaffirming the long-standing demand of the Italians for a university on Italian territory in Austria-Hungary.[29]

The Hapsburg government was reluctant to establish an Italian university for fear that it would become a center for irredentism. In 1899 it had established two chairs in Italian, in political economy and law, at the University of Innsbruck, but the German population was hostile to any instruction in Italian, and in May 1903, during the lecture of Giovanni Lorenzoni, professor of political economy, the Italians and Germans came to blows. If the Italians were not overpowered, it was largely because of the intervention of a muscular Russian student who was sympathetic to the Italians.[30]

The imperial government then proposed the establishment of an Italian law faculty at Rovereto. Cut off from the university organism, the faculty would soon have died a natural death, but the opposition of both the Italians and Germans prevented even the inauguration of the plan. Next, the government decided to transfer the faculty from Rovereto to Wilten, a suburb of Innsbruck. The initial lectures were given November 3, 1904, and De Gasperi, together with other Italian university students, gathered in Innsbruck to celebrate the inauguration of the Italian faculty. At the end of the first day of lectures, as the Italians poured into the streets of Innsbruck, they were greeted with shouts of derision on the part of the Germans. Soon a crowd collected, armed with canes and pistols, forcing the Italians to take refuge in two inns, the *Rosa d'Oro* and the *Croce Bianca*. Pursued by a mob which sought to storm the entrance, De Gasperi fled into the *Rosa d'Oro*, where another German group was ready to expel him. Only the arrival of a military detachment put an end to the melee.

The following morning, the governor of Tirol had all the Italian university students, numbering 137, arrested. The Germans scornfully posted a sign over the door of the Innsbruck prison, reading "Italian Law Faculty." The Italian deputies in the *Reichsrat*, notably Enrico Conci of Trent, immediately intervened to secure the release of the prisoners. De Gasperi was released on November 22, after nineteen days of imprisonment.[31] The following year, the Hapsburg government suspended the Italian law faculty at Wilten.

De Gasperi had long considered the establishment of an Italian university on Italian soil in Austria as essential to the fuller political, economic, and cultural development of the Italian minority; he had been willing to cooperate with the Liberals and Socialists in attaining such an objective.[32] The events at Innsbruck made him more determined than ever to work for an Italian university, but unlike the Socialists and Liberals, he was not insistent upon Trieste as the site of the university. He thought Trent could serve as a provisional site, and he regarded the formula of "Trieste or nothing" as an expression of the radicalism which he considered the bane of politics.[33] He asked for a repudiation of the policy of "all or nothing," affirming that: "It is necessary to understand once and for all that with a government such as ours . . ., to say 'all or nothing' means that we have had and will have the second part. For more than fifty years, this policy has been pursued, and what do we have? Nothing. Experience therefore teaches us that this strategy does not bear fruit."[34] This willingness to compromise, to face the realities of life, was to remain characteristic of his entire political career. The Italians of 1905 did not, however, share this point of view, and since Vienna refused to concede the establishment of a university at Trieste, the Italian minority remained without a university of its own.

In the same year that the government suspended the Italian law faculty, Germanizing Austrians formed the *Tiroler Volksbund* (Popular Tirolean League) to promote the Germanization of the Trentino. The activities of the league were quite varied: the organization of rallies, the dissemination of posters, the establishment of German cultural centers, and the free distribution of newspapers, especially the bilingual periodical, *Tiroler Wehr.* The league asserted, not without considerable truth, that it was necessary to know German in order to obtain a position in Tirol, either in private industry or in the public administration. It also alleged that the imperial government would give preferential treatment to the members of the *Tiroler Volksbund.*[35] The Trentini reacted strongly against the propaganda of the *Volksbund,* and during the next ten years De Gasperi was in the forefront of those who sought through speeches and writings to counteract the society's Germanizing endeavors.

CHAPTER II

DE GASPERI IN AUSTRIAN POLITICS

IN JULY 1905 DE GASPERI PASSED "WITH DISTINCTION" THE requisite examinations and received his degree in philology from the University of Vienna. His doctoral thesis was entitled "Die Glücklichen Bettler von Carlo Gozzi und ihre deutschen Bearbeitungen." His formal studies terminated, he could now devote more time to the social apostolate, which had become his mission in life. While combating Socialism, which he regarded as a degenerate form of social Christianity, he was careful not to treat it with contempt, averring:

> Friends, let us not scorn Socialism, but let us instead anticipate Socialism in social defense; let us anticipate it in the economic field. We, more than the Socialists, can combat injustice, regardless of its source; we, more than the Socialists, can and should oppose tyrannies of the big and the small; we, followers of a religion that has justice as its foundation! Woe to him who one day stops working in order to laugh at, to deprecate Socialism . . . .[1]

In September 1905 Bishop Endrici appointed De Gasperi director of *La Voce Cattolica*, thereby replacing Monsignor Guido De Gentili, who had manifested an excessive attachment to the Hapsburg monarch. Under De Gasperi the paper became a lively, combative journal, whose columns between 1905 and 1915 provide an invaluable index to the director's own life and thought. De Gasperi's words during these years convey little of the caution and restraint so characteristic of his later writings and speeches; instead, invective, irony, sarcasm, and occasionally even vulgarity leap out from the columns. Perhaps his biting tongue was provoked by the bitter attacks of his enemies, driving him to address Trentine Socialists as "giacobinucci" and Liberals as "Signori radicali" or "socialisti borghesi." He vigorously lashed out at their programs, particularly the anticlericalism that they had in common. He saw the two parties more or less in alliance with each other, and he wondered what had happened to the "struggle of the proletariat against the bourgeoisie." He was harder on the Liberals than on the Socialists, for Liberalism had produced not only an "inhuman capitalism" but also absolutism and laicization. He accused the Austrian Liberals of seeking to introduce into Austria-Hungary the laic laws of France, and he firmly announced the intention of Catholics to resist such legislation.

On the other hand, De Gasperi deeply resented the charge of clericalism levied against his journal and party by both Socialists and Liberals. He insisted that he was a "clerical" only in the sense of wishing to see religious interests defended and represented in the State. He denied any desire to establish a Church-dominated State, and by 1912 he was asserting that, in matters that were neither religious nor politico-ecclesiastical, political parties bore their own responsibility for their actions. On the eve of the First World War, then, the concept of the autonomy of parties was taking shape in De Gasperi's mind.

During his early months as director of *La Voce Cattolica*, De Gasperi was much concerned with proposals for the democratization of the imperial government. He supported universal suffrage, equality of colleges (i.e., electoral districts), and compulsory voting, all of which were under consideration in the *Reichsrat*. The Liberals favored universal suffrage, but not equality of electoral districts, while the Socialists opposed compulsory voting. Both equality of electoral districts (under the existing system an urban college carried more political weight than a rural college) and compulsory voting would augment the strength of the Catholic peasant masses.[2]

At a meeting of the *Unione politica* in December 1905, the directors decided to call their association the *Partito Popolare Trentino*.[3] The party was formally founded on February 12, 1906, but the *Unione* was retained as the organizational body. After animated discussions on the basic objectives of the movement, a program was hammered out which contained the essentials of Christian Democracy: political democracy, social reform, and administrative autonomy. In March 1906 De Gasperi changed the name of the paper to *Il Trentino* and made it the organ of the new party. He announced:

> *Il Trentino* remains the organ of those who desire to infuse the State and public life with the principles of Christianity, in which our people

find their history, their strength, their future. We shall champion energetically the national defense of our Italian land and the national elevation of our people. We shall be the organ of those who are instituting in our country the Catholic social movement and who work for and trust in the advent of Christian Democracy. . . . It seems to us that our journal has the right to call itself *Il Trentino* now that it has become, through the unceasing progress of the last few years, the voice of the great majority of our country and the organ of the *Partito Popolare*, which proposes to take in hand resolutely the interests of all. Like our journal, the party looks forward to the reconstruction of the unity of the Trentino on the triple basis of religion, national spirit, and democracy.[4]

Not all the members of the Diocesan Committee of Catholic Action, which was the legal owner of the paper, were in accord with the change in the title. With the dropping of the word "Cattolica" there appeared to be a loss of confessionality.

The socio-economic program of the paper and party included insurance against sickness, old-age pensions, more effective unionization, and a reorganization of communal finances, with the State and province contributing to communal expenses. The party also favored a decrease in the empire's military forces; in a speech describing the party platform, De Gasperi said that money lent by the State to the peasants would bear greater fruit than that expended on cannons and ammunition.[5]

In public administration the party stood for decentralization and for the administrative autonomy of the Trentino.[6] With respect to the nationality question, the party's task was defined as the education of the people "toward a positive national conscience, illuminating it politically and bringing it within the sphere of political responsibility."[7] Although a special effort would be made to educate the rural classes in politics, the party was to be interclass in structure:

> The *Partito Popolare* has been constituted with the firm intention of being in every way worthy of its own name. It does not wish to be a party of priests, nor of academicians, nor of pork butchers, but the party of the *people*.
>
> All of us have the obligation of working so that the *Unione politica popolare*, which is the party organization, becomes a great army not of raw recruits but of instructed soldiers.[8]

In preparation for elections to the *Reichsrat*, which were scheduled to take place in May 1907 and to be based on universal manhood suffrage, as provided for by a law which had become effective in January,

De Gasperi conducted a brisk and determined campaign. Speaking to a general assembly of the *Unione politica* in February, he called for "modern legislation" on behalf of the workers, the middle classes, and the farmers. He said the franchise should be extended to the popular classes not only for the *Reichsrat* but also for the provincial diets and the communal councils. Concerning the all-important national question, he reiterated the position of the party: "We desire the national integrity of the Trentino; we desire not only to conserve the linguistic patrimony but also to reinforce the national spirit of the people, creating in them a positive national conscience. . . ." For the actualization of the program, the party would call upon all "good Christians, brave Italians, sincere Democrats."[9]

A lively debate was carried on with both the Socialist and Liberal Parties. De Gasperi insisted that a true Socialist Party could not exist in the Trentino: Trentine Socialists were merely part of the Italian section of the international Austrian Socialist Party and, therefore, Trentine Socialists could not be true nationalists.[10] Topics discussed by Battisti and De Gasperi at public debates covered a wide range of topics, from electoral reform to religion.[11] In campaigning against the Liberals, De Gasperi called attention to the vagueness of their party platform, and he labeled their Liberalism as a "liberalismo di contrabando."[12] He accused both Liberals and Socialists of concealing their basic anticlericalism for the sake of winning votes. The same *L'Alto Adige* which now proclaimed respect for religion had favored lay schools, divorce, and civil marriage during the previous year.[13] These themes and the opposing principles of the *Partito Popolare Trentino* were reiterated in about five hundred meetings between February and May 1907.

When the elections took place, the *Partito Popolare Trentino* clearly won seven out of the nine seats allocated to the Trentino.[14] Those elected were Enrico Conci, Emanuele Lanzerotti, G. B. Panizza, Guido De Gentili, Bonfiglio Paolazzi, Baldasarre Delugan, and Albino Tonelli. In two colleges, Trent and Rovereto (both urban colleges), run-off elections were necessary; these resulted in the victory of the Socialist Augusto Avancini in Trent and the Liberal Valeriano Malfatti in Rovereto. Although he regretted losing Trent and Rovereto (in each college the Socialists and the Liberals had combined against the *Partito Popolare*), De Gasperi was elated by the over-all results.

The *Reichsrat* elections over, De Gasperi could devote more time to campaigning against the *Volksbund*. He regarded its racial nationalism as morally inadmissible and contrary, moreover, to the Hapsburg idea of a multinational empire. De Gasperi valued the Hapsburg monarchy for the very reason that Adolf Hitler, who was now visiting Vienna for the second time, was developing an intense hatred for it. In an effort to counteract the propaganda of the Pan-Germans, De Gasperi traveled throughout the small villages of the Trentino, and in countless talks in cottages and inns, upheld the *italianità* of the region. On July 3, 1907, the first page of his paper carried a lengthy article entitled "Il Momento Politico, Tirolo, Trentino, e I Germanizzatori." The article was provoked by a meeting of the *Volksbund* at Bressanone, during which De Gasperi had been characterized as "the bubonic plague of Tirol." In the article De Gasperi called upon the Austrian government to disavow the activities of the *Volksbund* and to recognize the equality of the Italian nationality with the German. He also stated that it was useless to expect the Trentini to repudiate their love of country: "In our breasts are the flames of love of country, flames which revive when the day darkens. Whether the weather be calm or stormy, we shall consign this living flame to future generations."[15] The German papers reacted very strongly, the *Tiroler Tagblatt* characterizing *Il Trentino* as the "most disgusting and the most contemptible of the irredentist sheets."[16]

International Catholic congresses were also of interest to De Gasperi. In August 1907 he journeyed to a Catholic congress held at Würzburg, which was attended by Italians, Frenchmen, and Austrians, as well as by the representatives of German cultural, labor, industrial, and charitable organizations. The congress lasted for four days and made a deep impression on De Gasperi. On the train to Würzburg, he made the acquaintance of Bavarians, and he listened with pleasure to their denunciation of the policy of Germanization. At the congress he found himself in vigorous agreement with the Center Party deputy who asserted that Catholics should be at the head of the social movement. He also made a note of the fact that Protestants could have attended all the sessions of the congress without hearing one offensive word. But what most edified De Gasperi was the German *volere di fare*. German Catholics were leaders: "Thus is verified the phrase of Pius X: '*Germania docet.*' If there were not these men who represent Catholicism in the most advanced form of modern civilization, where would we direct our eyes to refresh the spirit, where would we turn our hearts to become enthusiastic?"[17]

He spoke with many representatives of the Catholic states of Germany, and he became convinced that Modernism and everything that connoted deviation from orthodoxy were nonexistent; in matters of religion, the German laity recognized the authority of the bishops and of Rome. However, German Catholicism was not the only matter to engage the attention of De Gasperi during his visit to Würzburg. He was amused by the efforts of temperance workers, for "Würzburg is the city of wine with the splendor of gold and of beer which flows in torrents."

De Gasperi thought Trentine Catholics could well adopt the motto of German Catholics: *Vorwärts (Avanti)*. This was the period in which Franz Hitze, the Westphalian workmen's priest, was expounding the doctrine of "social deaconry" in both word and deed. Thanks to his work, the majority of Catholic workers were gathered into organizations which stood for constructive social policies and avoided narrow confessionalism. Hitze was one of the founders of the *Volksverein fuer das katholische Deutschland*, an organization which was to function up to its destruction in 1933 as an instrument for the social and political education of German Catholicism.

De Gasperi returned to Trent with renewed enthusiasm for the Christian social movement, and he considered conferences, books, and the press as efficacious means for the social education of the people. He continued to regard university students as the leaders of the social movement, and he urged them to be "democratic in thought and action," distinguishing themselves from others by the "consciousness of a lofty mission." He also urged them to avoid an "empty ideology" and the use of words that the people no longer understood.[18] But he did not think that study and observation were enough; it was also necessary to have contact with the people. Such contacts would be elevating to the students and would also serve to introduce them to the realities of life.[19]

Because it was so important to increase the number of educated leaders, De Gasperi persisted in his efforts to secure the establishment of an Italian university. At the tenth congress of the *AUCT*, held in September 1907, he drafted a resolution calling upon the Austrian government to institute an Italian university on Italian soil and directing the *Popolari* deputies to take up the matter in the *Reichsrat*.[20] As always, the cause was to be pressed according to the precepts of legality, for De Gasperi abhorred disorder and illegality. Writing in October 1907, he affirmed: "We have for *Law* and *Order* all that profound respect that we should have for these two words, written with capital letters. We nourish hatred for violence, regardless of its source, and we always condemn it. . . ."[21]

The papal encyclical *Pascendi*, which appeared in September 1907, met with De Gasperi's approval. He felt that there had been much confusion regarding basic principles and that this confusion had distracted energies that should have been expended on a Christian reconquest of society. Modernists had played into the hands of Catholics who were theologically orthodox but were opposed to the political and social advancement of the masses.[22] His approval of the doctrinal content of the encyclical does not, however, make him a traditionalist. Through the pages of *Il Trentino,* he urged Catholics to act like men of the twentieth century and to adopt a dynamic conception of life. To date it seemed to him that Catholics had been sleeping.[23]

At a general meeting of the *Unione politica* on October 29, 1907, De Gasperi, as secretary of the *Unione,* discussed the success achieved at the ballot box in May, and he attributed it to the adoption of a concrete program, which showed the people and especially the rural masses the connection between political action and the economic *risorgimento* of the Trentino. With the same program they would prepare for the elections to the provincial diet at Innsbruck, to be held in 1908. He asked, however, that more participate in the campaign; in the previous campaign the burden had fallen upon only a few. He also counseled fewer debates, questioning the value of face to face confrontations between members of opposing parties.[24] The campaign was successful, the *Unione* electing to the provincial diet all twelve of its candidates.

Political activity did not preclude union organizational work. In March 1908 De Gasperi organized in Pergine a meeting of Catholic labor unions from Pergine, Roncogno, Seregnano, Civezzano, Castagne, S. Vito, Susa, Frassilongo, Centa, Levico, and Caldonazzo. In an hour-long speech De Gasperi reviewed the history of the formation of labor unions. These, he said, had arisen at a time when it was necessary to combat Liberalism and Socialism, for the Liberals sought the laicization of life, and the Socialists, not only laicization but also abolition of private property. But a negative campaign was not enough now; it was necessary to demonstrate that Catholics were men of progress, interested in the elevation of the popular classes.[25]

By 1909 De Gasperi and his colleagues could well congratulate themselves not only on their electoral successes but also on their efforts in achieving socio-economic solidarity. The agricultural and industrial life of the Trentino was highly organized on cooperative lines, with about 180,000 persons affected by the cooperative movement. The *Sindicato Agricolo Industriale* brought together about 265 cooperatives and constituted the most solid economic nucleus of the region. The peasants were also protected by about 250 rural banks, especially designed to take care of the needs of an agricultural people.[26] Trent had two banks, the *Banca cattolica* and the *Banca industriale di Trento.* The former was founded in 1899 by the Trentine Diocesan Committee for Catholic Action to extend credit to the rural banks and peasant cooperatives. Subsequently it expanded its activities to include commercial and industrial undertakings. The *Banca industriale* was established in 1908 to provide loans for industrial purposes. De Gasperi served as its vice president.

In 1909, a year of economic depression for the empire as a whole, the Catholics of the Trentino constructed the Dermulo-Mendola railway line, and plans were made for a Trent-Tione-Lake Garda line. However, the imperial government, fearing the political consequences of a line which would be under autonomous administration, prevented execution of the plan by placing impossible conditions upon its construction.

One of the never-to-be-forgotten episodes in the life of De Gasperi during this period was his encounter with one Benito Mussolini. At the end of January 1909 a Socialist newspaper, *L'Avvenire del Lavoratore*, announced that Benito Mussolini of Forli had been appointed secretary of the local labor organization of the Socialist Party. The article stated that the new officer was a proven fighter, a specialist in anticlericalism.[27]

Mussolini arrived in Trent on February 9, and one week later spoke at a ceremony commemorating the anniversary of the death of the sixteenth-century heretic, Giordano Bruno.[28] Although not very happy in his new surroundings,[29] Mussolini threw himself into the work of organization, a work that involved a violent campaign against the "clericals" of the Trentino.

At this time Merano was beset by labor troubles. The first strike was that of the tailors, during the course of which the Catholic and Socialist trade unions cooperated. Next followed a dispute in the construction industry, and the Catholic unions again proposed a united front. Before accepting the invitation, the Socialists suggested that De Gasperi take part in a debate on "Socialism in History." The messenger of the Socialists delivered the invitation at the last minute and did not wait for a reply. Although the invitation was inconvenient, De Gasperi accepted it.

The discussion took place in a beer hall, the *Albergo alla Corona*, in Untermais, on Sunday, March 7, 1909, beginning at about two in the afternoon. The room was crowded with Socialist workers, many of whom were accompanied by their wives. Mussolini was the first speaker; in fact, he began before De Gasperi arrived. During the course of his talk he said that the workers should be educated in social revolution and that expropriation was absolutely necessary. He also stated that the activity of the Catholic Church could be divided into two periods, with 1890 the dividing line. Up to 1890 the Church had opposed the workers; after 1890, "a clever pope" ordered Christian Democracy. The latter was, however, nothing more than a fraud. De Gasperi's answer was an expression of his realistic outlook: "I am convinced that you will not achieve social revolution either tomorrow or next month. Do not think either of the expropriation of capital in the near future. What is of urgent concern is the struggle with the managers and the impending lockout because of the building crisis." He went on to urge solidarity between the Socialist and the Catholic labor unions. He declined, however, to engage in a debate with Mussolini, alleging a prior engagement in Bolzano which required him to catch the 3:30 train. The exit of De Gasperi was, according to the account in *L'Avvenire*, greeted with derision. Mussolini said he had no comment because such a "precipitous flight was in itself of great eloquence."[30]

In this encounter Mussolini was undoubtedly the winner, for De Gasperi's forte was not—and never would be—oratory. Tall, slender, bespectacled, with a swirling mustache, De Gasperi's appearance was imposing, but his voice and manner could not captivate an audience. His voice was harsh, a bit metallic, and his platform manner was devoid of impetuous gestures, of theatrical effects of any kind. Mussolini, on the other hand, was at his best before a crowd. With his head tilted back and his chin pushed forward, he knew how to whip himself and his audience into a frenzy of excitement.

Mussolini was in Trent until September 1909, when the Austrian authorities had him driven out, accusing him of inciting the commission of crimes and of circulating confiscated printed matter.[31] During his stay in Trent, he frequently attacked, by speeches and newspaper articles, the Church, *Il Trentino,* and De Gasperi. He referred to the latter as "a man of slovenly, ungrammatical prose, a superficial man who invokes an Austrian timetable to avoid an embarrassing debate."[32] Another time he rebuked De Gasperi, "doctor in what nobody knows," for his ownership of stock in the *Banca Cattolica*.[33] His language was so intemperate and threatening that De Gasperi must have been personally relieved to learn of his expulsion.

Mussolini's allegation that Christianity had impeded the worker in his quest for social improvement undoubtedly inspired some of De Gasperi's speeches during this period. In April 1909, speaking to the General Assembly of the Diocesan Committee of Trent, De Gasperi denied that Christianity constituted an obstacle to the worker who sought a better life. As evidence of the Church's interest in the common people, he cited the numerous economic and social organizations of the Trentino which were under Catholic auspices. But not satisfied merely to refute, he urged an ever greater social effort on the part of his listeners. He said thought must harmonize with the diffusion of culture; work with the progress of technology; and their own influence with the advance of democracy. Their social action had to be developed "with the cooperation of integral, sincere, practicing Catholics." Thus the prerequisite for effective social action was the regeneration of the individual. "Without the interior regeneration of the individual, we shall not succeed in the reform of institutions...."[34]

In this same year, 1909, De Gasperi was elected communal councilor of Trent. He was of the minimum age (twenty-eight) for election to the Communal Council, and he represented the First Corps of electors.[35] His many other obligations—direction of *Il Trentino,* vice presidency of the *Banca industriale,* management of the *Unione politica*—made it difficult for him to attend the sessions of the council, and he was frequently absent. However, the minutes of the sessions that he managed to attend reveal his wide range of interests. Thus in 1910 he voted in favor of the establishment of a special school in Trent for retarded children; he called for an investigation of the housing situation; and he complained that the librarian-archivist of Trent, a man of superior education, was receiving a salary that was no higher than that of a gendarme.[36]

As a member of the council De Gasperi proposed a reform of the electoral statute of Trent, so as to provide proportional representation of professions and occupations, direct women suffrage (under the existing law women who had the right to vote could exercise this right only by proxy), and a Fourth Corps of electors to represent the propertyless. Although the Liberals and Socialists combined against the proposal, preventing its immediate enactment, two years later a part of it was adopted in that a Fourth Corps was established.[37] Meanwhile, De Gasperi's sister Marcella was active in the formation of the *Associazione Femminile Tridentina* to prepare women to take part in the social activities of the day. The constitution of the organization was written by De Gasperi, in collaboration with the officers. De Gasperi firmly believed that women should participate in the public life of the nation, seeing in such participation no incompatibility with their functions in the home.

De Gasperi's study of provincial and local problems gave him a greater appreciation of the ideas and projects of Henry George. He had a great admiration for the American reformer, and he did not consider his ideas utopian; in fact, he regarded Henry George as "a man eminently practical, a reformer in the true sense of the word." While not subscribing to all of George's ideas, he approved of taxes on the unearned increment of real estate.[38]

With the same broad outlook that was to remain characteristic of him during his entire lifetime, De Gasperi interested himself also in the activities of Italian Catholics. He took note of the signs of a renaissance of Italian Catholicism, but he feared that after Giolitti (who had achieved a working partnership with Catholics) Catholicism would be hampered by the prejudice of the generation that had been trained in lay schools.[39]

In November 1910 De Gasperi attended the Italian Catholic Congress held at Modena. The proceedings made a favorable impression upon him, and describing the congress for his paper, he observed that there were no Modernists at Modena; there were only Catholics with "modern attitudes and methods." He added that neither rightists nor leftists were present, and in few congresses had he witnessed such vivid demonstration of obedience to the Holy Father.[40]

His contacts with Italian Catholics strengthened his pro-Italian foreign policy. De Gasperi favored the Triple Alliance, which he regarded as the best assurance that the Italians of the Hapsburg Empire would receive better treatment. He was cognizant of the fact that the Triple Alliance had never been popular in Italy, the latter having joined Austria and Germany only because of anger over the French occupation of Tunis in 1881. Nevertheless, he thought Italy could and should use the alliance to foster the objectives of her minority in Austria-Hungary. He hoped that Italy would increase her armed strength, so that her participation in the alliance would carry more weight. When the Italo-Turk War broke out in September 1911, De Gasperi supported the Italian position, and he criticized the portrayal of the Turks in Austrian newspapers as "innocent lambs." In his pro-Italian stance De Gasperi was undoubtedly influenced by Italian Catholics, who failed to see that the war was essentially imperialistic and who regarded it instead as a religious crusade.[41]

General elections to the *Reichsrat* were scheduled for June 1911. The campaign of the *Partito Popolare Trentino* was directed by De Gasperi, who was now thirty years of age and therefore eligible for election to the lower house. Running in the electoral college of Fiemme-Fassa-Primiero-Civezzano, De Gasperi called for "a democratic parliament that works for the people, not for militaristic and centralizing absolutism."[42] When the returns were in, he had amassed 3,116 votes out of the 4,275 cast, or 75 per cent of the total.[43] Other *Popolari* elected were Conci, De Carli, De Gentili, Grandi, Delugan, and Tonelli. The Socialists elected Battisti, and the Liberals, Malfatti. All the Trentine deputies, except Battisti, who ended up on the gallows at the Castle of Trent in 1916, remained members of the *Reichsrat* until the end of the First World War. Of the nineteen Italian deputies in the *Reichsrat*, ten were *Popolari* (seven from the Trentino and three from Friuli and Istria), six were Socialists, and three were Liberals.[44]

The new *Reichsrat* held its first session on July 17, 1911, and among its temporary secretaries was De Gasperi, who was also its youngest member. As secretary, it was De Gasperi's duty to administer to the Italian deputies the oath of loyalty to the emperor, and it greatly amused him to hear Battisti swear loyalty to Francis Joseph at the same time that he wore a scarlet tie and carried a red carnation in his buttonhole.[45] Battisti reacted to *Il Trentino's* sarcastic references to the incident by accusing De Gasperi of trying to pass himself off as a member of the aristocracy.[46] The charge stemmed from an error made by a parliamentary clerk who separated De Gasperi's name, then written as "Degasperi," into two words, "de Gasperi."

Parliamentary work began October 5, 1911. In a speech on October 13, De Gasperi pointed to the high cost of living in the Trentino, which he attributed to poor harvests, the prevalence of foot and mouth disease, prohibitive duties on imports of grain and meat from Italy, and governmental neglect. He castigated Vienna for inhibiting the development of the economic potential of the Trentino, and he demanded that the Trentini be permitted to exploit their hydroelectric resources as they saw fit. To date, the military authorities had given permission for the construction of a central electric station only on the condition that no Italian capital and no Italian workers be utilized on the project.[47]

Another item on the agenda of the Trentine *Popolari* was a perennial, namely, an Italian university on Italian soil. The government was now prepared to concede the establishment of an Italian law faculty at Vienna, but German deputies, especially from Tirol, opposed the plan. During the debates on the university question, De Gasperi explained that irredentism as understood by his party involved only spiritual and cultural links with the Italian nation; it was not irredentism in the historical sense. He also pointed out that the Italian deputies had pursued a policy of moderation, restraining the masses.[48]

In 1912, of far greater interest to the imperial government than the university question was the First Balkan War, which broke out in

September. De Gasperi was a member of the Austrian Delegation which convened at Vienna the evening of October 7, in order to hear a speech by Count Leopold von Berchtold, the foreign minister in the Austro-Hungarian government. On the following afternoon De Gasperi delivered an address which was heard by Berchtold and other members of the ministry. In it, he denounced the policy of the government in the Trentino, for it involved the confiscation of newspapers and films, the arrests of girls because the colors of their dresses could be combined to form the Italian tricolor, constant accusations of irredentism, and encouragement to the *Volksbund*. He concluded by warning that such treatment of the Italian minority would have unfortunate effects upon Austro-Italian relations. The talk was widely reported throughout the empire. In a private interview with De Gasperi in Budapest on November 18, Count Berchtold affirmed his personal interest in the grievances of the Trentini but asserted that military authorities did not permit the intervention of politicians in their zone, and the Trentino was considered within their own special jurisdiction.[49]

The Balkan Wars of 1912-1913 were extremely disturbing to De Gasperi, whose language became quite Marxian when he commented upon them. He saw European financial interests behind the Turks, and was convinced that the Ottoman Empire could not remain in the war a week without European capital. While thousands were dying, "European plutocracy celebrates its orgies in blood and barbarism." But if he was anti-Turk and anti-European, he was not pro-Slav. Behind the Slavic talk of Christian liberation, he saw only "pagan conquest."[50]

From 1913 on, De Gasperi had a sense of impending disaster. There was less sarcasm, more preoccupation in his voice. In spite of all the talk about universal brotherhood and human solidarity, it seemed to him that Europe was on a collision course. Armaments had become the chief topic of conversation, and De Gasperi complained that one was considered stupid if one could not converse intelligently on such topics as cannons, howitzers, dreadnoughts, and projectiles. Even Catholic parties had lost their sense of internationalism and had become infected by chauvinistic nationalism. He asked: "Will an imperialistic and nationalistic era follow the epoch of social concern?"[51]

In September 1913 De Gasperi made one of his infrequent trips out of the country; he went to The Netherlands to attend a meeting of the Interparliamentary Union at The Hague.[52] As the castles, cathedrals, and towers of the Rhine country disappeared from view, he entered what seemed like "an immense and silent plateau," pale green in color and broken by canals. The houses, painted green and red with white curtains framing the windows and tulips in the window boxes, gave the surroundings a peaceful air. To De Gasperi Holland seemed the ideal country for a pacifist congress.

Among the places that he visited during his sojourn at The Hague was the newly dedicated Palace of Peace. As he ascended the second floor, he was pleasantly surprised to come upon a bronze statue of Christ, but he was disconcerted to learn that it had been contributed not by a European country but by Argentina. Under his breath he said: "May your example serve to shake this unrealizing Christian society of Europe, which would have viewed with the greatest indifference the erection of a universal monument of peace devoid of any symbol of Christianity."

Descending the ornate stairs, he wondered why Catholics did not interest themselves in the cause of international peace. Was it, he thought, because some believed with Joseph de Maistre that "la guerre est divine en elle-même, puisque c'est une loi du monde?" Was it because Catholics feared that talk of peace was equivalent to acceptance of Tolstoi's pacifism? Was it because Catholics lacked a clear teaching on international law? He concluded that the latter could not be the answer, as there were the works of de Vitoria and Suarez. While meditating on the obligations of the Christian to the international community, he met Monsignor Alexander Gesswein, the head of the Hungarian Christian Social Party and president of a peace society. Monsignor Gesswein also expressed displeasure at the failure of most Catholics to interest themselves in the maintenance of international peace. He assured De Gasperi, however, that the few Catholics who had recently attended a pacifist congress in Holland were resolved to intensify their peace propaganda among their co-religionists in France, Belgium, Germany, and Austria-Hungary.

At home, in the Trentino, De Gasperi was involved in considerable controversy because of his attitude toward the Fiemme railroad project. A government project, the railroad was to connect Fiemme and Bolzano. Trentine Liberals and Socialists claimed that the tourist trade of the Trentino would be injured if Bolzano were the terminus, and that the railroad would, moreover, bring more Germans into the Trentino. But De Gasperi's position was that the railroad would aid the economic development of the Trentino. He was not deterred from supporting the project even after a meeting was held in Trent on May 7, 1913, during which about 2,000 persons shouted "Down with De Gasperi."[53] His stand on the Fiemme railroad was typical of his realism; later, in justification of his position he said: "When it seemed to us impossible to obtain more, we accepted the solution proposed as the lesser evil, with the intention of improving it today or in the future."[54]

Though more involved than ever in the affairs of the empire, De Gasperi remained in touch with local functionaries. According to an account he wrote for his paper, he once escorted the mayor of a small Alpine village on a tour of the *Reichsrat*. The mayor gave De Gasperi a rather difficult time. First he wanted to know why a modern parliament had to be housed in a structure that resembled the ancient Parthenon, complete with classical statues. Entering the stately chamber, the small-town mayor was astounded to note a total absence of decorum amid a babble of tongues. Not one of the 500 deputies appeared to be listening to the speeches being delivered, and De Gasperi patiently explained that speeches were not intended to be heard so much as to be printed and distributed. The mayor was even more mystified to learn that only the Ruthenians could understand the Ruthenian speaker who was then monopolizing the floor.[55]

In April 1914 De Gasperi was elected to the provincial Diet at Innsbruck by the college of Fiemme-Fassa-Primiero-Civezzano. The proroguing of the *Reichsrat* in March had enabled him to conduct a strenuous campaign, sometimes involving speaking engagements at three rallies in one day.[56] As a member of the Diet, De Gasperi voted against an increase in the number of provincial troops, and he condemned the continued militarization of the Trentino, ascribing to such militarization the decline of the region's economic life. He demanded that the government at least reimburse the innkeepers who saw their business decline because barracks were being erected close by; the shepherds who had to abandon the pastures to cannon shots; the consumers who had to pay more for their goods because they were forbidden to construct a road.[57] But the outbreak of the First World War was close at hand, and conditions in the Trentino were to become far worse than any De Gasperi could have imagined in the spring of 1914.

CHAPTER III

DE GASPERI DURING THE FIRST WORLD WAR

WHEN THE FIRST WORLD WAR BROKE OUT, DE GASPERI'S PAPER made no attempt to assess responsibility for the war; the reasons for it, stated an editorial, were known only to God, and this was "His Hour."[1] Another editorial, appearing just a few days later, expressed the wish that Italy would enter the war on the side of the Central Powers, and thus participate in the struggle against "Slavism."[2] In the succeeding weeks and months, however, the paper took a stand in favor of the neutrality of Italy. There was little or no possibility that Italy would enter on the side of the Central Powers, and a war between Austria and Italy would bring greater hardships to the Trentino. The subsequent growth of interventionism in Italy was alarming to *Il Trentino*, and in October 1914 it lamented the fact that intervention had become the chief topic of conversation among the "street brawlers" of Italy.[3]

In the meantime, in September 1914, De Gasperi made the first of his three trips to Rome during 1914-1915. Accompanied by Monsignor Guido De Gentili, head of the *Popolare* Parliamentary Club at Vienna, his objectives were to assure supplies for the Trentino and to ascertain the climate of opinion in Italy. For the latter purpose he went to see Baron Macchio, the Austrian ambassador to Italy, early in October. He told Macchio that the frequent movements of Austrian troops along the frontier, as well as the occasional thoughtless anti-Italian remarks of Austrian officials, were creating an atmosphere of extreme tension in the Trentino. Macchio replied that the military measures were inevitable in time of war and could be found along the frontiers of all belligerent countries. He assured De Gasperi that no responsible Austrian contemplated aggressive measures against Italy; such measures would be absurd when Austria was already engaged on two fronts.

During the course of the conversation, De Gasperi remarked that he had been surprised to find an atmosphere of calm prevailing in Italy. He had spoken with various persons, including men in politics, and everywhere he had found a desire to preserve peace. Regarding the Trentino, he assured Macchio that the people were loyal to the Hapsburg monarchy; in the event of a plebiscite, over 90 per cent would vote in favor of the monarchy.[4] While De Gasperi's figures may have been somewhat exaggerated and designed primarily to allay Austrian fears regarding the loyalty of the Trentini, it is undoubtedly true that a plebiscite at this time would have gone almost certainly in favor of the monarchy. The socio-economic ties of the Trentino were entirely with the empire, and the development of a "positive national conscience" had produced merely a desire for complete autonomy, not for incorporation in the Kingdom of Italy. The Italian government was well aware of the situation in the Trentino. A report to Sidney Sonnino, minister of foreign affairs in the Salandra government, stated that in the event of military action in the Trentino, the masses would manifest a "diffident passivity."[5]

During the autumn and winter of 1914-1915, the Berlin government strove to maintain good relations with Italy; no objection was offered to Italy's neutrality.[6] Germany sent to Italy a new ambassador, Prince Bülow, and also a distinguished representative of the Center Party, Matthias Erzberger. It was hoped that Erzberger would use his contacts with influential Italian Catholics to keep Italy in the neutral camp. Bülow and Erzberger repeatedly urged the German government to put pressure on Austria to make concessions to Italian national sentiment. The Austrian government was, however, deluded by the reassuring reports of Baron Macchio into thinking that no substantial concessions were necessary.

After his return from Rome, De Gasperi went to Vienna to sound out the directors of the Christian Socialist Party. Among the persons whom he saw in Vienna was Fünder, the editor of the influential *Reichspost*. Fünder had been kept informed of the informal talks which were taking place between Italy and Austria, and he told De Gasperi that Austria was prepared to cede the Trentino to Italy.[7] Armed with this important though unofficial information, De Gasperi in November 1914 made another trip to Rome. This time he had a private audience with the newly elected pope, Benedict XV, to whom he may have communicated the news he had received from Fünder, knowing that the

Pontiff did not wish to see an enlargement of the area of the war. Describing the audience, *Il Trentino* stated: "His Holiness, interesting himself fraternally in our condition, imparted . . . a special benediction to the families, to the widows and orphans of the war dead, to the wounded, to their families, and to all who have suffered directly the consequences of the war. He blessed the paper."[8] The audience evidently made a deep impression on De Gasperi, for a few days later he wrote a long article on it, entitled "A Stop at Rome," in which he described the intense desire of the Holy Father for the restoration of peace.[9]

The sentiments of De Gasperi and of Pope Benedict XV were shared by most Italian Catholics.[10] They did not judge "sacred egoism" as a principle that could justify war, and only a few Catholics favored aid to France and Belgium as having been unjustly attacked. On the other hand, they did not consider demands for the Italian areas of Austria-Hungary as unjust or immoral. By the spring of 1915, many of them had been won over to the cause of intervention on the side of the Allies. At the beginning of May, the Central Board of Catholic Action published an appeal which in substance favored such intervention. Some Catholics were hostile to the appeal, and the Vatican exhibited anxiety. Don Luigi Sturzo, then secretary general of Catholic Action, was attacked by the neutrality party because he accepted the principle of intervention (provided the Italian army could be more adequately prepared for war) and by the interventionist party because he rejected the principle of "sacred egoism."[11]

In the absence of contemporary documentary sources, it is impossible to be categorical concerning De Gasperi's attitude in the spring of 1915 toward Italian intervention. In view of his background and personality, it does, however, seem reasonable to suppose that his preference was still for a diplomatic settlement. In March 1915 he made a third trip to Rome, during the course of which he had an interview with Sidney Sonnino; in all probability, De Gasperi continued to urge a peaceful solution.[12] (Formal negotiations between Austria and Italy had begun in January 1915.)

What can be definitely stated regarding this third visit to Rome is that the Italian Ministry of the Interior was deeply suspicious of De Gasperi and kept a file on his arrivals and departures. He was suspected of engaging in contraband commerce and of seeking restricted information. The prefect of Rome was under orders to keep him under surveillance.[13] An unsigned memorandum in the files of the Ministry of the Interior reads:

> For what purpose the deputy Degasperi (pro-Austrian clerical, director of the paper *Il Trentino*, deputy at the Vienna Parliament, and son of an ex-gendarme) comes so frequently into the Kingdom and especially to Rome, we do not know precisely. We only know that other times he was at Milan and at Rome with one of his colleagues, also a deputy, a certain Paolazzi, a vulgar speculator-type, to try to obtain cereals and provisions for the Trentino, which undoubtedly would have ended up in military magazines. He spoke a short time ago with persons and officials in the Ministry of Agriculture and in the Ministry of Finance, but we believe that he got nothing, or very little. In Italy he is like a lamb, but once past the frontier he changes his voice and reports whatever he has been able to see or hear. It is certain, however, that he expects extraordinary things regarding the Trentino . . . .[14]

De Gasperi had not been in Rome very long before he found himself isolated and avoided even by those who had previously encouraged him in his pacific mission. When he left Rome, toward the end of March, Guido Miglioli, the Catholic Left leader who shared his aversion for war, was the only one to see him off at the station. Impulsively Miglioli said to De Gasperi, "Stay in Italy." De Gasperi's answer was characteristic: "I cannot; my job and duties are elsewhere."[15]

The concessions that Austria was prepared to make to Italy could not compare with those offered by the Allies. On April 26, 1915, Italy signed the secret Treaty of London, whereby she was promised, in return for her participation in the war, not only the South Tirol but Trieste, a large part of the Istrian Peninsula and of Dalmatia, Valona in Albania, islands in the Aegean seized in her war against Turkey, and compensation in Africa if England and France annexed territory there after the war. Furthermore, the Papacy was to be excluded from the peace negotiations. On May 4, 1915, Italy denounced her alliance with Austria-Hungary, and on May 24, entered the war against her.

The entry of Italy into the war was greeted enthusiastically even by Catholics, and on June 6, 1915, the district of Borgo was festooned with flags. It was reported that when the Pope was asked if he had any objections to the tricolor draping the windows of the district, he answered, "If the others exhibit the tricolor, you do the same."[16] But in spite of the patriotism shown by Catholics, the government remained suspicious, and it feared that Catholics abroad would endeavor to intervene in Italo-papal relations. In April 1916, the Italian ambassador to the United States reported that Catholics had become very powerful in the United States and that the "Irish fanatics" who constituted the nucleus of American Catholicism were hostile to Italy.[17]

The First World War

During the early days of May 1915, when the Hapsburg government sensed that an Italian declaration of war was imminent, the Trentino was declared a fortress, with the military authorities assuming absolute control. Their powers included the right to evacuate "suspect" Italians, according to lists prepared for some time. The trains that brought to Trent carloads of soldiers returned to their destinations filled with civilians who had been compelled, often on a few hours' notice, to abandon families, jobs, and property.

The municipal administration of Trent requested De Gasperi to go, together with Deputy Mayor Giuseppe Menestrina, to Salzburg, headquarters of the military command entrusted with the "Refugee Operations," to ascertain the intentions of the military with respect to the evacuation of the Trentino. They arrived at Innsbruck on May 22 and, two days afterward, they were received by the Lieutenant of Tirol, Count Toggenburg. Normally Toggenburg was a very polite official, but on this occasion, probably because he had already been informed of the Italian declaration of war, he was extremely rude. He informed the Deputy Mayor that he was being conscripted into the army, and he forbade De Gasperi to proceed to Salzburg.[18]

Returning to Trent, De Gasperi reached an important decision concerning *Il Trentino*. The last issue had been that of May 22, which had been censored because it carried the headline "The Decisions of the Italian Parliament." From the outset of the war, blank spaces had frequently appeared in the columns of the paper, and such items as it carried consisted of official communications or excerpts from German newspapers. De Gasperi knew that with the Italian entry into the war, the paper could not survive except as a pro-Hapsburg paper. On May 25 a printed notice advised the readers of *Il Trentino* that because of the shortage of workers, the paper was temporarily suspended.[19]

The Liberal paper, *L'Alto Adige*, had suspended publication on May 22. The Socialist paper, *Il Popolo*, had suspended publication in August 1914, when its editor Cesare Battisti fled to Italy.[20] The only paper that remained in circulation after May 1915 was a government paper, *Risveglio Trentino*, subsequently known as *Risveglio Austriaco*.

The war profoundly affected the entire constitutional and legal structure of Austria-Hungary. Not only did the army increase in political power, but imperial edicts replaced some of the civil law code and the paragraphs relating to civil liberties in particular. The constitutional checks on the powers of the military also disappeared, at least in the Austrian half of the monarchy. While the Hungarian Parliament met in regular session in Budapest, the Austrian at Vienna had been prorogued since March 1914; not until May 1917 was it to meet again. In the meantime, the parliament building was being used as a military hospital.

For the Trentini, deportations were the severest consequence of the suspension of parliamentary life. Those forced to leave their homes were either confined to concentration camps or dispersed in colonies among the villages of the interior of the monarchy. So much confusion prevailed in the transportation arrangements that frequently families were separated. Men who were sent to the front—all men from 18 to 50 were subject to the draft—were frequently ignorant of the location of their families. Those in concentration camps received food and lodging from the government; those in *diaspora* received a small subsidy. Deputies shared the fate of their fellow Trentini; six members of the Diet at Innsbruck were sent to the notorious concentration camp, Katzenau, near Linz.

When the exodus was completed, about one third of the population of the Trentino had been uprooted. There were 1,405 Trentini in Bohemia; 19,717 in Moravia; 12,956 in Lower Austria; 12,317 in Upper Austria; 20,000 in Styria; 2,000 in Salzburg; and undetermined thousands in Hungary. In addition to the officially evacuated Trentini, there were thousands who voluntarily left their native homes, having found the military authorities in the regions close to the Italian frontier too restrictive. These included 6,000 in the northern valleys of the Trentino; 7,500 in the German regions of Tirol, and 30,000 in Carniola.[21]

The policy of expelling Italians from the regions adjacent to the Italian border was applied not only to the Trentini but also to the Italians of the Adriatic provinces. It was the intention of the Hapsburg government to house all refugees in concentration camps, and during the autumn and winter of 1915-1916, camps were erected at Leibnitz, Mitterndorf, Pottendorf, and Braunau. Only technical difficulties and the reopening of parliament in 1917 prevented the government from carrying the plan to completion.[22]

Exempt from military service for medical reasons, De Gasperi's most important wartime work was to provide aid to the displaced Italians. In June 1915 Vienna had permitted the establishment of the *Comitato di soccorso per i profughi meridionali* (Committee for Assistance to the Southern Refugees), for the purpose of visiting refugee camps and colonies and making recommendations. The *Comitato* was under the patronage of Archduchess Maria Josepha, and its head was Max Vladimir Beck, president of the Supreme Court of Accounts and former premier. The committee was divided into two bodies, the *Grande comitato*, consisting of 333 members, and the *Comitato ristretto*, consisting of 56 members. The *Grande comitato* found the financial means to carry on the relief operations and determined the norms for the dispensation of aid. The smaller committee executed the directives of the first and compiled reports on the aid disbursed.[23]

The establishment of contacts with the refugees was the work of a few delegates, to each of whom a specific area was assigned. De Gasperi, who was appointed to the *Comitato ristretto* and designated a delegate, was to visit refugees in Bohemia, Upper Austria, the camp of Braunau, and a few communes in Salzburg. Every month the *Comitato ristretto* met under the presidency of Beck to discuss the reports of the delegates, and frequently De Gasperi was the principal speaker.

The primitive conditions that prevailed in the camps appalled De Gasperi, and he sought to improve them. Assisted often by Trentine priests who had voluntarily followed their parishioners into exile, he directed the formation of local committees, which provided not only material aid to the refugees but also undertook the construction of churches and schools. By the middle of 1917, 140 schools had been established, frequented by 16,000 pupils. Cooperation between the local committees and the parent committee also produced workshops, laboratories, and hospitals. Upon the recommendation of the parent committee, the supplying of materials and foodstuffs, originally in the hands of private speculators, became the responsibility of the government.[24] De Gasperi served without pay and at great personal inconvenience.[25] Fearful of confinement if he returned to the Trentino, where the military authorities were accustomed to taking the law into their own hands, De Gasperi avoided that area until the summer of 1917, when, after the reopening of parliament, he visited his family, then living in Caverena in the Val di Non.

At the end of 1916 the governing circles of Austria-Hungary had reason to be confident. Serbia and Montenegro had been overrun, and the Russian offensive of the summer of 1916 had long since frittered away. The Central Powers were in occupation of practically all of Galicia and the Bukovina, as well as Warsaw and Brest-Litovsk. The Allies, meanwhile, were bogged down in Salonika. Italy was making no progress on the Alpine front, while Rumania, who had entered the war encouraged by the Brusilov offensive, was overrun by the end of the year. But the situation behind the lines was much less favorable to the Hapsburg Empire. The minorities were seething with discontent, and food shortages were becoming acute, particularly in the Austrian half of the monarchy.[26]

It was at the end of 1916 that responsible men throughout the world turned to thoughts of peace conferences or at least to a definition of war aims. On November 21, 1916, Emperor Francis Joseph died, and his successor, Karl I, promised his subjects an early peace. He began secret negotiations for a separate peace, but he was unsuccessful and the price he paid for his attempt was a higher degree of subjection to Berlin.[27]

While Karl strove to achieve peace, revolution toppled the Czarist regime in Russia. Probably in no other country did the revolution make such a profound impression than in Austria-Hungary: the ease with which one of the strongest monarchies in the world collapsed was alarming, and the men of Vienna began to search for ways to mitigate the national and social unrest that was becoming so pervasive in the empire.

The convocation of the *Reichsrat* was considered the first step in allaying discontent. At the opening session Karl promised to rule constitutionally; in return, he asked that moderation be observed, at least as long as the war lasted. The minorities, however, were determined to take advantage of the situation to press their demands for a reorganization of the empire, particularly in view of the fact that the premier, Heinrich Clam-Martinitz, in his speech to parliament, had held out no hope that the end of the war would see better treatment of the minorities. The Czechs asked for the establishment of a federal state in which all autonomous national units would have equal rights. The Yugoslavs demanded the union of all terrtiories inhabited by the Slovenes, Croats, and Serbs in a state which would be independent under the Hapsburg dynasty. The Ruthenians clamored for a "state unity of all the Ruthenian territories."

The *Popolari* of the Trentino refused to make any declaration. Either they wished to deny loyalty to the Hapsburg monarchy by declining to be satisfied with even a reorganized empire, or else they felt that a declaration was useless at that time, for the emperor had recently stated that Tirol would remain indissolubly united with Austria.[28] De Gasperi frequently used parliament as a forum to advertise the sufferings of the Italians of Austria-Hungary. On June 12, 1917, he presented an interpellation in which he described the manner in which Italians had been treated since the outbreak of the war with Italy. Priests, doctors, lawyers, men and women of all classes and ages: all had been torn from their families and had been taken far from their native villages to be placed in concentration camps or other places of confinement, in spite of the fact that no law authorized such deportations. Not only adults but also children, idiots, deaf mutes, and the blind had been interned. Soldiers who had been wounded at the front and had thereby become disabled were among those interned. No one was able to learn the precise reason for his confinement, nor was he given an opportunity to first take care of personal or family matters. When the internees arrived at their destinations, they frequently found that the camps were woefully unprepared to receive them. Conditions were so bad in some camps that there were even cases of suicide. De Gasperi concluded by requesting a governmental inquiry into the manner in which so many Austrian citizens of Italian nationality had been interned or confined, on the conditions prevailing in the internment camps, and on the measures taken in expiation and reparation of the injustices and illegalities committed.[29]

In the Budgetary Commission, of which he was a member, De Gasperi introduced a resolution calling for the immediate liberation of all citizens who had been unjustly or illegally confined or interned. The resolution passed unanimously;[30] although it had no binding effect on the government, De Gasperi had won a moral victory.

On September 28, 1917, during discussion on the budget, De Gasperi delivered his strongest discourse against Austria. He pointed out that in the preceding two months less than 2 per cent of the detained or confined had been permitted to return to their homes, in spite of a governmental directive to the military recommending the adoption of "liberal criteria." He described the Trentino as being in the grip of terror, and he characterized the Lieutenancy of Innsbruck as the center of the terror. He denounced the attempts then being made to Germanize the Trentino by removing all signs in Italian and substituting German signs. He asserted that the spirit of liberty would arise from the bones of the dead, and he predicted that one day all injustices and cruelties would be avenged. He concluded: "That day must come. This war has already had one result, a result that precedes the decision that may be obtained on the battlefield—the victory of the principle of national democracy."[31]

Less than a week later, an incident in the Italian camp at Wagna in Styria brought tempers to the boiling point. Istrians and Friulians for the most part had been assigned to this camp, which numbered 18,000 at its height. Early in October 1917 two soldiers returned from the front to visit their families. One was in a state of intoxication, and the other was mentally deranged. The sentinel refused to admit the soldiers, and in the ensuing scuffle, the soldiers were beaten by other guards. In the meantime, a large crowd, composed mostly of women and children, had gathered to support the soldiers. To disperse the mob, the gendarmes began to fire shots, one of which hit and killed a young boy, the son of a widow who had four other sons at the front.

The Wagna incident had repercussions far and wide. The refugee committee named a committee to ascertain responsibility for the shooting. De Gasperi was named presiding officer of the investigating commission, and he brought the matter to the attention of parliament. He presented a report to parliament in which he demanded an investigation of the conduct of the gendarmes involved in the incident, the conveyance of apologies to the family of the dead boy, the condemnation of the administration of Wagna, and the employment at the camp of officials who spoke the Italian language.[32]

The month of October 1917 was the most difficult of the war for the Trentine deputies. On their way to Vienna for the meeting of the *Reichsrat,* they saw trains moving south to deliver the *coup de grace* to Italy. On October 24 the Italians suffered an overwhelming defeat at Caporetto, and thus ended the offensive that General Cadorna had begun in August in the hope of winning Trent.

On December 20, 1917, the *Reichsrat* ended its deliberations for the year. Both the internal and external situation of the monarchy had greatly deteriorated during the preceding year. The winter of 1917-1918 was unusually severe, and by the end of December Vienna was covered by several feet of snow. Worse than the fuel shortage then prevalent was the food shortage, which was now reaching famine proportions. In January 1918 a reduction in the flour ration in the Austrian half of the monarchy led to a mass strike in Vienna, which spread to Lower Austria, Styria, Upper Austria, and Brno, the Moravian capital. From this time on, strikes, mutinies, and hunger demonstrations became chronic in the monarchy.

The crisis of the monarchy became deeper as a result of the peace negotiations with Russia at Brest-Litovsk in the winter of 1917-1918. The Poles, hitherto considered a bulwark of the monarchy, agitated strongly against the proposed assignment of the district of Kolm to the Ukraine. At a meeting of the *Reichsrat* on February 20, 1918, Baron Goetz, the leader of the Poles, asserted that Polish eyes had finally been opened to the duplicity of Hapsburg diplomacy.

The unrest of the minorities spurred the Pan-Germans of Tirol to greater efforts. On May 9, 1918, the members of the *Volksbund* convoked a congress at Sterzing, where they pledged implacable war against Italian irredentism and spelled out the Tirolean demands in the event of Austrian victory. In organizing the resistance of the Trentini, De Gasperi decided to enlist the aid of Bishop Endrici, in spite of the fact that the latter had been confined by the Austrian authorities to a monastery at Heiligenkreuz because of his pro-Italian attitude. At the end of May De Gasperi had an interview with the Bishop, informing him that Conrad was preparing an offensive against Italy and that the *Volksbund* was accordingly encouraged in its anti-Italian stance. The Bishop replied by addressing a pastoral letter to his diocese. Evading the Austrian censorship, De Gasperi succeeded in having the letter read in all the churches of the Diocese of Trent. The letter deplored the intemperate language used at the Congress of Sterzing and it urged clergy and laity to remain firm in defense of the liberty and dignity of the Church. It ended with a plea that Mass be celebrated on June 7, the Feast of the Sacred Heart, for the Bishop's intentions. On the appointed day, in spite of governmental attempts to secure a cancellation of the service, an impressive number of Trentini, including De Gasperi, gathered in the Cathedral of San Vigilio, thereby manifesting their attachment to their exiled bishop.[33]

It was at this time that Austria and Germany were making desperate efforts to end the war. The Treaty of Brest-Litovsk (March 1918) had released the men and supplies needed for an onslaught against the Allied positions on the Western front. Between March and July the Germans were highly successful; Paris was brought within the reach of German guns. Meanwhile, beginning in mid-June, the Austrians launched an offensive that was designed to break through the Piave. The offensive failed, however, and the Austrians suffered one of their worst defeats. On June 23 the Italian general, Armando Diaz, announced that the Italian Army had sustained the offensive of the Austrians from the Tonale to the Piave, on a front of more than one hundred and fifty kilometers.

By mid-summer the German offensive on the Western front had petered out, and by the end of September Ludendorff was demanding that Germany make peace and armistice offers to the Allies. A week later, Prince Max von Baden, the new chancellor, requested President Wilson to arrange the conclusion of an armistice. The failure of the German Army caused the defection of Berlin's allies. On September 14 Emperor Karl published a peace manifesto without consulting Kaiser William II; although it was ignored by the Allied statesmen, it clearly indicated that Vienna was ready to desert Berlin.

On the Italian front, where most of the Austro-Hungarian combat forces were concentrated, both Austria and Italy were on the defensive. It was here, however, that the morale of the Hapsburg army was broken and its strength dissipated in two unsuccessful attacks spread over too long a front. The number of deserters began to increase very rapidly. Against this background of military defeat, Baron Max von Hussarek, Austrian premier since July 1918, announced early in October that the Emperor was prepared to cede autonomy to the nationalities. But it was too late; the various nationalities spurned the offer. In a speech in parliament on October 4, De Gasperi, after again denouncing the treatment of the Trentini, frankly stated that the question of sovereignty over the Trentino would be decided by force of arms.[34] On the same day, Karl asked Wilson for armistice terms.

The downfall of the monarchy was now imminent. The role of the Allied governments in the demise of the monarchy must now be briefly surveyed. Before Germany's final offensive, the Allied statesmen had reached no decision on the break-up of the Hapsburg empire, and they did nothing to encourage the subject minorities to rise up against the Hapsburgs. Point 10 of the Fourteen Points called for the "autonomous development" of the peoples of Austria-Hungary, not for the dismemberment of the empire. By the autumn of 1918, however, the situation had radically changed, as a result of the ambitions and propaganda of Hapsburg exiles, notably the Czech exiles. On June 29 the French had recognized the right of the Czechoslovaks to independence, and on August 14 the British had acknowledged the Czechs as an Allied nation. On September 3 the United States had followed suit and had recognized the Czech National Council as a "de facto belligerent government." On October 19 American Secretary of State Robert Lansing, in reply to the Hapsburg peace note, clearly stated that the tenth point of Wilson's January address had been superseded by subsequent developments.

The Italians, no less than the other nationalities, had embraced the principle of national self-determination. Speaking in parliament on October 11, De Gasperi announced: "The Trentine population expects from the conclusion of peace recognition of the principle of nationality and its practical application to Italians who are presently living in Austria. It is convinced that the Austrian government in accepting Wilson's Fourteen Points has already recognized this principle."[35] Continuing, he affirmed that if a plebiscite were to be held in the Trentino, the overwhelming majority would approve of this principle. His statement concerning the outcome of a plebiscite contradicted his remarks to Macchio four years previously, but the events of the intervening years had had their inevitable consequences. The privations and vexations of the war, together with the propaganda of national self-determination, had produced in the Trentini a profound desire to sever all connections with Austria. Military rule in the Trentino and concentration camps and colonies throughout the empire seemed to symbolize the attitude of the Hapsburgs toward the Italians, and the latter now wished to join the Kingdom of Italy. On October 15 the Italian deputies presented to the Delegations an interpellation in which they stated that the acceptance of Wilson's proposals by the Central Powers signified for the Italians political union with their co-nationals.

A day later Emperor Karl published the Manifesto whereby he proclaimed the transformation of Austria into a federal state. But by this time the empire existed in name only. When parliament met on October 22, the Ruthenians announced that they would not recognize Count Burian, the minister of foreign affairs, as their representative at the peace conference. Czechs and Slovaks declared that they already had a government of their own. The Yugoslavs stated that they did not consider themselves subject to the Vienna government.

The *Popolari* from the Trentino had already stated their position. Nevertheless, to leave no doubt on the matter, on October 24 they formed, together with the Liberals of the Trentino, Trieste, Pola, and Gorizia and a *Popolare* from Istria, the National Italian *Fascio*, with Conci as president, Rizzi (Liberal from Pola) as vice-president, and De Gasperi as secretary.[36] At the October 25 meeting of parliament, Conci repeated in the name of the *Fascio* the declaration made ten days previously in the form of an interpellation to the Delegations:

> Basing ourselves on the postulates of President Wilson, recognized and accepted by the Central Powers, we declare that we consider all the Italian territories, up to now subject to the Austro-Hungarian Monarchy, with no exception, as virtually detached from the territorial nexus, and for this reason the Italian deputies have not assumed the task of entering into negotiations with the monarchy or with the representatives of the nationalities still subject to Austria for the purpose of giving a new orientation to the State . . . .[37]

Thus ended the work of the Trentine delegation at Vienna. On October 24 an Italian offensive had begun at Vittorio Veneto and by November 3 Italian troops were in Trent. De Gasperi was now thirty-seven years of age: his Austrian life was at an end.

During the last days of October, De Gasperi, Conci, and Malfatti (the Liberal deputy from the Trentino) went to Switzerland to establish contact with the Italian government. Their objectives were to obtain immediate aid for the Trentini, who were literally dying of hunger, and the repatriation of refugees and demobilized soldiers. They arrived at

Berne on October 31, where they were received by the Marquis Paolucci de' Calboli, the counselor of the Legation. They submitted to him a memorandum which outlined the points to be considered in signing an armistice with Austria.

In granting the deputies a passport for the voyage to Switzerland, the Vienna government may have been thinking of instituting negotiations for a separate peace. Czechs, Yugoslavs, and Poles were also given permission to go to Switzerland. Here the Liberal deputies, Rizzi of Pola and Gasser of Trieste, joined De Gasperi, Conci, and Malfatti. Thus with the collapse of the Austrian armies at Vittorio Veneto, the five were able to enter Italy and negotiate directly with the Italian government. They reached Rome the evening of November 6, and were enthusiastically greeted by representatives of the government and of patriotic societies. Appearing on the balcony of the Braschi Palace with them was Vittorio Emanuele Orlando, the Italian premier. Technical talks were begun immediately to facilitate a rapid incorporation of the new provinces into Italy.

CHAPTER IV

DE GASPERI IN ITALIAN POLITICS 1919-1922

BY THE TIME DE GASPERI HAD BECOME A SUBJECT OF KING Victor Emmanuel III, Christian Democracy in Italy had attained maturity. Its origins and development must be briefly reviewed, for it bears both comparisons and contrasts with its counterpart in the Austrian monarchy.[1] Christian Democracy in Italy had its immediate origins in the Church-State quarrel that accompanied political unification. Pope Pius IX encouraged the formation of Catholic organizations, under the direct authority of the hierarchy, to defend the Church against the Liberal despoilers. In 1868 the *Società della gioventù cattolica italiana* (Italian Catholic Youth Society) was founded, and in 1874, in Venice, the first Catholic congress took place. At the second congress, held in Florence in 1875, the *Opera dei Congressi* was constituted; it was to direct most Catholic activities until 1904.

The congress movement was under the control of "intransigent" Catholics, i.e., Catholics wholly unreconciled to Italian unification and desirous of restoring the political and economic position of the Church. They regarded the Liberal Italian State as the very embodiment of evil. From the beginning, they manifested concern for the masses as victims of the same class, the bourgeoisie, that was exploiting the Church. The publication of *Rerum Novarum* in 1891 further stimulated their interest in socio-economic questions, and soon Christian cooperatives, savings banks, and benevolent societies were increasing at a rapid rate all over Italy, but especially in the North.

The efforts of the intransigents who aimed at a Catholic conquest of society were not always appreciated by bishops, some of whom regarded these Catholic enthusiasts as little better than demagogues. Furthermore, the prelates, having been appointed with the consent of the Italian government, were not unanimously opposed to reconciliation with the Italian State. Outstanding among those favoring reconciliation was Geremia Bonomelli, bishop of Cremona from 1871 until his death in 1914. In 1882, when Pope Leo XIII asked Bonomelli whether he would consider the participation of Italian Catholics in political elections as opportune, the Bishop answered in the affirmative. In 1885 he submitted to the pontiff a memorandum in which he pointed out the impossibility of restoring the Papal States; he urged instead an increase in the moral stature of the papacy.

By the end of the nineteenth century, a basic division had developed within the Catholic congress movement; it was between those who favored a Catholic mass party, with a program and ideology of its own, and those who regarded Catholic organization merely as a papal weapon in the war with the Italian State. However, the supporters of a Catholic mass party were not united. One group, the moderates, led by a young lawyer, Filippo Meda, saw no incompatibility between the Liberal, parliamentary Italian State and Roman Catholicism. Their desire was not so much to destroy the Italian State as to baptize it. The other group, the extremists or Christian Democrats, was headed by a young priest from the Marches, Don Romolo Murri, and was bitterly antagonistic to the existing State. The Murri adherents thought in terms of a mass party based on the Catholic economic and social organizations. These Christian Democrats published their program in 1899. Their principal demands were: (1) formation of corporations for the various professions and occupations; (2) democratization of political life through the introduction of proportional representation, the initiative, and the referendum; (3) social legislation to regulate labor conditions and to provide a greater measure of security in sickness and in old age; (4) protection of the small landowners and of the agricultural laborers; (5) reform of the tax structure, including the introduction of a progressive income tax; (6) development of religious education; and (7) general and progressive disarmament. These Christian Democrats were regarded as radicals because for the free play of economic forces they wished to substitute the statutory organization of corporations. Furthermore, when necessary, the State was to enforce the new order.[2]

Both the Meda and Murri factions looked for inspiration to Giuseppe Toniolo, the Venetian-born professor of political economy at the University of Pisa. Toniolo's basic premise was the primacy of ethics in the socio-economic sphere. The Christian social order, according to his teachings, has its foundation in three sets of social institutions: private, civil, and juridical. The private institutions are the individual, the family, and private property. The civil institutions are the hierarchical class organizations and the territorial associations. For those in commerce and industry, the hierarchical class organizations take the form of corporations of arts and crafts; for those in agriculture, there are separate associations for landowners and laborers. The settlement of classes in specified territorial zones is the responsibility of the territorial associations. The juridical institutions are the Church and the State, two societies distinct yet harmonious. The separation of the two would be detrimental to the public welfare. Christian Democracy is "that civil order in which all the social, juridical, economic forces, in the plenitude of their hierarchical development, cooperate proportionately for the common good and, in the last analysis, to the prevailing advantage of the lower classes."[3] Toniolo's conception of the socio-economic order was essentially static and too much influenced by his study of the guild system of Tuscany. Nevertheless, his teachings enjoyed a tremendous vogue among Christian Democrats, and it is very likely that he contributed ideas to the encyclical *Rerum Novarum.*

During the last years of the reign of Leo XIII, both extreme and moderate Christian Democrats were opposed by the older leaders of the congresses, the intransigents of the Veneto. These stood for the status quo primarily, and their idea of a reconquest of society was political rather than social. Their social organizations in the Veneto were considered merely as a papal auxiliary in the battle with the Liberal State.[4] So great was the dissension within the congress movement that one of the first acts of the new pope, Pius X, was to dissolve the *Opera dei Congressi,* replacing it, after 1906, with three national unions, each independent of each other: the *Unione popolare,* to diffuse Christian culture; the *Unione economico-sociale,* to coordinate the activities of social and economic organizations; and the *Unione elettorale,* to provide directions for elections. Toniolo was appointed head of the *Unione popolare.* Each union was controlled by the Papacy.

During the same year that he dissolved the congresses, Pius X permitted the suspension of the *non expedit* in those electoral districts in which anticlerical candidates might win in the absence of Catholic voting. In a few cases, Catholics were permitted to run for seats, but it was to be understood that if elected, they would sit as *cattolici deputati* and not as *deputati cattolici,* to emphasize the fact that there was no

Catholic party.[5] The progress of Socialism made churchmen realize that Catholic electoral intervention was necessary to safeguard the remaining rights of the Church. In 1905 the encyclical *Il Fermo proposito* gave official sanction to modification of the *non expedit*.

The general elections of 1909 brought the question of Catholic participation in politics to the fore once again. Acting through the *Unione elettorale*, the Vatican gave precise instructions. The principal conditions for Catholic participation in the elections were: (1) in their diocese's electoral district, there must be a militantly anticlerical candidate; (2) against such there must be a candidate (Catholic or non-Catholic) who must promise to refrain from attacking religion; and (3) there must be a great probability of victory for the anticlerical candidate should the Catholics abstain from voting. The result of Catholic participation was the election of twenty-one deputies who were Catholics. In 1913, after general elections had again taken place, Count Vincenzo Gentiloni, president of the *Unione elettorale*, revealed the existence of a pact between himself and Giolitti, under the terms of which Catholics were permitted to vote for Giolittian candidates, provided they agreed to abide by certain principles which would safeguard the rights of the Church.[6] Under the pact 228 majority deputies had been elected with Catholic support.

Catholics were still disunited. From 1910 on, the Catholic movement had a Left group made up of such Christian Democrats as Giuseppe Donati, Guido Miglioli, and Giovanni Gronchi. The Left wing represented the labor and peasant unions for the most part. The Right wing, the Clerico-Moderates, had as its leaders such men as Count Giovanni Grosoli, Marquis Filippo Crispolti, and Marquis Carlo Ottavio Cornaggia; it represented agrarian property for the most part. The Clerico-Moderates controlled the bulk of the Catholic press through the *Società Editrice Romana* (Roman Publishing Society, or the so-called Trust), which was headed by Grosoli. The chief spokesman for this group was Filippo Meda, who acted as a mediator between the different currents of Catholicism. The differences between the two groups were not pronounced.[7]

Meanwhile, Italy's ruling class, the Liberal bourgeoisie, was entering the crisis stage. This class had held power since unification and had never been renewed. While they called themselves Liberals, their party was essentially conservative. It stood for a restricted suffrage, governmental centralization, laicization, and distrust of working-class movements. It showed, moreover, an excessive concern for the protection of property.

Italian Politics, 1919-1922

The advance of Socialism[8] and the entry of Italy into the First World War forced Christian Democracy to seek greater integration with national life. In pursuit of this goal, Christian Democrats were aided by the fact that many ecclesiastics were now more friendly toward them. Confronted with individualism on the right and Socialism on the left, churchmen felt that a Christian Democratic political movement might help defend the Church's ultimate interests and also assume those social services which the Church was no longer in a position to carry out.[9] The war increased the prestige of Italian Catholics, for the official leadership of Italian Catholicism had supported the war effort, and Meda, as minister of finance in the war governments of 1916-1919, had been regarded as the unofficial representative of Italian Catholicism. The war also accelerated the new economic and political forces in the nation, rendering Catholic isolation all the more impossible.

When a few weeks after the end of the war, Don Luigi Sturzo, then head of Catholic Action, asked Cardinal Gasparri, the papal secretary of state, if the Vatican was prepared to rescind the ancient official prohibition against Catholic participation in political life, an affirmative answer was given. Late in November, forty men assembled in Rome and decided on the formation of the *Partito Popolare Italiano.* On January 18, 1919, from the Hotel Santa Chiara in Piazza Minerva in Rome, the executive committee launched its now famous appeal, "A tutti gli uomini liberi e forti." The platform of the new party called for proportional representation, women suffrage, an elective senate (to represent national academic, administrative, and trade union organizations), the widest decentralization, liberty and independence for the Church, extension of land ownership, and social legislation. It also demanded that the League of Nations recognize national aspirations, hasten the advent of universal disarmament, abolish the secrecy of treaties, effect the freedom of the seas, and promote social legislation.[10] The Roman Question was not mentioned, for the founders of the party did not feel that it should become involved in matters that were strictly ecclesiastical.

Primary credit for the organization of the party belongs to Don Luigi Sturzo. This Sicilian priest had made his entry into the Catholic apostolate as an associate of Murri, but unlike the latter he did not conceive of an alliance between a party and the formal Church; and unlike the latter he did not fall into the Modernist heresy. During the pontificate of Pius X he had served as municipal administrator in the commune of Caltagirone, in Sicily. Though opposing the intransigent leadership of the Catholic congresses, he was content to wait until a more propitious time before attempting to secure the formation of a political party. At the beginning of the war, Pope Benedict appointed him head of Catholic Action. In 1918 Sturzo promoted the formation of two unions which subsequently became strong supporters of the party that he founded, the Confederation of Cooperatives and Rural Banks, and the Italian Confederation of Laborers.

With the formation of the *Partito Popolare* Don Sturzo severed his connections with Catholic Action. The *Unione elettorale* was dissolved, and the remaining Catholic Action groups became exclusively religious in scope. Don Sturzo insisted that his party be nonconfessional; he was willing to admit into it anyone who would accept its platform. He considered it dangerous to make Catholicism the point of differentiation, for it might bring into the party those who were unwilling to accept the political, economic, and social principles for which the party stood. On the other hand, church affiliation with the party might embroil the Church in issues that were not strictly religious or moral.

Many recruits for the new party came from the ranks of Catholic labor. During the war the number of workers in Catholic unions had greatly increased, and in 1918 the *Unione economico-sociale* was succeeded by the above-mentioned Italian Confederation of Laborers, which paralleled the national organization of the Socialist unions. The Catholic unions gave the party their general support without becoming formally affiliated with it. Some union leaders, however, such as Giovanni Gronchi and Achille Grandi, became party leaders.

From the beginning the party had a Right and a Left wing. The Right wing had as its leaders Stefano Cavazzoni, Count Grosoli, and Fathers Agostino Gemelli and Francesco Olgiati. The two priests objected to the nonconfessional character of the party, to what they termed its "negative Christianity." In a pamphlet published on the eve of the first congress of the party, they stated that Catholicism should be the point of differentiation and that the Roman Question should be a matter of open concern to the party.[11] The extreme Left wing, headed by the Marxist-oriented Miglioli, favored collectivism and class war. Both Left and Right wings failed, however, to modify the platform when the first National Congress of the *Partito Popolare* convened in Bologna in June 1919. This first congress was presided over by De Gasperi.

Up to this time De Gasperi had been concerned primarily with Trentine problems and politics. One of his first acts upon returning to the Trentino had been to resume the publication, on November 23, 1918, of *Il Trentino*, which he renamed *Il Nuovo Trentino*. Until 1926, when

Fascist pressure forced him to resign, De Gasperi served as its director. As before the war, his columns employed forthright, direct language, but comparing the De Gasperi of the 1919-1926 period with that of the 1905-1914 period, one does note a change in pitch. The tone is more muted, more concerned, as though De Gasperi sensed that there was no real escape from the calamity that was descending upon Italy.

After the entry of Italian troops into Trent, the region became subject to military government, the *Governatorato di Trento*, which began to function on November 4, 1918. Military government lasted nine months, and was unpopular from the start, especially with the Trentini who had followed the leadership of the *Partito Popolare Trentino*. The decrees of the military government changed from day to day, or so it seemed, and frequently one decree contradicted another. The military government was also criticized because it failed to tackle the problem of reconstruction, and, worse still, it permitted the internment of several thousand Trentini who had served in the Austrian army. The ex-soldiers were sent to camps in Isernia, Castellamare Adriatico, Savigliano, Urbania, Alessandria, Bari, Barletta, and even Sardinia. Several months elapsed before these former soldiers were permitted to return to their homes in the Trentino.

To the solution of the many problems besetting the war-ravaged Trentino, De Gasperi's journal sought to make a contribution. It urged the most rapid repatriation of soldiers and refugees, the reconstruction of the devastated areas, and the concession of the greatest amount of autonomy to local officials and institutions. The military authorities were not appreciative of these suggestions, and frequently censored the news carried in the paper. In April 1919 De Gasperi wrote:

> With all our energy we protest against a censorship which suppresses every word in defense of the interests of the country....
>
> Give us the opportunity to prove, particularly in view of the fact that the Germans are watching us, that our political redemption does not mean passage from one domination to another but rather liberation from one overlordship to be taken into a family of brothers and equals....[12]

De Gasperi also protested against reprisals against those Trentini who, "threatened by bayonets," had carried out the orders of Austrian authorities; he demanded that the criterion be "justice, not reprisals."[13] His protests were inspired by the fact that a purge was then being conducted against all those who had not been sufficiently pro-Italian and anti-Austrian before and during the war. A new aristocracy seemed to be in the process of formation, composed of those who had been blatantly irredentist. Styling themselves the "Patriots," their hatred of Austria was carried to the point of demanding that Austrian university degrees be denied recognition by the Italian government.[14] De Gasperi's moderate temperament had no patience with such extremism, and he opposed a purge in 1919-1920. After the Second World War he was to use his influence to prevent a wholesale purge of all former Fascists.

To assist the military government in understanding local problems and grievances, the Italian government permitted the establishment of a *Consulta*, composed of six *Popolari*, three Liberals, and two Socialists, the members being designated by their respective parties. The *Popolari* included Monsignor De Gentili, De Gasperi, and Conci; the latter was president of the *Consulta*, and De Gasperi was secretary. If the *Consulta* had originally thought in terms of making specific recommendations to the military authorities, it was soon set straight on its competence. The head of the military government, Lieutenant General Pecori-Giraldi, refused to accept the *Consulta* other than as "an interpreter . . . of the interests, needs, and desires of the population."[15]

The report of the military government to Rome for the May 1-July 31, 1919, period is instructive. The *Consulta* was designated as an "organismo sterile," and the *Partito Popolare* was charged with "allowing few opportunities to go by without attacking the government." The party was also accused of keeping the region in a state of agitation, thus retarding the solution of urgent problems. The party sought the preservation of the old order for the purpose of "maintaining its own domination, especially in scholastic and religious matters," and it stood for provincial and communal autonomy. On only one point did the military government find itself in agreement with the "clerical party" and that was on the need for proclaiming an amnesty.[16]

In August 1919 the Governorship of Trent gave way to the General Civil Commissariat, headed by Luigi Credaro. The appointment of Credaro was a disappointment to De Gasperi and to the majority of the Trentini. An educator by profession, Credaro was lacking in administrative and political experience, and he was, moreover, an exponent of lay schools. When he took steps that seemed to portend a laicization of the schools of the Trentino, De Gasperi, Conci, and De Gentili sent him a strongly worded protest.[17] A similar protest came from Bishop Endrici when compulsory religious instruction was abolished in the secondary schools.[18] With respect to autonomy, however, Credaro supported the *Popolari*: as early as October 1919 he wrote to the premier, Francesco Nitti, to say that he did not think that the autonomy of the Trentino would constitute a threat to the Italian State.[19]

De Gasperi was not so absorbed by Trentine problems, particularly the question of autonomy, as to ignore national and international affairs. When in April 1919 the Italian delegation left the Paris Peace Conference because Italy was being denied satisfaction of its claims to Fiume, *Il Nuovo Trentino* expressed its solidarity with the Italians.[20] Although the bickering at Paris was ominous, De Gasperi affirmed: "We still hope for a just and lasting peace and in a new era of social justice. The old capitalistic society has crumbled...."[21] The preliminary terms of peace were a disappointment, for they failed to conform in their entirety to the Fourteen Points. As De Gasperi saw it, Wilson had come under the influence of David Lloyd George, who wished to "consolidate and extend the world domination of England." Wilson had also given in to Georges Clemenceau, who believed in the old European political system. The League of Nations was being transformed into an alliance of the victors, and with such transformation, "a beautiful dream ended."[22]

In June 1919 De Gasperi went to Bologna to take part in the first National Congress of the *Partito Popolare Italiano*. By this time the party had 56,000 card-carrying members, distributed among 850 sections.[23] On the day that the congress opened, a general strike was in progress, and only with difficulty did the delegates succeed in obtaining food and lodging. The streets were full of people who carried red banners and shouted Marxist slogans. When the congress got under way, Don Luigi Sturzo, the party's political secretary, invited De Gasperi, whose *Partito Popolare Trentino* he had long admired, to preside over the sessions. The presidency of De Gasperi was enthusiastically voted by the delegates, and amid prolonged applause, De Gasperi said: "I thank you for this honor; I thank you all the more because it amounts to the conferral of full citizenship upon redeemed Trentino, even before the international congress and the official proclamations accomplish this deed." He pledged himself to work for the "greatness and prosperity" of Italy.[24]

The first day of the congress was devoted to a discussion of the party's nonconfessionality, the morality of which had been disputed by some members. Don Sturzo defended nonconfessionality, and while De Gasperi does not appear to have spoken publicly on the matter, his sympathies were undoubtedly with the political secretary. Fifteen years previously, by changing the name of *La Voce Cattolica* to *Il Trentino*, he had diminished the confessionality of the paper and of the party it represented.

On the last day of the congress, Guido Miglioli arrived from Cremona. A neutralist during the war, he began his talk to the assembly by discussing the question of responsibility for the war. When he made what were interpreted as aspersions on the Italian army, some of the delegates openly displayed anger. De Gasperi intervened, stating that if the words of Miglioli had offended him, the son of a territory redeemed by the Italian army, he himself would have left the hall. Continuing, Miglioli explained that he had meant to attack only militarism.[25]

The Congress of Bologna decided that the party should refrain from making any alliance or compromises with the other parties in the forthcoming (November 1919) parliamentary elections, fighting for its program and its candidates with "absolute intransigence." Because the Trentino had not yet been juridically incorporated into Italy, De Gasperi was unable to present himself as a candidate for the Italian Chamber of Deputies.

De Gasperi spent the autumn of 1919 organizing the Trentine branch of the *Partito Popolare Italiano*, which now superseded the *Partito Popolare Trentino*. The party soon numbered 13,340 members, distributed among 183 sections. The interests of De Gasperi and his followers were not narrowly Trentine: speaking at a meeting of the Constituent Assembly of the Trentine branch of the party on October 12, 1919, De Gasperi was applauded when he stated that it was the mission of Italy to work for the renovation of Europe according to the precepts of fraternity, law, and justice.[26]

The war and its attendant horrors were probably still vivid in the mind of De Gasperi. In August 1919 he had visited a mountain in the Trentino which had been the scene of a sanguinary battle between the Austrians and the Italians. Ascending the grey-colored mountain that was almost devoid of vegetation, he had seen everywhere spent shells and scraps of lead and iron. At the top of the mountain he had come upon a mass of bones that had been bleached white by the burning sun. It had occurred to him that it would be a good idea if the bones were gathered together and a memorial erected. Out of the sacrifices of one war, perhaps a new world would arise, dedicated to fraternity and liberty.[27]

Through editorials and public speeches, De Gasperi also worked for the reconstruction, economic and political, of the Trentino. He argued that the Trentine people should not have less under the Italian government than they had had under the Hapsburgs, and he urged communal and provincial autonomy and the retention of such Austrian legislation as had been beneficial to the Trentini, such as workers' insurance laws and agricultural regulations.[28] On October 27, 1919, he sent to Nitti a resolution of the Trentine *Popolari* which stated that the situation in the Trentino was becoming intolerable and that the financial and economic clauses of the recently concluded Treaty of St. Germain (September 1919) did not adequately protect the interests of the region.[29]

In the meantime, the national leadership of the *Partito Popolare Italiano* eagerly looked forward to the opportunity of testing its strength at the polls. A law passed by the Italian Parliament in the summer of 1919 provided for modified proportional representation and constituted an electoral change which gave the mass parties an edge over the caucus groups of the Liberal politicians. The *Partito Popolare* was a mass party; it was interclass in structure, its membership embracing Christian Democrats, Clerico-Moderates, middle-class intellectuals, trade unionists, and large and small property-holders. Strong support for the party was to be found particularly in the ranks of the trade unions and the lower clergy. Geographically, the greatest strength of the party was in the North, where study clubs and workers' associations helped to publicize the party and its program. To many conservatives the new movement seemed to represent "Black Bolshevism" in spite of the fact that the campaign witnessed much violence on the part of the Maximalist Socialists against the *Popolari*.

The election returns were among the most extraordinary since the foundation of the Kingdom of Italy. For the Liberals they constituted an "electoral Caporetto." The Fascists, who had been making considerable progress since the foundation of the *Fascio di combattimento* in March 1919, failed to elect a single candidate, Mussolini receiving only 50,000 votes. For the *Popolari*, on the other hand, the results represented an amazing triumph: 100 seats out of 508. Unfortunately, however, not only had they not won enough seats to enable them to form their own government but they faced the hostility of the Liberals and Socialists. Giolitti resented the supersession of the Gentiloni Pact as much as he resented Don Sturzo, the Sicilian who talked so much of decentralization.

The strongest single party to emerge from the elections was the Socialist Party, which won 156 seats. True to their doctrinaire principles, however, the Socialists refused to accept their constitutional responsibility. At the same time, they were failing to make a success of revolution, and the vacillating policy of the party was to play into the hands of the Fascists.

The *Popolari* decided to support a Nitti government, but the latter turned out to be a great disappointment. Nitti failed to carry out any of the reforms proposed by the *Popolari*, and he openly favored the Socialists, hoping to gain their support. When, at the beginning of 1920, the Socialist unions called strikes of the postal, telegraph, and railroad workers, the Catholic or "White" unions, backed up by the party, kept the public services in operation. Nevertheless, the "White" unions were rewarded by being abandoned to the reprisals of their Socialist companions, with whom the Nitti government negotiated. De Gasperi was annoyed with Nitti, not only because of his lack of gratitude toward the Catholic unions but also because he had taken no action regarding the autonomy of the Trentino, in spite of assurances of a sympathetic attitude toward the matter.[30]

From April 8 to 11, 1920, De Gasperi was in Naples, attending the second National Congress of the *Partito Popolare*.[31] The party now had 255,000 members, distributed in 3,173 sections. The most lively discussion at this congress concerned agrarian reform, but the problems of the Trentino were closer to De Gasperi's heart. He sponsored a resolution which called for speedy ratification of the Treaty of St. Germain, the bestowal of constitutional rights upon the populations to be annexed, and the adoption of administrative, technical, and financial measures for the reconstruction of the economic and social life of the redeemed territories.

Concerning the existing government, an order of the day stated that the *Popolare* group could not support a ministry that showed itself incapable of guaranteeing the liberties of the "White" organizations. Miglioli proposed collaboration with the Socialists, but Meda opposed the suggestion. *Il Nuovo Trentino's* comment on the issue of collaboration was that "until the Socialists give up their attempt at an absolute mastery over the organization of classes, it is vain to hope for parliamentary collaboration between *Popolari* and Socialists."[32] At the end of the congress, a National Council composed of twenty-seven members was elected. The majority of those elected were of centrist orientation, and De Gasperi was one of these. He was also made a member of the Directory of the party, whose other members were Sturzo, Giuseppe Micheli, Alessandro Pennati, Giovanni Viola, Giovanni Uberti, and Gustavo Colonnetti.

In May the Nitti government fell when the *Popolari* withdrew their support. The King then offered the premiership to Meda, but the latter declined it on the ground that the party did not have a sufficiently strong basis in the country to enable it to assume the responsibility of government. After an attempt to form another Nitti government failed, Giolitti constituted a ministry. He agreed to combine the demands of the *Popolari* for agrarian reform and freedom for the Catholic schools with his own program for administrative and fiscal reform.

On July 6, 1920, De Gasperi and Conci had an interview with Giolitti in which the latter stated that as soon as the French ratified the Treaty of St. Germain he would introduce a bill for the formal annexation of Venezia Tridentina and Venezia Giulia. De Gasperi and Conci came away from the interview under the impression that the Giolitti government would advance the cause of Trentine autonomy.[33] They were destined to be disappointed: in August 1920 the Italian Parliament voted annexation, together with treaty ratification, but no grant of autonomy was made.

Meanwhile, Fascism had resumed its march in spite of its setback at the polls in 1919. By the early months of 1921 Fascists were attacking Socialist unions and cooperatives in North and Central Italy, on the pretext of saving the nation from a Socialist revolution. In the hope that the reaction against the Left would enable him to enlarge the center majority, Giolitti called for a new election. It was held under conditions of increasing Fascist violence, which Giolitti did little to abate. Having included Fascists in the "national bloc" of parliamentary candidates, hoping to tame and utilize them, he was not in a position to take more than defensive measures against them.

The strategy of Giolitti turned out to be a great error. The Socialist Party was weakened by the election, but not as much as Giolitti had expected. It gained 122 seats, as opposed to its previous 156; on the other hand, the Communist Party, an offshoot of the Socialist Party, gained 16 seats. The *Popolari* improved their position, gaining 107 seats. The national bloc captured a majority of the seats, but into the Chamber of Deputies 35 Fascists now entered; to these were joined 10 Nationalists. After the opening of the XXVI Legislature on June 11, 1921, Giolitti resigned, to be succeeded in July by Ivanoe Bonomi, who was to serve until the end of January 1922. The *Popolari* supported Bonomi, expecting to achieve under him at least a partial realization of their program.

Among the five *Popolari* elected by the Trentino in the 1921 elections was De Gasperi. He was elected president of the *Popolare* parliamentary group, but the real leader of the group was its secretary, the Lombard conservative Stefano Cavazzoni. De Gasperi made his first speech in the Italian Parliament on June 24, 1921. After expressing gratitude for the liberation of the Trentino, he asked for the restoration of the local autonomy of the former Austrian provinces. He also requested the continuation of those Austrian social institutions, laws, and customs which had been beneficial to the workers. Always a believer in direct language, he sought to illustrate the need to reform the Italian bureaucracy by pointing out that certain postal operations which had required only two hours under Austrian rule now required eight and a half hours under Italian rule. Whereas three employees had sufficed in the railroad ticket office in Trent, now twelve were needed.[34]

During the course of De Gasperi's first speech, Giuseppe Mingrino, a Socialist, had shouted: "At the Viennese Parliament, you voted for military expenditures against Italy." About a month later, Silvio Flor, another Socialist, made a similar charge, accusing De Gasperi of having bowed reverently before the flag of the Hapsburgs and of having maligned Cesare Battisti.[35] In the hope of ending charges of wartime subservience to the Hapsburgs, De Gasperi retorted: ". . . compared with other parties, we comported ourselves in the Austrian House in a manner that left no doubt, so that during the war, as well as during the Versailles negotiations, adversaries said that at all times we had desired the collapse of Austria and the reunion of the land with the Nation [Italy]."[36]

To the charge that he had voted in favor of military expenses, he pointed out that it was legitimate for Italian deputies in the Austrian Parliament to vote for military bills when Italy and Austria were both members of the Triple Alliance and when military collaboration between the two countries was within the realm of possibility. However, he himself had voted in the Austrian Parliament for a military bill only once, and then not for credits but for a reduction in the term of the military enlistment. During the war, he had always voted against military expenses.[37]

De Gasperi was not favorably impressed by the workings of the Italian Parliament. In Vienna, in spite of the babel of tongues, some respect for form prevailed; at Montecitorio, personal insults and verbal brickbats were freely exchanged. To intimates he once confided: "I thought I was in parliament. I was mistaken; I found myself in an equestrian circus."

The most important question to confront the Italian Parliament in 1921 was how to restore public order. From March 31 to May 31 the number of Fascist sections had climbed from 317 to 1,001, and the number of members from 80,476 to 187,098.[38] Violence had increased correspondingly, particularly in the Trentino.[39] Unfortunately the Chamber that had emerged from the elections of 1921 gave little indication that it comprehended the grave problems, such as unemployment, inflation, and the Fascist threat to the integrity of the State, that awaited legislative solution. Interrogations concerning Fascist violence always elicited the same response from the ministerial benches: the government was ready to condemn "all violence, whatever its origin." Of action, there was little.

During the session from June 11 to July 31, De Gasperi and his fellow *Popolari* succeeded in securing the passage of bills to reform the bureaucracy, modify the tax on wine, and provide some means of tackling the problem of unemployment. They failed, however, to secure approval of their program of agrarian reform. When parliamentary labors were resumed on November 24, 1921, the *Popolare* group obtained only recognition of the urgent necessity to discuss the bill on *latifundia*.[40]

In foreign policy the *Popolari* stood for the pacification of Europe as quickly as possible. Whether or not Bolshevik Russia should be recognized was a matter of considerable controversy in governmental circles. At the Naples Congress the establishment of normal relations with Soviet Russia was proposed. In parliament De Gasperi expressed himself as being in favor of the establishment of economic relations with the Soviet regime.[41] Formal diplomatic recognition would remain in abeyance.

During the four months that parliament was not in session, De Gasperi's most important political activities were a trip to Germany and participation in the third National Congress of the Popular Party. De Gasperi's German trip can be understood only in relation to the party's foreign policy. Broadly pacifist and internationalist, the party envisaged the formation of an International composed of all European parties of Christian Democratic inspiration as a means of achieving a world order based upon peace and justice.[42] In the late summer of 1921 De Gasperi, together with Sturzo, Stefano Jacini, Prince Rufo Ruffo della Scaletta, and a journalist, Francesco Bianco, went to Germany to study the new republican institutions and to ascertain whether or not there existed in the new Germany a mentality that would provide the psychological and spiritual bases for an international popularist understanding.[43]

De Gasperi was impressed and encouraged by what he saw during his German trip. A universalist spirit existed which made an *internazionale popolare* practical and desirable. He reached this conclusion after conversations with persons in every walk of life: the heads of the German Center Party, including Chancellor Karl Wirth, the representatives of industry, including the Krupp directors, labor leaders, heads of the Socialist Party, and representatives of the Church, including the Archbishops of Munich and Cologne and the Bishop of Ratisbon.

Among his hosts was Konrad Adenauer, mayor of Cologne, with whom he was to collaborate after the Second World War in the creation of a new Europe.

De Gasperi appears to have been particularly edified by the social attitudes and policies of the Center Party. In the Wirth coalition government, the minister of labor was a priest, Heinrich Brauns, who, according to De Gasperi, was promoting social legislation in a manner that elicited the admiration and cooperation of all parties. De Gasperi was also pleased by the fact that Catholics were behind the moves to inaugurate a more equitable social order and were supporting the social clauses of the Weimar constitution for that purpose.

Examining the collaboration between Centrists and Socialists, he pronounced it fruitful; it seemed to him that the Centrists had succeeded in bringing Socialists permanently into the mainstream of national politics. He characterized the end as "worthy of every effort." He asked the politicians of the Center Party many questions about this collaboration. He was assured by Wirth that Socialists were loyal and could be trusted to keep their word. De Gasperi did not conclude from the fact of Centrist-Socialist collaboration in Germany that a similar collaboration could take place immediately in Italy between the *Popolari* and the Socialists. In Italy the situation was markedly different, and the "lines of convergence" were missing. Nevertheless, De Gasperi was subsequently to make the effort to bring about such collaboration.

His German experiences and impressions were undoubtedly still vivid in his mind when he attended the third National Congress of the *Partito Popolare Italiano* at Venice from October 20 to 23, 1921.[44] This congress represents a definitive stage in the history of Popularism. As Bologna symbolizes the victory of aconfessionality and electoral intransigence, and Naples a dynamic openness with respect to the problems of national reconstruction, particularly in the field of agrarian reform, so Venice represents the response of the party to the crisis of the liberal State.

The political report was delivered by Mario Cingolani, a deputy who had been one of the founders of the party. Cingolani was preoccupied with answering the charge that the party, though participating in all ministries since its electoral victory in 1919, nevertheless, had failed to realize a single fundamental objective. He observed that the line of political action followed by the party during these years was determined not so much by its program as by a dual necessity: to reinvigorate the parliamentary institution, which had entered a critical period, and ward off the hostility of both the Democratic and Maximalist Socialist groups. Cingolani maintained that the party had achieved a measure of success insofar as it had forced other parties to clarify their positions. Regarding the Socialist Party, he expressed the hope that it would enter into responsible participation in government, in collaboration with the *Partito Popolare*.

Cingolani was followed by De Gasperi who discussed relations between the State and labor unions and between Socialism and *Popolarismo*. Influenced undoubtedly by what he had witnessed in Germany, he stated that organized economic groups would inevitably obtain political representation in the government. With regard to Socialism, De Gasperi affirmed that only two alternatives existed: either convert the Socialist masses to *Popolarismo* or win the Socialists "through the realism of the responsibilities of government." He personally believed in the possibility of the second alternative. He concluded his talk by asking the party to base all activities on the criteria of liberty and universal suffrage.

Giovanni Gronchi, the experienced labor leader, declared himself skeptical on the possibility of collaboration with the Socialists. He said he judged the example of an alliance between the Socialists and Centrists in Germany as inconclusive. On the other hand, he declared himself sympathetic to the idea of a labor party. Miglioli interrupted to express the opinion that the formation of a labor party was impossible. Concerning Socialist-*Popolare* collaboration, he stated that such cooperation had to take into account three great phenomena: the predominance of the landowners, the fact of Fascism, and parliamentary reactionism. He concluded his discourse by supporting a resolution introduced by Francesco Luigi Ferrari that banned all collaboration with the forces of the Right.

Another important theme at Venice was administrative decentralization, including the establishment of autonomous regions. The principal speaker on the subject was Luigi Sturzo, but De Gasperi also took up the cry for autonomy. He sponsored a resolution calling upon the government to restore to the new provinces their local autonomy through a reconstitution of the respective Diets.[45]

At the conclusion of the debates the principles that the party considered essential for collaboration with "responsible political groupings" were enumerated: (1) liberty and respect for the Christian conscience; (2) restoration of the national economy and finances; (3) recognition of labor organizations and of the equality of those supported by the *P.P.I.* with other organizations, without privileges for the

Socialist unions; (4) restoration of the authority and functions of the State (political freedom, action against factions, organic decentralization); and (5) a foreign policy capable of creating international ties based upon justice and solidarity with all nations.

Throughout 1922 opportunities arose to apply these principles. At the end of January the Bonomi government fell when the Fascists and the Giolittian Democrats withdrew their support, hoping thereby to bring Giolitti back to power. The *Popolari,* however, refused to accept Giolitti, distrusting his ability to oppose Fascist violence and illegality and recalling his ambiguous conduct toward Fascists in 1920-1921.[46] The King offered the premiership to Meda, but fearful as always of responsibility, the latter declined it without so much as consulting De Gasperi or Sturzo. In February Luigi Facta, one of Giolitti's lieutenants, "an honest character, but limited, and without directing aptitude,"[47] formed a government. More out of weariness brought on by the prolonged crisis than out of confidence in his ability, De Gasperi and Cavazzoni accepted Facta.

De Gasperi was at pains to show the divergence between the *Popolari* on the one side and the Nationalist and Fascist Right on the other. *Il Nuovo Trentino* stated:

> As opposed to this Right, the *Popolari* are a party of the Left. In the politics of everyday, they want common law protected, and they do not admit the legitimacy of reprisals and punitive expeditions. . . . They recognize the value of labor unions and of the cooperative movement, and in fact cooperate in their greater development. The Fascists instead too often lend themselves to the support of the proprietary class. . . .
>
> Finally the Right, blind worshiper of the unitary State, is opposed to all political and administrative decentralization and renounces all local autonomy, considering it destructive to the national framework. Can we, proponents of decentralization, of autonomy . . . orient ourselves toward the Right?[48]

In another issue the so-called conservatives were designated as "subversives" who were contemptuous of law and of the State.[49]

One of De Gasperi's most effective speeches in parliament during this period was directed against the Right:

> . . . we must declare that the formula concerning the reintegration of the "national function of the State," accompanied by interpretive utterances given in these days, which even go so far as to question parliament and to desire a dictatorship, which characterize our efforts for

social reform as "disastrous and costly reformist experiments...," this formula with such interpretive comments in both word and deed is one which we cannot accept.[50]

De Gasperi considered the "tacit or admitted complicity" of the Liberal Party in Fascist deeds as a crime which could not be judged severely enough. As for the Socialist Party, it was, with its policy of *nullismo*, destroying its own life as effectively as Fascism was seeking to do. He was unable to comprehend why the Socialists neither made revolution nor accepted the responsibility of government.[51]

As Italy approached the Fascist era, De Gasperi decided to give up his bachelorhood (he was now forty-one) and marry Francesca Romani, who was to be his greatest comfort in the difficult years that were ahead. Born in the Valsugana in 1894, Francesca was one of eight children. Her father, a business man in Borgo Valsugana, died while the children were still young, and upon the oldest son, Pietro, devolved the responsibility of caring for the younger children. De Gasperi first met Pietro around the turn of the century, when both were students in Vienna. The friendship continued beyond student days, and in 1914, when he visited Pietro in his home in Borgo Valsugana, he met Francesca for the first time. It was a meeting which Francesca did not forget, if only because De Gasperi's face was swollen from a toothache and was covered with a handkerchief.

After De Gasperi became involved in Italian politics, he hesitated to court her. In the summer of 1921, he wrote to her: "Do you think that I shall ever have a respite from this public service that sometimes seems to be my cross and is instead my mission or destiny? And that a man in my position has the right to ask another person to adapt herself to this tyranny that will continue to impose itself inexorably?" But in his mind human and divine love were indissolubly united, and he asked Francesca to be his companion in following Christ: "I am not a bigot and perhaps I am not even as religious as I shoud be, but the personality of the living Christ pulls me, enslaves me, and comforts me as though I were a child. Come, I want you with me, to be drawn to that same attraction, as though toward an abyss of light."[52] He found it difficult to write words of love at the same time that he was being distracted by parliamentary battles such as had never before taken place in the Italian Parliament; nevertheless, he succeeded in persuading Francesca to "adapt herself" to his way of life. On June 14, 1922, the marriage was performed in the parish church in Borgo Valsugana. There followed a three-week honeymoon that took them to Venice, Rome, Naples,

Capri, and Sicily. After their return they settled down in Trent on Via Torre Verde, in the same building that housed the printing press of *Il Nuovo Trentino*. De Gasperi did not resume his seat in Montecitorio until July 5. He could afford a three-week absence from parliament, for Cavazzoni remained the real leader of the *Popolari*. Unfortunately, Cavazzoni had philofascist leanings.

De Gasperi's entry into married life coincided with the crisis period of Italian parliamentary democracy. What happened in October 1922 was largely determined by the events of the summer of 1922, and these must now be briefly reviewed.[53] In mid-July Miglioli gave in parliament a highly dramatic account of Fascist outrages in his native Cremona.[54] The speech touched off a demonstration among the *Popolari* and Socialist deputies and the Facta ministry toppled.[55] A ministerial crisis ensued which lasted until the early days of August.

Meanwhile, a *Popolare*-Socialist entente seemed to be within the realm of the possible, much to the disgust and apprehension of Mussolini. Within the Socialist Party the trend among the reformist element, led by such men as Filippo Turati and Claudio Treves, was in favor of collaboration with the *Popolari*. On June 2 the Socialist parliamentary group approved by a strong majority a resolution favorable to collaboration. The Maximalists, however, loudly objected to cooperation with bourgeois parties to save a bourgeois state. On June 14 the National Council of the Socialist Party disavowed the resolution of the parliamentary group, condemning every form of collaboration. Nevertheless, during this month and in July Sturzo had talks with Turati, Treves, Giuseppe Modigliani and Giacomo Matteotti in the Soderini Palace. Since any entente had to be in accordance with the principles set down at Venice, Sturzo, as well as a majority of the *Popolari*, was skeptical concerning collaboration.[56]

When the Facta government fell, Sturzo was annoyed with the *Popolari* deputies for their role in bringing down the government; he did not think that the events of Cremona warranted a ministerial crisis. After attempts to form ministries under Orlando and Bonomi failed, the King turned to Meda. Although Sturzo invited him to "sacrifice himself," the cautious *Popolare* declined, alleging that an official position would interfere with his legal practice! A more probable reason for the refusal is that Meda realized that only force could re-establish law and order, and he had no stomach for such a policy.

Facta was called once again to form a government, thereby becoming the "Romulus Augustulus" of Italian democracy. Meanwhile the Socialists were playing into the hands of the Fascists by engaging in a general strike, which Sturzo termed "morally a crime, politically an error."[57] The Fascists were thus afforded an excuse to expand their military operations, which were directed as much against "White" unions and *Popolari* headquarters as against the Socialists. Between September 30 and October 2, Fascists occupied the headquarters of the Civil Commissariat in Trent; on October 5, Credaro submitted his resignation.[58]

No *Popolare*-Socialist coalition emerged. The ideological differences were too great to be bridged, and the general strike alienated whatever support the reformist Socialist element might have had among the *Popolari*.[59] The possibility of an accord had never been popular among some elements in the party; on September 18, eight *Popolari* senators sent a letter to Sturzo to denounce attempts on the part of the *Popolari* deputies to seek an accord with the Socialists. Within the ranks of the Socialists, the Maximalists were equally adamant against collaboration.

On October 27, as alarming reports reached Rome of Fascist concentrations in many provincial cities, the Facta cabinet convened and decided to resign. On the 28th Facta sought, not too insistently, to have the King proclaim a state of siege, but Victor Emmanuel refused, not wishing to provoke a civil war. Furthermore, he had no confidence in Facta's ability to handle the situation. The following day, a royal telephone call summoned Mussolini from Milan.

On the morning of October 28 De Gasperi was crossing the Roman countryside in a train. At Orvieto, in front of the Cathedral, he purchased a postcard on which he wrote: "Seeking in the works of past greatness a comfort for the anxious waiting of today."[60] Twelve days earlier, his paper had stated that Fascists had to be taken into the government if civil war were to be averted.[61]

Christian Democracy had not been strong and experienced enough to prevent a Fascist victory, but Einaudi's assessment of it is valid: "On balance, the contribution of Christian Democracy to political life from 1919 to 1922 was a positive one, for it stressed the need of renovation and of modernization in the life of the country, which as later events will prove, were long overdue."[62] The work of *aggiornamento* was to be resumed after 1945, under the able direction of Alcide De Gasperi.

CHAPTER V

DE GASPERI AND THE FASCIST REGIME 1922-1929[*]

THE FIRST GOVERNMENT FORMED BY MUSSOLINI WAS A coalition, including not only Fascists but also Nationalists, Liberals, and *Popolari*. The six *Popolari* chosen by Mussolini were Vincenzo Tangorra as minister of the treasury, Stefano Cavazzoni as minister of labor, Ernesto Vassallo as undersecretary of foreign affairs, Fulvio Milani as undersecretary of justice, Giovanni Gronchi as undersecretary of industry and commerce, and Umberto Merlin as undersecretary for the redeemed territories. Recognizing the need for men experienced in public affairs, Mussolini was willing to accept the collaboration of non-Fascists in this initial stage.

A dilemma had confronted the non-Fascists: if they worked with Mussolini, they might become responsible for policies inconsistent with their own; if they refused collaboration, they might arouse the anger of the blackshirted chieftain, thus provoking an intensification of Fascist violence. At the villa of Prince Rufo Ruffo della Scaletta, the leading *Popolari* had convened during the days of crisis to decide whether or not to participate in Mussolini's government.[1] Don Luigi Sturzo opposed any understanding with the Fascists, but Cavazzoni and De Gasperi had decided to sanction participation. A communique issued October 30, 1922, explained the action taken by the party leaders:

[*] Portions of this chapter appeared in my article "Alcide De Gasperi and the Fascist Regime, 1924-1929," *The Review of Politics*, XXVI (1964), 518-530.

> Given the extraordinary circumstances in which it was necessary to reach a decision, it was not possible to consult the group in the regular manner, nor to bring together the party directory. The members of the directory present in Rome authorized the participation of the designated in the new cabinet, considering it essential today to make every effort to achieve a rapid restoration of legality. Furthermore the new government intends to maintain the system of proportional representation, except for improvements in form suggested by experience, and it proposes to put an end to all manifestations in national life that cannot be reconciled with legality and constitutionalism. Such assurances result from the precise and loyal declarations (made to the Honorable Cavazzoni and De Gasperi) that Mussolini has had occasion to make, adding that as far as proportional representation was concerned, the Fascist party had never taken any decision contrary to it.[2]

In spite of the optimistic tone of the communique, the party was merely acquiescing in a *fait accompli*; the party was, as De Gasperi later admitted at the party congress at Turin, in a state of "passive resignation."[3] It is not likely that he personally felt the Fascist Revolution could be tamed, that it could be brought to the path of constitutionalism.[4] From the very outset he refused to regard the March on Rome as justifiable. *Il Nuovo Trentino* editorialized: "Revolution is made or it is not made; it is explained or it is not explained; but it is not justified." As De Gasperi saw it, the formal epilogue of the revolution was the entry of Mussolini into the government; the substantial epilogue would be achieved only when squadrism came to an end.[5]

In a letter to the *Popolari* who had entered the government, De Gasperi outlined the purpose of collaboration: ". . . we trust that you will succeed in accomplishing a renovating and durable work, inspired by our social and financial program, which as never before has demonstrated itself so much in consonance with the exigencies of the situation and the interests of the country."[6]

Two weeks later, De Gasperi acquired ample grounds for doubting whether the *Popolari* could accomplish a "renovating and durable work" as part of Mussolini's government. On November 16, 1922, in a speech in parliament, Mussolini affirmed that "revolution has its rights" and he characterized the Chamber of Deputies as "dull and grey."[7] Rising up the following day to answer Mussolini, De Gasperi deplored the crude and revolutionary language employed by the Premier, and he defended the work of the Chamber of Deputies. He pointed out that the crisis had developed in part from the excessive concentration of power in the central organs of the government.

Against the centralizing state, the *Partito Popolare* had proceeded with proposals of legal reform. The Fascist Party, on the other hand, had attained its objectives through direct and violent action, using methods that were contrary to the ethical and political criteria of the *Popolari*. De Gasperi concluded his speech with a summary of the program of his party: political amnesty, administrative decentralization, autonomy for the new provinces, a strengthening of the labor unions, and a defense of liberty and legality.[8]

The dangers of collaboration were sharply delineated by Don Luigi Sturzo in a speech given in Turin on December 20, 1922. It was the Secretary's first public pronouncement since the March on Rome, and consequently it attracted widespread attention. Don Sturzo warned that the party could lose its autonomy and ideological consistency in an alliance with Mussolini. The next four months saw a heated intraparty controversy concerning collaboration. The Right wing of the party, led by Stefano Cavazzoni, had complete faith in Fascism and in Mussolini. If Fascism had not accomplished all the good that had been immediately expected, it was because of the difficult times through which the country was passing. The party should make no demands on Mussolini; it should pose no conditions for collaboration; rather it should suspend its own life and its own program in order to advance Mussolini's program of national reconstruction. The Left wing, led by such men as Francesco L. Ferrari and Gerolamo and Luigi Meda, as well as Guido Miglioli, took the position that Fascism was a phenomenon which did not correspond in any manner to the political and ethical principles of *Popolarismo* and hence it favored the end of collaboration.

The party secretariat may be said to represent a Center position. While personally disliking collaboration, Sturzo did not want a sudden break with Mussolini for fear of provoking a crisis within the party; rather he wished to demonstrate that an accord with Fascism was not possible because Fascism did not respect the norms regulating collaboration.[9] He did not regard collaboration as an evil *per se*. At a party meeting in Rome on March 23, 1923, he said that just as the party had cooperated with Liberals and Masons in the past, so could it cooperate with the Fascist Government for the purpose of solving national problems. "Today, to deny collaboration to the government would be absurd, since it would lead the country to civil war. Since the *Partito Popolare* has always subordinated its desires to the collective wellbeing, there is no road other than that of sustaining the government, always, however, maintaining intact the physiognomy of our party."[10]

Meanwhile the Fascists worked incessantly to provoke divisions in the *Partito Popolare*. Two days before the opening of the fourth National Congress at Turin in April 1923, the Right-wingers or the so-called Clerico-Fascists voted for an order of the day which demanded the expulsion of the Left from the party.[11] When the congress convened on April 12, 1923, it was obvious that collaboration was the chief issue. As an exponent of the Center position, De Gasperi stressed that *Popolare* collaboration in Mussolini's government was a "collaboration of emergency, a collaboration without collaborationism," undertaken as the lesser of two evils and predicated upon the preservation of the ideological autonomy of the party. He defined "collaborationism" as "a tendency," and "collaboration" as a "state of fact." He defended the conditional support given to Mussolini's government, affirming that the *Popolari* had joined in the vote of giving Mussolini full powers to reorganize the financial and bureaucratic system only in return for Mussolini's pledge to respect law and to resist illegality, even Fascist illegality. At the same time De Gasperi reiterated the complete ideological autonomy of the party, and he denounced, partly to alert the Right wing, the squadrist attacks against the "White" organizations. He presented to the congress the following order of the day, which was approved by a large majority:

> The fourth National Congress of the *Partito Popolare Italiano*, acquiescing in De Gasperi's report and the directives of the central organs of the party: (1) *approves* of the participation of the *Popolari* in the present ministry as an appreciable way to the insertion of the Fascist Revolution in the constitution, and intending that their presence can and should efficaciously cooperate in effecting the country's political and financial restoration, the rebirth of moral and religious values, social pacification, and national discipline . . .; (2) *obligates* the parliamentary group to undertake the most intense and valid defense of proportional representation and directs the National Council to be vigilant so that the party, independently of the electoral system, maintains intact its autonomy and its political electoral figure clearly distinct from every confusion and compromise with other parties.[12]

From this congress on, De Gasperi acquired greater control over the *Popolare* parliamentary group. Mussolini was angered by the order of the day and demanded the resignation of the *Popolari* from the government, all the more so because although the Right wing of the party, led by such men as Egilberto Martire and Livio Tovini, was expanding and moving in the direction of insertion in the Fascist Party, local branches of the *Partito Popolare* were engaging in anti-Fascist activities.[13]

Against the anti-Fascists, repression or organized violence was freely utilized, extending even to the centers of Catholic Action and to the clergy. In August 1923 the local authorities of the Trentino forbade the holding of the twenty-fourth annual congress of the *AUCT*, in spite of a personal appeal made to Mussolini by De Gasperi and his brother-in-law, Pietro Romani, deputy from the Valsugana. The pretext was that Valsugana Fascists intended to meet at the same time and place as the Catholic association, and consequently there was danger of a disturbance of the public order.[14]

Although the Church protested when Fascists committed acts of violence against Catholic institutions or clergy, its policy was to dissociate itself from the *Partito Popolare*. The elevation to the papacy of Pius XI had been a fact of tremendous import for the *Partito Popolare*. As Jacini points out, the socio-economic formation of Pius XI was typically Lombard and conservative. As a Lombard, he had during his youth witnessed the conflict between Milanese intransigents and Catholic Liberals, and he desired above all a conciliation, on the politico-juridical terrain, with the Italian State. An autonomous party, composed of Catholics, might hinder such a reconciliation. As a conservative, he felt a certain diffidence toward the social and economic goals of Christian Democracy, of which the *Partito Popolare* was in part at least the political expression. Furthermore, he had a positive horror of Bolshevism, having had firsthand experience with it in Warsaw, and thus he had an instinctive sympathy toward those forces that seemed most energetically opposed to Bolshevism.[15] As for Italian bishops, though they were appalled by squadrist violence against the Church, they were, generally speaking, sympathetic to Fascist appeals for unity against the Left.

Since his priestly character was incompatible with politics, it was only a matter of time before Don Sturzo would have to retire from the party leadership. On June 25, 1923, *Il Corriere d'Italia*, a "Trust" organ published an interview with Monsignor Enrico Pucci, already an intermediary between Fascism and the Vatican, in which Pucci implied that Sturzo was embarrassing the Church.[16] On July 10 Sturzo resigned as political secretary, motivated also by veiled threats of Fascist reprisals against the Church. He remained active in the party until October 1924, when he was forced to go into exile. From July 1923 to May 1924 the party secretaryship was replaced by a triumvirate composed of Giulio Rodinò as president, Giovanni Gronchi as secretary and Giuseppe Spataro as vice-secretary.

Simultaneously with the resignation of Don Sturzo, the Chamber of Deputies was discussing the Acerbo project for electoral reform. As originally drafted, the measure would have assigned to the party that received a plurality of votes in a parliamentary election an absolute majority in the Chamber. De Gasperi had characterized the project as "indigestible,"[17] but aware of the schism within his own party and fearful of defections, he attempted a compromise, informing Mussolini that the party would accept the electoral reform if the government amended the bill so that at least 40 per cent of the vote would have to be won by a party before it could claim an absolute majority of the seats in the Chamber. Mussolini rejected the proposal, cognizant of the fact that he enjoyed the upper hand. The Liberals were favorable to the Acerbo project, while Amendola and Bonomi were averse to provoking a ministerial crisis. Meanwhile the Fascist press threatened a resumption of revolution if the Chamber rejected the electoral reform. On July 12 Meda weakened De Gasperi's position by sending an open letter to his colleagues, asking them not to assume responsibility for the political situation that would be created by rejection of the project.

On July 15, 1923, at the conclusion of the general discussion, Mussolini threatened dissolution of the Chamber in the event of a negative vote. Seeking to widen the schism within the *Partito Popolare*, he requested the collaboration of the opposition. De Gasperi then convoked the *Popolari* deputies, who voted to abstain from voting when the bill had its first reading. The decision was taken by the group after a lively discussion, ending with a vote of 41 for abstention and 39 against abstention. De Gasperi's vote was among the 39 opposing abstention, for he wished to vote against the measure.[18]

In the Chamber De Gasperi announced the decision of the group: they would abstain from voting on the first reading but would retain full liberty to vote against it later if amendments were not introduced. To De Gasperi's surprise, Cavazzoni suddenly announced that he and eight other *Popolari* favored passage of the bill.[19] These were the votes that Mussolini required for passage. As finally enacted, the bill provided that the party receiving 25 per cent of the total vote was entitled to no less than two thirds of the seats in the Chamber. The remaining third would be distributed among the other parties according to the principle of proportional representation.

De Gasperi obtained the expulsion of the *Popolari* deputies who had broken party disicipline and had voted for the Acerbo proposal. The process of separation of the Right wing from the party was now complete. In 1924 these Rightist deputies, together with some *Popolari* senators, formed the *Centro Nazionale Italiano* and supported the Fascist electoral list in the parliamentary elections of that year. Except for such persons as Meda, Giorgio Montini, and Giovan Maria Longinotti, the pro-Fascist *Popolari* were the old Clerico-Moderates. In general the Lombard financial circles, the Bank of Rome, and the "Trust" chain assumed pro-Fascist positions.[20] Giuseppe Donati, the editor of the party organ, *Il Popolo,* made a scathing attack upon the pro-Fascist *Popolari:*

> These gentlemen—whether they are acting consciously or unconsciously, whether in good faith or bad faith, does not interest us—defend Fascism and the Fascist Government principally because it is a system of political reaction (they will probably call it *national discipline*) that has important repercussions of a socio-economic character. . . . Here religious principles form the banner for the social and economic contraband with which the boat is loaded. This arouses our indignation.[21]

Because of a fundamental divergence of principles and tactics, it was not possible for the three constitutional parties, i.e., the *Popolare,* the Amendola Democratic, and the Di Cesarò Social Democratic, to come to an understanding with the four nonconstitutional parties, the Unitary Socialist, the Maximalist Socialist, the Communist, and the Republican. The directory of the *Partito Popolare* announced that the party would participate in the election with its own national list in order to contribute to "a restoration of normal political and constitutional life." The battle against the centralizing and pantheistic state would continue.[22]

In spite of the fact that the odds were against him, De Gasperi conducted a vigorous campaign. To the Fascist charge that the party defended Socialism, De Gasperi replied that he had combated both theoretical and practical Socialism for too many years for anyone to give credence to the accusation. He insisted, however, that under certain circumstances cooperation with Socialists was legitimate. When the Trentino was under Austrian rule, Socialists, Liberals and *Popolari* had fought together for the autonomy of the region. He added that many who were now wearing the Fascist insignia had once been Socialists.[23] In a speech at Verona at the beginning of March, De Gasperi asserted that the prerequisite for *Popolare* collaboration in government was the prevalence of liberty. This involved the end of squadrism and the maintenance of proportional representation, but Mussolini had so far failed to keep his promises on these two points. In the chamber elected as a result of the new elections, the *Popolari* would act as a Center party, opposing the Fascist dictatorship on the one side and every suggestion of a proletarian dictatorship on the other. The program of his party would be summed up as "neither reaction nor Socialism, but a system of liberty and administrative justice."[24]

In a speech in Venice at the end of March, De Gasperi denied that the Catholics of the *Partito Popolare* were subversive. The motto of the party was "libertas" and this went beyond the immediate vindication of political liberties: it signified the liberation of citizens, of associations, of communes, and of local units from the excessive centralization of the State.[25] In Trent De Gasperi pointed out that the Fascists who were now loudly proclaiming their Catholicism were the very ones who had declared war on religion in 1919.[26] Here on De Gasperi's home territory, the Fascists were conducting a strong campaign, bringing in an impressive array of orators. According to De Gasperi's newspaper, each day automobiles arrived with an "indefinite number of agitators."[27]

The result of the elections, held April 6, 1924, was to give four and a half million votes to the Fascists and three million to the Opposition parties. The *Popolari* elected only thirty-nine deputies, but in view of the Fascist campaign tactics, it is perhaps surprising that they succeeded in electing as many as they did. De Gasperi was elected from Venezia Tridentina.[28]

In May 1924 the National Council of the party elected De Gasperi political secretary, thus uniting in one mandate the presidency of the parliamentary group and the party secretaryship. Giuseppe Spataro became vice secretary. At the time of his election De Gasperi was still residing in Trent, but upon being notified of his election, he came to Rome and took an apartment on Via Ripetta, close to the party headquarters at No. 102. Under De Gasperi the party continued along the line of moderate legal opposition. He may be said to personify the center, while Giorgio Montini of Brescia represented the conservative wing, and Giovanni Gronchi the Left wing. The influence of Sturzo remained strong, however, and De Gasperi had all to do to maintain his independence in the face of the multiple and methodical interference of Don Sturzo, even after the latter went into exile.[29]

Fascist violence did not abate after the April electoral victory. Catholic clubs and "White" cooperatives continued to be sacked and destroyed, and the editorial presses of many Catholic papers were invaded. Squadrist attacks were particularly devastating in northern Italy, and the Trentino witnessed more than one scene of Fascist outrage. The atmosphere in this area had been hostile to Fascism from the outset, and in May 1924 the Ministry of the Interior had considered it necessary to seek information concerning the "grave condition of Trentine Fascism."[30] According to the report of Giuseppe Guadagnini, prefect of Trent, Fascism had failed to make headway in the Trentino for two reasons: (1) Fascism appeared as a foreign phenomenon, having been brought into the region by persons, "not always the best," from the older provinces of Italy, and (2) the relative absence of subversives in the Trentino made the people unmindful of the need for Fascist rule.[31] In other reports from the local authorities, De Gasperi's paper was characterized as an "enemy of Fascism," and the Ministry of the Interior was requested to send funds immediately in order to keep the Fascist paper *Brennero* in circulation and thus counteract the influence of *Il Nuovo Trentino*.[32]

The most serious act of violence in the Trentino took place on May 31, 1924. That night, at about ten o'clock, the village of Sopramonte was invaded by about thirty Fascists, armed with revolvers and clubs. Going from door to door, the armed thugs beat up villagers and spread terror. On June 2 De Gasperi arrived to console the wounded and to conduct a personal investigation into the cause of the attack. He discovered that the invasion had taken place in retaliation against the town's disarming of Fascists who had arrived in Sopramonte with cudgels on May 25.[33] In the Chamber of Deputies on June 7 and 12 De Gasperi protested against the Fascist attack on Sopramonte, demanding assurances that such an incident would not be repeated. Finzi, the undersecretary of state for the interior, replied that the "brawl" had resulted from the refusal of some "subversives" in Sopramonte to permit the establishment of a Fascist Party section.[34]

If the Sopramonte incident aroused the indignation of the anti-Fascist deputies, the ensuing Matteotti affair shocked the conscience of the entire nation. Giacomo Matteotti, secretary of Filippo Turati's Unitary Socialist Party, had delivered in the Chamber on May 30, 1924, a strong attack on the newly elected Fascist majority, giving specific instances in which Blackshirts had used physical violence to influence the vote. The speech had aroused angry retorts both in parliament and in the Fascist press, and suggestions of physical reprisals had not been absent. On June 10 Fascist toughs led by Amerigo Dumini, an experienced *squadrista*, kidnapped Matteotti near his home along the Tiber River, stabbed him in a car, and then left his body half-buried in a grove fourteen miles from the capital. The mutilated corpse was not found until several weeks later, but as soon as the forcible capture of Matteotti became known, the worse was expected.[35]

For the first time since forming his government Mussolini feared for his political power, so great was the revulsion produced by the incident.[36] Although he promised punishment for the culprits, many members of the lower house were not impressed, and on June 27 about 150 *Popolari*, Republicans, Socialists, and Constitutional Democrats withdrew from the parliamentary chamber and retired to another auditorium of Palazzo Montecitorio. Here the anti-Fascist bloc heard a speech by Turati, commemorating Matteotti. Because of Turati's reference to the stand of Gaius Gracchus and the plebs around the Temple of Diana on the Aventine Hill, the withdrawal of the bloc from parliament became known as the Aventine Secession.[37] De Gasperi was in full accord with the secession, which was both a moral protest and an attempt to oust Mussolini by provoking a government crisis. In April 1925 he explained to a meeting of the Tiber section of the party that the *Popolari* had retired to the Aventine and had adhered to the Opposition bloc only when they recognized the futility of parliamentary action, and when, moreover, the antithesis between their program and that of the dominant party was too acute to be ignored.[38] Meanwhile, Giolitti, Salandra, and other former members of the government were either silent or continued to give Mussolini their support.

On July 1, 1924, Donati's *Il Popolo* published an interview with Turati in which the Milanese deputy, taking advantage of the anti-Fascist solidarity created by the Aventine Secession, called upon the *Partito Popolare* and the Unitary Socialist Party to take the same path, each party, however, retaining its own distinctive characteristics and program.[39] Through the columns of his newspaper De Gasperi announced the readiness of the *Partito Popolare* to cooperate with other Opposition parties as a consequence of the Matteotti crime. He went on to say that the absence of a real coalition of the Opposition parties did not preclude the possibility of *Popolare* participation in a ministry in which there were also Socialists. In other countries, such as Belgium, Germany, and Poland, Catholics would have been lacking in their civic duty if they had failed to take part in ministries which included Socialists.[40]

On July 16, in a discourse in Rome to the provincial party secretaries who had been especially convoked for the purpose of discussing relations with the Opposition parties, De Gasperi said: "The gradual process of clarification with respect to Socialism which has come in the postwar years in all the countries of Europe must be sought and favored even in Italy, as an important element in politico-social normalization."[41] As a consequence of his speech, which was delivered in his usual dry, concise manner of speaking, the assembly adopted a resolution which sanctioned both the principle of the political autonomy of the party and the possibility of establishing closer tactical relations with the Socialists.[42]

A *Popolare*-Socialist union, proposed by De Gasperi and Turati as an alternative to Fascism, did not evoke a sympathetic response in the Church. The influential Jesuit review, *Civiltà cattolica*, was sharply critical of the proposed collaboration, which was termed as "neither convenient, nor opportune, nor licit." The Italian situation, the review stated, was not comparable to that of other countries. In Austria and Germany the Catholics either found the Socialists in power or the arbiters of power. To save their nation from worse ills, Catholics joined governments that had already been constituted. The *Partito Popolare* was founded to effect a Christian restoration of society, and such an objective could not be achieved in union with a party that opposed the social and religious order.[43]

Pope Pius XI was similarly disturbed by a party that claimed to be of Christian inspiration but was willing to consider an alliance with Socialists. In a statement to university students on September 8, 1924, the Pope made no secret of his aversion for such an alliance:

> The collaboration of Catholics with Socialists in other countries is also cited; but here there is confusion, due to insufficient experience, between two totally different sets of circumstances. Apart from the differences in environment, and in historical, political and religious conditions, it is one thing to find oneself face to face with a party that has already attained power, and it is another thing to open the way to provide the possibility for that party to arrive at power; the matter is essentially different.
>
> It is truly painful to the heart of the Holy Father to see good children and good Catholics divided and fighting each other. Why, in the name of Catholic interests, oblige others or hold oneself obliged to adhere to a quarter where nonconfessionalism is made a program, which in itself might lead to ignoring even the Catholic confession itself.[44]

Following his open expression of disapproval of the strategy of the *Partito Popolare*, the Pope dispatched a circular to all bishops, urging them to instruct their clergy to remain outside of all political parties and to refrain from contributing to party newspapers. Although the ban applied to all political parties, the circular was interpreted as being directed against the *Partito Popolare*.[45] Apparently, the Pope did not recognize the right of the party to be autonomous and nonconfessional.

Though De Gasperi considered the party autonomous and nonconfessional, his loyalty to Rome was so deeply ingrained that he could not bring himself to defy the Pope, particularly in view of the fact that

Pius XI had made the matter quasi-moral. After September 1924 De Gasperi no longer pursued the goal of a *Popolare*-Socialist coalition. Very different was to be his reaction thirty years later (1952), when the Vatican favored a coalition between Christian Democrats and all nonleftist parties, including the Neo-Fascists, in order to block a Communist victory in local elections. A more experienced and self-assured De Gasperi then defied church intervention.

Within a month of Pius XI's address to the university students, Don Sturzo was invited to leave Italy by Cardinal Gasparri, who provided him with a Vatican passport. Sturzo left Italy for London on October 25, 1924, and thus became in effect the first of the great anti-Fascist leaders to leave the country. Yet De Gasperi was still optimistic. Speaking to a Trentine party meeting on October 15, he said that the primary obligation of the *Popolari* was to uphold the constitutional system by exercising its rights as an Opposition party. In parliamentary as in real wars, the party that wins is the party that shows the most resistance.[46] On November 2, 1924, ten days before the scheduled reopening of parliament, De Gasperi took part in a meeting of the Aventines in Room B of Montecitorio. Together with about a hundred deputies, he announced that he would not take part in parliament as long as the situation denounced on June 27 perdured.[47]

It was at this time that the Fascist press launched a determined attack upon the party and its leader. Alleging a Socialist-*Popolare* pact, *Il Popolo d'Italia*, edited by Arnaldo Mussolini, Mussolini's brother and journalistic mouthpiece, sneered:

> The Socialist-*Popolare* alliance which in spite of papal disapproval maintains its pact is the culmination of absurdity. Look among all the exhibits of mythology and you find nothing that surpasses the horror and grotesqueness of a similar union. And how classify differently the attempt to unite in the sands of compromise the Gospel and the *Social Contract*, Canon Law and historical materialism, Catholic dogma and free thought? The trap, concealed in this compromise, is dangerous. The Socialist-*Popolare* alliance is too clearly of a Masonic nature.[48]

Beginning October 24 and continuing for the next few months, De Gasperi became the chief target for the attacks of *Il Popolo d'Italia*. The fact that he had been born in the Trentino became a matter of reproach, and an old accusation, that of being *austriacante*, was revived: "During the war, while Cesare Battisti was on the Italian front fighting against Austria, and while the real head of the Catholic people of the Trentino was persecuted by Austria and relegated to a concentration camp, De Gasperi enjoyed the comfortable position of Austrian deputy, neither persecuted nor suspected."[49] Subsequent issues alleged that De Gasperi had done nothing to alleviate the sufferings of the interned, that he had done nothing to prevent Italians from being sent to the front in Galicia (as though such had been within his power). That he himself was not conscripted was, according to *Il Popolo d'Italia*, proof that he was a trusted agent of the Hapsburg government.[50] The November 22 issue pontificated: "The Honorable De Gasperi has truly all the characteristics of an Austrian politician, or better still, a Hapsburg politician: mediocre intelligence, second-hand culture, but a vast and subtle cunning."[51] Typical headings for the articles against De Gasperi were: "With Austria Always, with Others, Never," "De Gasperi the Austrian," and "The Austrian Government Trusted in De Gasperi."[52]

Through his newspaper and through testimonials of friends De Gasperi endeavored to refute the charges of being *austriacante*.[53] He had his trusted friend and party colleague, Igino Giordani, publish a pamphlet, *La verità storica e una campagna di denigrazione*, containing documents in refutation of the charges brought against him.[54] According to Prefect Guadagnini, the publication passed almost unnoticed.[55]

By the beginning of January it was obvious to the anti-Fascist parties that the struggle against Fascism had entered its final phase. On January 8, 1925, the Aventine deputies issued a manifesto declaring that:

> The ultimate phase of the conflict between Fascist domination and the country has begun. The constitutional and normalizing mask has fallen off. The government tramples upon the fundamental laws of the State. . . .
> The Aventine is neither sedition nor conspiracy; it is a resolute, irrepressible protest of the representatives of the people, who have come together from diverse parties after the most atrocious crime of the regime.[56]

Late in January, when the National Council of the *Partito Popolare* convened to discuss relations with the other parties, it voted in favor of maintaining the understanding.[57] But by spring, it was clear that the Aventine's political strategy, i.e., the provocation of a ministerial crisis that would topple Mussolini, had failed. The nation, considered as a whole, was indifferent to the Aventine Secession. De Gasperi warned in vain: "The Aventine dies, if not today, then tomorrow, but with it dies also Montecitorio."[58] If the Aventine failed, it was partly, as Piero Gobetti, the "Liberal revolutionary," asserted, because it had no real leader. The situation was static, and the Aventine was the "Dreyfus case of the Italians."[59]

An appeal of the anti-Fascist leaders to the Crown proved fruitless.

On the twenty-fifth anniversary of the accession of Victor Emmanuel III and on the same day as the anniversary of the Statute of 1848, the Opposition sent to the King an address of homage and good will, reminding him of his constitutional oath and of Italy's liberal past. The papers which published this address were confiscated, and when *Il Corriere della Sera, La Stampa, Il Giornale d'Italia,* and twenty-five other dailies sent him a petition protesting against the systematic violation of freedom of the press, the King merely informed them, through his adjutant general, that their memorandum had been transmitted to the premier. However, he agreed to receive the heads of the Opposition at the Quirinal on June 11, 1925. Amendola, Di Cesarò, and De Gasperi endeavored to convey the gravity of the parliamentary situation, and although Victor Emmanuel listened carefully, he failed to give any indication that he had been persuaded by their arguments. Exchanging impressions later on, the three men were convinced that nothing was to be gained in that quarter.[60]

A few days later, from June 28-30, 1925, the *Partito Popolare* convened in Rome to hold its fifth and, as it turned out, its last National Congress. More than five hundred delegates crowded into the hall on Via Monte della Farina. On the stage were a crucifix and the Italian flag; the president's box was adorned with a portrait of Don Luigi Sturzo and a huge bouquet of white carnations. Tremendous applause greeted the entry of the heads of the party: De Gasperi, Gronchi, Cingolani, and Tupini. After a letter from Don Sturzo had been read, De Gasperi delivered his final report, which had one theme—to hold firm. It was evident that although he recognized that the battle had to be temporarily abandoned, he wished to sketch plans for the battle of the future. His opposition to the Fascist regime was based upon the essential incompatibility of Fascism and natural law:

> It is undeniable that the theoretical and practical principles of Fascism contrast with the Christian concept of the State, according to which the natural rights of personality, family, and society exist before the State. The contrast is not between Fascism and Liberalism but between Fascism and certain fundamental exigencies of modern political organizations; it is the contrast between the State based on law which has developed in modern constitutions and the old Police State which attempts to reappear in disguise and which holds over Catholic institutions the sword of Damocles.

Then he called attention to the continuation of persecutions: "Argenta and Castel San Giovanni where two priests were killed; Brianza, Faenza,

Gubbio, Meldola, Trani, Brembate, Pisa, Padua, Olesine, right up to their final devastation, represent only some among the many names that recall violence against Catholic institutions." In conclusion he said: "Let all Democrats, Liberals, and Socialists learn that our party, even when it battled against them, battled in defense of liberty.... There exists the doctrine of Christ before every other idea, and if everyone of these ideas should fail, there would always remain the Christian affirmation of the liberty of the human person."

At the end of the debates, the Honorable Gino Brenci, winner of a medal for military valor, ascended the platform to present to De Gasperi a parchment, signed by all present, and a bouquet of flowers bound together with a tri-colored ribbon. The gifts were proferred as symbols of solidarity with De Gasperi, of protest against the campaign of calumny that had been launched against him. Enthusiastic applause greeted the presentation of the parchment, and De Gasperi accepted it with deep emotion on behalf not of himself but of "the heroic people of Trent."[61]

The best description of the appearance, character, and personality of De Gasperi at this time comes from the pen of Gobetti:

> Undeniably, Alcide De Gasperi, who until a few months ago was only a proconsul is today a chieftain. The congress was in his hands. Tall, thin, erect, his neck longer and more solid because he wears one of those high rigid collars which seem to lend him dignity though no longer in style, his eyes survey everything. From the stage he surveys the tactics, listens to the orators, and has signs of approval or dissent for even the most humble speakers who tire the assembly; nevertheless, it seems that he is bridling his impatience, that he is not happy with this oratory, that he is thinking of tomorrow's work.... He alone wanted this congress, he wanted it in order to obtain a confirmation of his work, and having obtained it ..., he is engrossed with promises for the prosecution of the battle. If it seems during certain discussions that he dominates the congress, that he wishes to impose his own responsibility as head even upon the heretics, one must remember that his education has been antioratorical. De Gasperi is a man who knows how to have pride. His mouth open, with a smile that is bitter, or disdainful, or contemptuous, he is always ready with a lively interruption, with an energetic retort. He is bored with adulation, compliments, with useless phrases. He does not know how to pretend indulgence. He does not need noisy popularity and appreciates instead the assent, the meditated opinion of others. Nevertheless, accustomed to deciding, he does not have a taste for discussion.
>
> ... rustic austerity and simplicity are at the base of the realism of

De Gasperi, and therefore his politics take refuge from rhetorical ideology to understand democracy in its most ordinary meaning as a struggle in defense of the most abandoned classes who seek not protection but justice and independence and who do not wish to submit to oppression.[62]

Thus it was at the Congress of Rome that De Gasperi appeared as a real leader, but by this time all prominent members of the Opposition parties were in danger of their lives. Donati had been forced to leave Italy in June, even before the congress. His paper, *Il Popolo*, suspended publication in November. When De Gasperi went to Montecatini for health reasons, he was quick to note that Tuscan squadrism was still very active. Knowing that Amendola had made reservations at a hotel in that city, he wrote to advise him that the environment was not conducive to the personal safety of opponents of the regime. The letter arrived too late: on July 20, 1925, Amendola was dragged from his car by thirty *squadristi* who beat him so brutally that he never recovered. Soon afterward, he migrated to Cannes, where he died on April 7, 1926.

Meanwhile the Aventine had come to an end, even in a formal sense. The Maximalist Socialists withdrew in September 1925, the Republicans in October, and the *Popolari* in November. At a meeting of the National Council in November, it was decided that the *Popolari* deputies should return to the Chamber of Deputies for the purpose of "defending from the parliamentary tribune the program and ideas of the party."[63] The *Popolari* sought to return to the Chamber of Deputies on January 16, 1926, taking advantage of a memorial service scheduled that day for the recently deceased Queen Mother. The *Popolari* succeeded in entering the hall, but once the official ceremony was over, the Fascists forcibly obtained their withdrawal.

On December 14, even before the ill-fated attempt of the *Popolari* to resume their parliamentary duties, De Gasperi had resigned the secretaryship of the party.[64] In January 1926, he reluctantly gave up the direction of his paper. Writing to his colleagues on January 22, he averred that he was leaving the journal "with inexpressible anguish but with the intention of rendering it one last service." Characteristically his letter ended, "I beg pardon for my impatience. I have loved you, and from afar I shall follow your work day by day, just as one follows the fate of companions in arms."[65]

The records of the Italian Ministry of the Interior indicate that from at least March 1926 on, De Gasperi was under police surveillance, with his arrivals at Rome and departures from it closely scrutinized by Public

Security agents.⁶⁶ In May 1926 the Questura of Rome noted that De Gasperi had shipped to Borgo Valsugana the furniture from his apartment on Via Ripetta.⁶⁷ Having withdrawn from politics, De Gasperi had seen no further need for maintaining an apartment in Rome. In June De Gasperi rejoined his family in the Romani house in Borgo Valsugana. Shortly after his arrival in the Trentino, he requested a passport in order to go to Vichy for a health cure, Montecatini no longer being safe for a person of his political background. Prefect Guadagnini advised his superiors not to grant the passport, arguing that the presence in Vichy of a person as politically important as De Gasperi would convey to the outside world the impression that security was lacking in Italy. Mussolini agreed with the reasoning of Guadagnini, writing across the Prefect's communication "No passport."⁶⁸

Meanwhile opposition to the regime appeared to be mounting. Non-Fascist newspapers still in circulation employed irony or sarcasm in referring to Fascist claims, and in the province of Rome the Prefect reported "an intense anti-Fascist propaganda."⁶⁹ More alarming to the government were the attempts to assassinate the Duce. In September 1926 the anarchist Gino Luccetti attempted to assassinate Mussolini in Rome, and in October a fifteen-year-old boy, Anteo Zamboni, who belonged to an anarchist family, fired at Mussolini as he passed through Bologna.

Fascists were not slow in retaliating. Taking note of the use of irony as a weapon, Mussolini sent a telegram to all prefects in which he ordered the careful perusal of newspapers and the confiscation of those which derided the government.⁷⁰ In Trent, during the night of October 31 and November 1, a band of Blackshirts assaulted and occupied the headquarters of the Catholic associations and papers of the city. In spite of the protests of Archbishop Endrici, the principal exponents of Catholic Action were expelled from Trent.⁷¹

Sooner or later, De Gasperi was bound to be caught up in the countermeasures employed by the Fascist regime. During the night of November 5-6, police agents went to his home in Borgo Valsugana, and with the pretext of protecting him from Fascists who were on his trail, they persuaded him, together with his brother Augusto, to get into a waiting car which supposedly would take them to the train in Padua or Vicenza. At Bassano del Grappa a group of Fascists entered the car and drove it to the Fascist headquarters in Vicenza. Here the De Gasperi brothers were interrogated by a self-appointed tribunal which charged them with "austriacantismo" and anti-Fascism. When a member of the tribunal asked Alcide De Gasperi the reason for his refusal to accept Fascism, the reply was: "It is the concept of the Fascist State that I cannot accept, for there are natural rights which the State cannot trample upon. I cannot accept the annihilation, the disciplining, as you say, of liberty."[72]

Fortunately for the De Gasperi brothers, a friendly Fascist, Luciano Marzotti, a member of parliament, happened to be on the scene. With the pretense that he would personally attend to the punishment of Alcide De Gasperi, he took him and his brother to his own house in nearby Valdagno, and on the following day, he had them escorted to Verona where the two brothers took the train for Milan. In Milan Alcide De Gasperi remained hidden for some time in the house of Signora Carpaneda, the daughter of the *Popolare* deputy, Arturo Baranzini. In the meantime, Fascist papers had published their version of the interrogation at Vicenza, according to which De Gasperi had reconsidered his attitude toward Fascism and had praised it. In reply, De Gasperi sent a letter to several journals, stating that while he had condemned the attempts on the life of Mussolini, the story of his reconsideration concerning Fascism was "a pure invention." The letter was not, however, published in any newspaper.[73]

On the same day as his arrival in Milan, De Gasperi received news of the expulsion of the Aventine deputies from the Chamber of Deputies. On November 9, 1926, the Chamber adopted the Turati (Augusto)—Starace—Farinacci resolution, which declared that the electoral mandate of the Aventine deputies had lapsed. These deputies were accused of having used their parliamentary prerogatives to subvert the powers of the State.[74] On the same day the prefect of Rome decreed the dissolution of the *Partito Popolare Italiano*.[75] In retrospect the conclusion is unavoidable that the Aventine Secession was a mistake, for De Gasperi and the other Opposition leaders put themselves out of action for sixteen months, unwittingly giving Fascism an opportunity to consolidate itself with a minimum of opposition. The only value of the Aventine protest was that it forced Fascism to reveal itself as totalitarian.

The motion to deprive the Opposition deputies of their electoral mandate was adopted simultaneously with the "Exceptional Decrees." These covered a wide range of activities: some provided for the suppression of all antinationalist newspapers and parties; others canceled passports and prescribed severe penalties for clandestine expatriation. Still others established the Special Tribunal for the Defense of the State and expanded the system of administrative justice. The death penalty was decreed for those who sought to assassinate either the king or the head of the government.

The Special Tribunal for the Defense of the State, whose members were appointed by Mussolini, began to function on February 1, 1927. Two weeks later, a Ministry of the Interior directive ensured that the tribunal would be kept occupied. Noting that "manifestations of aversion toward the national order and the highest persons of the regime have become frequent," the Ministry instructed prefects that persons responsible for such manifestations should be brought within police custody.[76]

By this time De Gasperi had become the object of a nation-wide search. After leaving Milan he had gone to Rome where he assumed the name of Professor Paolo De Rossi. He escaped detection by moving from place to place, living at one time in the home of the lawyer and former *Popolare*, Ivo Coccia, on Via Pompeo Magno, then in the furnished room of his brother-in-law Pietro Romani at 40 Via XX Settembre, and finally in another furnished room at 70 Via Napoleone III, with the family of Vincenzo Sciurba, a postal employee who was not involved in politics. His wife Francesca joined him in the last residence. This was an extremely difficult period in De Gasperi's life. Fearful of becoming objects of suspicion to the Fascist authorities, people who had known De Gasperi for decades shunned any contact with him. For this reason De Gasperi was especially appreciative of the kindness of Coccia, who was also under surveillance. One evening Fascist agents arrived while De Gasperi was conversing with Coccia in his professional studio, adjacent to the family residence. Fortunately the guards did not recognize De Gasperi who, pretending to be a client, slipped out quietly. Coccia informed the guards that he had not seen the former deputy from the Trentino in some time and would himself be interested in learning his whereabouts.[77]

In the friendly atmosphere of the Coccia home, De Gasperi met representatives of the German Center Party, who had come to Italy to obtain first-hand information concerning the situation in Italy. De Gasperi warned the Germans to take care lest history evolve in a similar manner in their own country.[78] De Gasperi's contacts with the Germans became known to some government informer who, elaborating on the known facts, reported that De Gasperi and Angelo Mauri, another ex-*Popolare* deputy, acting on behalf of Don Sturzo and Prince Rufo Ruffo della Scaletta, had gone to Berlin to carry on propaganda against Italy. De Gasperi and Mauri were described as having urged the German foreign minister, Dr. Gustav Stresemann, to draw closer to France and away from Italy.[79]

Unable to continue living without regular employment and in constant fear of detection, De Gasperi decided to leave Rome and go to Trieste. In a city where he was relatively unknown, he would be in a better position to plan for the future. It is quite possible that he even contemplated going into exile; many of his friends were urging him to do so. Coccia made the arrangements, obtaining from the Touring Club membership cards made out to Professor Paolo De Rossi and his wife. To avoid being recognized and stopped at Rome's Termini Railroad Station, De Gasperi and his wife made plans to proceed to Orvieto by car, and there take a train for Trieste. Prince Rufo Ruffo della Scaletta placed his car at the disposition of the De Gasperi couple. The plan was to fail, however, because a journalist who was visiting the Ruffo household became aware of the preparations and alerted the police.

On Friday, March 11, 1927, De Gasperi and his wife left Rome at 2:00 P.M., and at 4.30 P.M., they boarded train No. 44 at Orvieto, after having purchased two second-class tickets for Trieste. Meanwhile, Arturo Bocchini, Mussolini's chief of police, having been informed of De Gasperi's imminent departure, sent a telegram to the prefects of Ancona, Pisa, Florence, Bologna, and Zara, informing them that De Gasperi had left or was about to leave Rome with the intention of clandestine expatriation. The prefects were to take all appropriate measures to intercept De Gasperi and to prevent such expatriation. He informed the prefects of Fiume, Venice, and Trieste that De Gasperi would probably seek to leave Italy from the region of Fiume.[80] In a later telegram to all prefects, Bocchini warned that De Gasperi would probably try to enter Yugoslavia at Susak.[81]

At 11.07 P.M., as train No. 44 pulled into the station at Florence, it was met and boarded by two Public Security agents, Achille Strazzuso and Ettore Bacialli, and by the commander of the railroad police, Ferdinando Mancini. In a compartment of the second class, they spotted De Gasperi and his wife. Upon their request for identification, De Gasperi immediately turned pale but admitted his identity, producing an expired passport as evidence. Taken to the local Questura for questioning, De Gasperi said that he and his wife were going to Trieste for a "few days of relaxation" prior to returning to Borgo Valsugana. The personal search disclosed that De Gasperi was carrying 6,659 *lire*, a passport issued August 7, 1921, visiting cards for Professor Paolo De Rossi, a Touring Club card made out to Paolo De Rossi and bearing the photograph of De Gasperi, and another Touring Club card made out to Francesca De Rossi Prati with the photograph of Francesca De Gasperi. These items were confiscated, as were also personal jewelry, a notebook, a suitcase containing clothes, a handbag, and a summons apparently issued by the Tribunal of Rome on March 3, 1927, instructing De Rossi to appear in court on March 19 to testify in a suit against a Rosa Calisti. During the interrogation De Gasperi freely admitted having adopted the alias of Paolo De Rossi in order to avoid political reprisals.[82] After the examination at the Questura of Florence, De Gasperi and his wife were taken to the Murate and Santa Verdiana prisons respectively, while the authorities awaited further instructions from Rome.

Informed of the apprehension of De Gasperi, Mussolini sent a penciled note to "Caro Bocchini," directing that the De Gasperi couple be immediately brought to Rome.[83] On March 12 Bocchini informed all prefects that they were to forbid the publication of the news of the detention of De Gasperi, for such publicity might alert Pietro Romani and Augusto De Gasperi, whose arrests had also been ordered.[84] On the same day De Gasperi and his wife were brought to Rome, De Gasperi being consigned to the Regina Coeli prison and his wife to the Mantellate (for women).[85]

On March 13 Pietro Romani was arrested in Florence. In his statement to the police, he said that he was on his way to Borgo Valsugana, preparatory to undertaking a business trip to Brazil. He insisted that he was not involved in politics, having withdrawn in 1924, and that he had not seen his brother-in-law during the previous three weeks.[86] He too was taken back to Rome and placed in a cell of Regina Coeli. As in the case of De Gasperi, newspapers were forbidden to carry news of the arrest.[87] Bocchini was so pleased with the efficiency of his agents in Florence that he provided for the distribution of 550 *lire* among them.[88]

The government immediately began to prepare its case against De Gasperi. A paper in the files of the Ministry of the Interior lists the following items belonging to De Gasperi or Romani as exhibits to be used in court: (1) two maps, one of Trieste and the other of Fiume, found among De Gasperi's possessions; (2) a map of Trieste found in the suitcase of Romani; (3) the Touring Club cards; (4) the railroad tickets; (5) two suitcases belonging to De Gasperi but carried by Romani; (6) a book of checks belonging to Romani; and (7) notes for a probable publication by De Gasperi.[89]

All persons listed in De Gasperi's notebook became the subjects of investigation. For those believed to be in foreign countries, the investigation was conducted by the Ministry of Foreign Affairs.[90] The search eventually extended to England, Austria, Paraguay, Rumania, Switzerland, Germany, and France. Meanwhile the homes of De Gasperi's closest friends and relatives were subjected to a thorough search. On March

16 the police went through Sella, the summer home of Ida Romani, De Gasperi's mother-in-law, without, however, finding any incriminating evidence.[91] A search of Augusto De Gasperi's home in Trent failed to uncover either owner or incriminating evidence.[92]

In the Regina Coeli prison Pietro Romani was interrogated to determine whether or not he had been an accomplice in the alleged attempted clandestine expatriation of Alcide De Gasperi. Although he admitted that he had placed his room at 40 Via XX Settembre at the disposition of his brother-in-law from the middle of January to the middle of February, he satisfied the police that he had not been an accomplice and consequently he was released.[93]

De Gasperi was not permitted to see his wife or brother-in-law before making his statement to the police on March 19.[94] On March 20 the two Public Security agents before whom the statement was made, Guido Leto and Giuseppe D'Andrea, prepared a memorandum for the chief of police. It stated that except for the map of Fiume and an obscure letter carried by De Gasperi and addressed to a certain "Riccardo" whom De Gasperi refused to identify, nothing had emerged from the exhaustive investigations and interrogations to cause suspicion that a crime had been committed. The agents recommended that Signora De Gasperi and her brother Pietro Romani be immediately released; they made no recommendation regarding De Gasperi other than that the superiors decide what should be done with him.[95]

Mussolini's orders were to release Signora De Gasperi and her brother but to hold De Gasperi for trial. The Premier condescended, however, to grant his prize prisoner permission to go to Trent to visit his father, who was reputed to be dying.[96] On March 21 De Gasperi left for Trent, accompanied by police agents and technically in a state of arrest. He remained with his father until April 26, by which time his father's condition had changed for the better. While De Gasperi was in Trent, Bocchini informed the Ministry of the Interior that no elements of crime were evident in the investigations, although the intention of clandestine expatriation could be assumed.[97] Nevertheless, on April 1 the Ministry of the Interior decided that a trial should be held, particularly in view of the report that when the new Yugoslav minister arrived in Rome, De Gasperi had twice gone to see him.[98]

Although the delay in bringing the case to court severely tried De Gasperi's patience, he sought resignation. The letters that he wrote to his wife during the period of his imprisonment provide an intimate glimpse into his character and personality. Writing to Francesca on April 26, 1927, he said: "Dear Francesca, when every effort is made and nothing succeeds, then it means that Providence for inscrutable reasons has so disposed things, and let us pray that good may come of it for us and for others."[99] He failed to obtain "provisional liberty" while awaiting trial, and he was segregated from the other prisoners even when going out for air. His time was spent in prayer, meditation, and reading. The religious books from which he derived the most consolation were the *Confessions* of St. Augustine, the *Imitation of Christ*, and the Psalms of David. For relaxation he enjoyed reading history books and English adventure stories. While awaiting nightfall, his thoughts often went back to his previous visits to Rome—his audience with Pope Leo XIII in 1902, his interview with Sidney Sonnino in 1915, the triumphal entry into Rome in 1918, and then the years of feverish work on behalf of the *Partito Popolare*. Now, enclosed in a small cell, he could no longer see Rome and its monuments, but his love for Rome remained unchanged: "and still I love you, as I love Italy. . . ."[100]

De Gasperi's trial began May 18, 1927, in Section Thirteen of the Penal Tribunal of Rome, with Doctor Luigi Guidone as president and Amedeo Marini and Carlo Violanti as judges. De Gasperi was charged with violation of Article 160 of the Law of Public Security, forbidding clandestine expatriation, and of Article 278 of the penal code, forbidding the forgery of the signature of a public official. The latter charge was based on the fact that the summons found on De Gasperi contained a forged signature. The charge of attempted clandestine expatriation was pressed even after it became known that De Gasperi had not seen the new Yugoslav minister, the latter having arrived on March 12, a day after De Gasperi had been taken into custody.[101] During the trial, Filippo Meda defended him ably, and De Gasperi felt confident of acquittal. The court's verdict on May 28 of guilty and its sentence of four years of imprisonment and a fine of 20,000 *lire* came as a terrible blow to De Gasperi.[102] That morning he had left his grim cell certain that he would never return to it; so convinced had he been of acquittal that he had not bothered to make arrangements for his dinner, which was usually brought in from the outside. Describing to Francesca his first night in the cell after conviction, he wrote: "God, what a night. I saw Father, from whom it would not be possible to conceal what had taken place, fall dead. I saw you sick and all belonging to me in affliction and desolation, my children poor and you almost a poorly dressed widow. When the Lord so desired, dawn came and then lifting my eyes to the strip of blue sky above, I began to cry. . . ."[103]

In July 1927 the Court of Appeal heard De Gasperi's appeal of the verdict. Setting aside the forgery count and declaring that there were extenuating circumstances for the attempt at clandestine expatriation, the Court of Appeal reduced the term of imprisonment to two and a half years and the fine to 16,666 *lire*.[104] In May 1928 this decision was upheld by the Court of Cassation, which refused to entertain a further appeal.[105]

Until July 1927 De Gasperi was a prisoner in Branch VIII of Regina Coeli. His cell, dank and bug-infested though *a pagamento*, contained a bed, chair, and table. On the table he placed family photographs, holy pictures, and books. The nonreligious authors included Balzac, Gioberti, Dostoievsky, and Maupassant. It was a lonely existence, and because of censorship it took anywhere from nine to twelve days for letters to reach him. Sometimes, placing his head in his hands, he sat before pictures of his family, and blotting out the present and future, he thought only of the past. Toward the end of June, the heat in his cell became unbearable, and as he crowded into a corner seeking some shade, he saw reflected on the ceiling a checkerboard caused by the rays of the sun coming in through the barred windows. He thought of the gridiron of St. Lawrence.

In July his stomach and digestive troubles required his transfer to the Ciancarelli Clinic in Rome, which was like limbo compared with the hell of Regina Coeli. His room was clean, and when he sat in the garden or on the terrace, he could enjoy cooler air. During the next few months, the lack of company granted him ample opportunity for reverie and meditation. His wife was in Borgo or Sella and could not come every month. He thought a great deal about her, wondering if he could ever repay her for all she suffered on his account. His thoughts also took him to Sella, their summer home, where the sun was almost always shining. It was not difficult for him to visualize quartz glittering in the waters of the valley, "like the gold of the Nibelungs in the Rhine," and to see in the carollas of the wild flowers the faces of his children.[106]

The sound of a church bell also served as an impetus to De Gasperi's prayerful reveries. In front of the clinic was a convent, surrounded by greenery. From his room, De Gasperi could glimpse a rose window, behind which was the altar. The bell sounded every hour, and each time the black and white habits of the nuns rustled among the shrubs as the nuns made their way to the chapel. De Gasperi was reminded of the eternal mysteries, and he was then able to view with more equanimity the collapse of his work and the "evaporation of his hopes like the evaporation of a fog."[107]

When he reflected upon the past, he inevitably came to the same conclusion: he could not have done otherwise. Writing to his wife, he observed:

> I have resisted . . . to the very end, on the advanced trench to which duty called me. But it was my very own conscience which imposed this upon me—my own convictions, dignity, self-respect. . . . There are many who go into politics as a short excursion, as amateurs, and others consider it—and such it is for them—an accessory of secondary importance. But for me, ever since I was a child, it was my career, or rather my mission. It did not matter that I had to give up my mandate, abandon my journal, impose silence upon my lips and claustration on my feet. . . . I shall always remain a "popolare," the De Gasperi of his youth or of his mature years, just as a surgeon remains a surgeon even if he changes hospitals, and an engineer remains an engineer. I have not been lacking in matters of prudence, and the duties of father and husband suggested demobilization in due time. But to change, I would have had to cease to exist, to deny existence, to repudiate myself.[108]

One day he wrote on the walls of his cell "Blessed are those who thirst after justice." The guard compelled him to erase these words from the walls, but they could not be erased from his heart, where they had been written since childhood. They summed up the program of his life, a program which had obliged him to "work for the elevation of the humble and the justice and rights . . . of the common people."[109] Asking himself whether he should have sustained his ideas with less zeal, he answered, "I would certainly have done so if sometimes those who call themselves Catholics, like myself, and often with better appearance of representing Catholicism, had not applauded success so much and had not by their attitude given the impression that the Church had abandoned the vanquished, an accusation against which I had rebelled all my life."[110] With these thoughts in mind, he could neither renounce his past nor despair of the future.

His days in the clinic were not without amusement and occasional tenderness. De Gasperi had guards ("protectors" he called them) day and night and he became quite friendly with some of them. They confided family troubles to him, and sometimes one would smile benevolently and say: "I have a cousin who received fifteen years for homicide." Before leaving, one *carabiniere* brought him a flask of wine and sweets. Another, returning for a visit, brought him a ricotta. Their kindness led De Gasperi to remark that Machiavelli had been wrong in his evaluation of human nature, that he had incorrectly judged human nature because he had studied only the upper classes, which had been corrupted by unbridled ambition. For himself, he was of the opinion that these people were basically good and that they liked him because, consciously or unconsciously, they recognized his interest in the poor.[111]

Despite distractions caused by operations which were in progress night and day in the room below him, De Gasperi managed to read and to prepare articles on corporativism and on the German Center Party. Thus time flew quickly and he did not think of his own troubles. Furthermore, it was only by writing so-called historical articles and then publishing them under a pseudonym that he could continue to make his influence felt. During the course of 1928–1929 the *Rivista internazionale di scienze sociali e discipline ausiliarie* carried two of his articles under the name of G. Jaspar: "Un Maestro del corporativismo italiano" and "Le Direttive politico-religiose del 'Centro' Germanico (1871–1928)."[112] If their language was necessarily veiled, the articles nevertheless conveyed De Gasperi's messages.

In "Un Maestro del corporativismo italiano," De Gasperi traced the career of the French Catholic leader, René de la Tour du Pin who, together with Albert de Mun, founded the Catholic workers' movement in France. De Gasperi criticized Du Pin for his royalist proclivities and also for his roseate interpretation of the Middle Ages. Du Pin saw the medieval world as "all light and no shadow," an ideal world, like the world of Rousseau or the collective state of Socialism. Recalling the turbulence of medieval factions, De Gasperi asked whether it was not better to count heads than to crack them. Discussing corporativism, he noted—undoubtedly to refute Mussolini's claim to the establishment of a socio-economic system consonant with papal teachings—that Pope Leo XIII did not speak of a corporative regime in *Rerum Novarum* nor did he concern himself with the socio-political edifice which the social Christians had considered a prerequisite for the renovation of society.

In his article on the German Center Party, De Gasperi traced the historical evolution of the party and by implication drew analogies with the *Partito Popolare Italiano*. He pointed out that Windthorst, the founder of the Center Party, accepted the modern state constitution and wished his party to be aconfessional. During the imperial period, the Center Party played a decisive role in German politics, particularly with respect to the achievement of social reforms. Under the Weimar Republic the party continued to show interest in the socio-economic problems of the German nation. During the drafting of the Weimar constitution, the leaders of the Center Party participated in the formulation of its socio-economic articles and upheld the fundamental principle that property has obligations. Also worthy of praise, according to De Gasperi, was the Center Party's acceptance of a republic, the principle of the sovereignty of the people, and the separation of Church and State. The latter could be easily endorsed by the party, for the Weimar constitution did not create a state hostile to Christianity. Separation of Church and State in Germany was very different from separation as found in France, Portugal, or Mexico.

The article also surveyed the relations of the Centrists with the Socialists. The collaboration, said De Gasperi, was an instrument in the reconstruction of a new Germany, for the Center Party was able to exert a moderating influence on the Socialists, persuading them to give up their negative and revolutionary role. The Weimar coalition of Socialists, Centrists, and Democrats had been fruitful. De Gasperi's conclusion was that while the Center Party had never succeeded in becoming a truly interconfessional party, it had performed inestimable services on behalf of the German nation by its positive outlook and its devotion to constitutional government. Undoubtedly he envisioned an Italian Christian party performing the same service for Italy.

De Gasperi's research and writing was interspersed with the reading of daily newspapers. On December 22, 1927, his hopes rose when he read that conditional liberty had been granted to about three hundred and thirty who had been "interned," including numerous ex-deputies. For both internal and external reasons, he expected other amnesties, and perhaps he would be released. That he did not intend, however, to renounce his principles is obvious from a letter he wrote to his old friend from Trent, Giovanni Ciccolini. In response to Ciccolini's letter, commending him for his battle on behalf of the principles of Christian Democracy, he affirmed:

> No, I am not a martyr, but perhaps I can admit, without being boastful, to being a confessor of our ideas. I have proclaimed them and I still proclaim them in this time of peril, when they become even dearer to me and more sacred, like a treasure that is carried to safety along the edge of a precipice. It is the only wealth that is left to me, and it is made finer and more crystalline in the purifying fire of sacrifice. Perhaps some people, noting the visible fortune that accompanied me on the road of life, misinterpreted our social and political Christianity, seeing it linked with a certain comfort and surrounded by some favor and prestige. I am happy that now honest adversaries need not be scandalized by fortune and may judge the beauty and fecundity of our idea, now stripped naked and the sole mistress of my spirit. I am even happier, in fact, proud, of the moral solidarity of our friends. A storm has descended upon us and we have all emerged more or less battered. My breast does not enclose the soul of a hero, nor does the interior light of a saint illuminate me; nevertheless, praised be the Lord who makes me understand how just it is that in the disgrace that has befallen all I, who was in the highest positions, by an equal compensation should now drag myself along in life, the most worn out and the most bat-

tered among the others. There is no merit in being among the first, when one marches under a triumphant sun and a banner accustomed to victory. There is perhaps some merit in dragging oneself in the mud of life, after the rout. But why do I speak to you of marches and movements, when my camp is a small room, with thoughts as my fellow soldiers.[113]

Inactivity was distasteful to De Gasperi, whose temperament had always been that of "Martha rather than of Mary." He wondered if the days of feverish political activity would ever return, and if they did, how much salty water would first have to be traversed. His immediate fear, however, was that he would return to Regina Coeli, a fear which was not unjustified. Shortly after his wife's visit late in January 1928, the Court of Appeal inquired of the clinic whether or not De Gasperi was well enough to return to Regina Coeli. The doctor in charge of the clinic returned a negative response, but for several days De Gasperi saw himself back in the dreary cell at Regina Coeli, stripped like a thief and deprived of so many objects of comfort. Everytime he heard the rumble of a motor-lorry, he would run to the window to see if a police van had come to take him back to Regina Coeli. After the fear had passed, De Gasperi returned to his research activities. Having lost hope in either an amnesty or further reduction in penalty, he continued to work on a book, later to become known as *I Tempi e gli uomini che prepararono la "Rerum Novarum,"* and by May 21, 1928, he had completed the first draft. Writing to his wife a month later, he said: "I am going through a period of torpor; I neither pray nor study seriously; I neither hope nor despair; I neither enjoy myself nor suffer privations."[114] The numbness ended July 10, when he was suddenly informed that his imprisonment was terminated, though he would remain subject to the surveillance of the authorities.[115] He owed his release to the intervention of the Archbishop of Trent. During the inauguration of a monument in Trent to Cesare Battisti, Archbishop Endrici asked King Victor Emmanuel III to pardon De Gasperi. The King made no reply, but a few days later, the proper authorities were informed of the royal pardon.[116]

Upon his release De Gasperi took up lodgings in the Hotel Santa Chiara, for he had been ordered to remain in Rome. On August 1, De Gasperi asked for permission to reside in Borgo Valsugana until he had found employment in Rome. In reply Bocchini gave him permission to go to Borgo for fifteen days (eventually extended to a month), subject to the usual surveillance to prevent clandestine expatriation.[117] De Gasperi returned to Rome September 17, once again taking up residence at the Hotel Santa Chiara. The surveillance now became tighter than ever, with agents posted night and day in front of his hotel room. Writing to the director general of Public Security, he explained that such shadowing impeded his efforts to find work, and he requested a less ostentatious vigilance, one which would take into account his economic exigencies and at the same time serve the purpose of the regime.[118] On October 8 the shadowing was suspended, but surveillance continued in such a manner as to ascertain at least three times a day the presence of De Gasperi in Rome.[119]

The autumn of 1928 was perhaps the most difficult period in De Gasperi's life. He lived alone in a *pensione*, hotel life having become too expensive for his depleted finances, and he was grateful for the food packages that Don Giulio Delugan of Trent, his old friend and journalistic collaborator, sent him from time to time. Perhaps the greatest cross De Gasperi had to bear was social ostracism. A person of intense loyalty to his friends, he discovered that this loyalty was not always reciprocated. Writing to Don Giulio, he lamented: "If you only knew how lonely I feel in this Rome that is so populated." In search of work, he climbed many stairs, asking if he could do some translating or tutoring. He encountered many humiliations, an occasional kind word—but no offers of jobs. Blaming himself, he asserted: "My capital sin in life was pride, and the Lord has punished me; but precisely because I have grown proud, how difficult it is today to receive, seek, and feel obligated."[120]

A few friends remained loyal, and one of the most important of these was Archbishop Endrici, who not only provided financial assistance but sought for De Gasperi a position in the Vatican Library.[121] But the position could not materialize immediately, because unknown to De Gasperi and to most persons in both Church and State delicate negotiations were then under way between the Vatican and Mussolini with a view to ending the Church-State controversy. If Pope Pius XI had given De Gasperi a position, such an act of charity might have been interpreted by Mussolini as a rebuke to himself, and the negotiations on the Roman Question might have been suspended. Not until April 1929, after the signing of the Lateran Pacts, could Archbishop Endrici's recommendation bear fruit. In the meantime, De Gasperi continued to suffer from hunger, humiliations, and loneliness.

Early in December 1928 De Gasperi obtained permission from the authorities to go to Borgo for the Christmas holidays. When he returned to Rome in mid-January, he was accompanied by his wife and their older daughter, Maria Romana. They arrived in Rome as the

Lateran negotiations were drawing to a close, and by this time it was widely rumored that a pact was about to be signed by Mussolini and the Vatican. Although some of his friends were "desolate" at the prospect of such an agreement, De Gasperi was "pleased" that the long conflict was about to be terminated.[122]

Signed February 11, 1929, the Lateran Treaty consisted of three parts: the Treaty proper, the financial settlement, and a concordat. The treaty recognized the sovereignty and independence of Vatican City, the financial agreement promised the Pope seven hundred and fifty million *lire* in cash and one billion *lire* in government bonds, and the concordat gave the Church a privileged position in the country. In addition to settling the status of the clergy, including the appointment of bishops, the concordat gave wide powers to the Church in such matters as marriage and education. The teaching of the Catholic religion was to be part of the curriculum of both elementary and secondary schools, with teachers and books approved by Church authorities. From a historical point of view, however, the most important of the concordat's provisions was Article 43, whereby the Italian State recognized the organizations dependent on Italian Catholic Action "insofar as they carry out their activity outside of any political party and under the direct dependence of the Church hierarchy for the spreading and realization of Catholic principles."

When the pacts were announced, some of the former *Popolari* expressed their indignation to De Gasperi. That the Pope should enter into an agreement with a regime that had been at least indirectly responsible for the destruction of so many Catholic organizations and buildings no doubt seemed incomprehensible. But De Gasperi's attitude was that the higher good of the Church required a settlement of the Roman Question, and that even Don Luigi Sturzo would have signed if he had been pope. He realized that the agreement was politically beneficial to the Fascist dictatorship, but this did not diminish his confidence in its essential worth.[123] The only part of the Lateran Pacts which caused De Gasperi some misgivings was the concordat, for he feared that collaboration might lead to a popular identification of Catholicism and Fascism.[124] In mid-March De Gasperi's apprehensions concerning collaboration increased when Luigi Colombo, the president of Catholic Action, urged Catholics to vote for the Fascist list in the forthcoming elections.[125] De Gasperi's opinion was that a "bad beginning" was being made.[126]

The elections were a victory for Mussolini, who soon adopted a more arrogant attitude toward the Church. His speech to the Chamber of

Deputies on May 13, 1929, was so insulting to the Church as to almost wreck the Lateran Accords. After declaring that "within the State the Church is not sovereign, nor even free . . . because it is subordinate, both in its institutions and its members, to the general laws of the State," Mussolini went on to discuss the Roman Question and its settlement in the "least lyrical and most frigid of speeches." He boasted that the final solution had been "Italian," with a complete renunciation of all previous papal claims. The Vatican was "that State which we, with a spontaneous act of our will as Fascists and Catholics, have created." The final portions of the speech were concerned with the concordat. In analyzing its provisions, Mussolini evidently wished to show that the State had suffered no diminution of its authority. In the matter of education, he claimed priority for the State, and he pointed out that the extension of religious instruction to secondary schools had been accompanied by his "categorical refusal to extend it to the universities." Mussolini ended his discourse, which had been very well received by the Chamber, with the warning: ". . . the regime is vigilant; nothing escapes it. Let nobody think that the smallest bulletin of the smallest parish is not known to Mussolini. We will not permit the revival of parties and organizations which we have destroyed forever."[127] On May 25, however, Mussolini made a more conciliatory speech in the senate, and on June 7 ratifications were exchanged. De Gasperi personally benefited from the signing of the pacts, for on April 3 he entered the Vatican Library as a cataloguer. For his new position he was indebted to both Archbishop Endrici and to Monsignor Mercati, the prefect of the Vatican Library. From his Vatican "exile," which was to last fourteen years, De Gasperi continued to write under pseudonyms, thus keeping alive though muted the message of Popularism.

CHAPTER VI

THE YEARS OF OBSCURITY

THE NEXT DECADE AND A HALF OF DE GASPERI'S LIFE WERE spent in relative obscurity, the Fascist regime taking note of him only on rare occasions. An intransigent with respect to Fascism, De Gasperi was content to lead a secluded life as an employee of the Vatican. Because of his political past, he could not, at least in the beginning, be utilized in the public areas of the *Biblioteca Apostolica Vaticana*, and consequently he was assigned to the cataloguing division, located in the basement of the library. Although the position was humiliating to one of his background, nevertheless, he was happy to have it and he considered it a good beginning.[1] His salary was small (1000 *lire* a month to begin, rising to 1,900 by 1939), but he was able to supplement it by writing articles under pseudonyms or by preparing translations of scholarly works, such as those of Ludwig von Pastor, René Fülop Miller, and Romano Guardini. An Aristotelian by training and temperament, De Gasperi found Guardini's discussion of Platonic philosophy difficult to comprehend, and on one occasion he resolved not to undertake the translation of any more of his works.

After the first eight months of service in the Vatican, De Gasperi was no longer optimistic regarding the future. Writing to Don Giulio Delugan at the end of 1929, he confided: "The new year does not open with new prospects. I continue my solitary labors, and while good health now enables me to endure them with less physical labor, the flexion imposed on the spirit and its pride makes me often drip and clatter like a boiling pot."[2] He made enough money, however, to bring the entire family together in a small apartment at 6 Via Monte Santo.[3]

In the mid-thirties, after two more children had been born, the family moved to 21 Via Bonifacio VIII, a biscuit-colored five-story apartment building located in a dilapidated section of Rome. It had the advantage, however, of being within the shadow of St. Peter's Basilica, which in effect became De Gasperi's "parish," and within walking distance of the Vatican Library. This remained the De Gasperi residence until the early 1950's.

De Gasperi's hours in the library were from 8:30 A.M. to 1:00 P.M. Under the guidance of Igino Giordani, another ex-*Popolare* who was employed by the Vatican, he learned the art of library classification according to the Library of Congress system. Whether he ever mastered the art is a matter of debate; in later years, after he had once again become famous in politics, his former colleagues in the catalogue room said that his cards were models of how they should *not* be prepared.

Every so often, De Gasperi would push back his glasses to watch from the window the movement of the Swiss Guard in the adjoining courtyard of Belvedere, or to engage in *chiacchiera* with his fellow workers. The conversations almost always ended in a discussion of politics, with De Gasperi holding forth in his usual dry manner, without bitterness or rancor and with no reference to his own personal experiences. Of his own political past, he recalled it only by insisting on the retention of the title of "onorevole."[4] As an employee of the Vatican Library, he was able to read books that were not available to the Italian public. One day a book arrived from Switzerland; entitled *Sixty Years of Heresy*, it was the autobiography of Fritz Brupbacher, the Zurich Socialist. De Gasperi read it with great interest, and contrary to all library regulations, made pencil notations in it.[5]

The over-all performance of his duties must have been satisfactory to his superiors, for De Gasperi was given tasks of increasing responsibility. From 1934 to 1937 he was entrusted with the organization of an international exposition of the Catholic press. Seventy rooms of the Pigna were given over to the exhibits, which were divided into three sections. The first was intended to illustrate the development of journalism, with particular reference to the Catholic press; the second was a survey of the Catholic periodical literature of the individual countries of the world; and the third contained the periodical publications of religious congregations and orders, mission literature, Catholic Action publications, and the journals of the Oriental rites.

De Gasperi was the collaborator of the secretary general of the exposition, Monsignor Monti. His special function was to organize the participation of the exhibitors of Europe and America, and in the course of the work he had to deal with forty-five national committees, composed of the best known representatives of the Catholic Press.[6] It was a work which enabled him to expand his contacts and widen his horizons. It was not, however, without its humiliations. On one occasion he confided to his diary: "Great humiliations suffered in the committee. If one day my daughters read these lines, they will know that I have endured these things only for the family and for them. This winter especially I felt the chains of my servitude. Man does not live by bread alone; but every time that De Gasperi wishes to make himself esteemed, if only in the circle of friends, he is rejected. . . . May the Lord pardon me and aid me."[7] The president of the directing committee was Count Giuseppe Dalla Torre, director of the *Osservatore Romano*. He was a sincere and loyal friend of De Gasperi's but because of the environment in which he worked, he frequently had to exercise extreme caution in order to assure freedom for his paper.

At the request of the prefect of the Vatican Library, the Spanish Benedictine Father Anselmo Albareda, Pope Pius XI appointed De Gasperi secretary of the Vatican Library, effective June 1, 1939. Albareda had been unaware of De Gasperi's political past, having become prefect only in 1936. Having heard his predecessor in the post, Eugene Tisserant, praise the scholarship of De Gasperi, he had decided to make him his assistant. When he went to Pope Pius XI to obtain his approval, the Pontiff was startled, and said: "We have taken him out of Regina Coeli." Then putting his hands to his temples, he remarked: "What will the people on the other side say about this?" But regardless of what "the other side" would say, the Pontiff gave his consent. De Gasperi was profoundly moved by the appointment, coming as it did after years of loneliness and frustration.[8] As secretary of the Vatican Library he was in a position to receive more guests. Among his callers were such persons as Ivanoe Bonomi, Benedetto Croce, Tommaso Gallarati Scotti and Meuccio Ruini.

That De Gasperi's thoughts were not concerned exclusively with library problems is evident from a perusal of his writings during his Vatican "exile," which, considering his position, were quite voluminous. Because they are a good guide to his political thought during these years, they must now be surveyed.

In *I Tempi e gli uomini che prepararono la "Rerum Novarum,"* a work begun in prison and published in 1931 under the pseudonym of Mario Zanatta, De Gasperi presented Bishop Ketteler, Cardinal Mermillod and Cardinal Manning as the precursors of the Christian social movement, and he traced the origins and development of this movement in Austria,

Germany, France, and Italy. With particular reference to Giuseppe Toniolo, he said that while Italians had been the last to arrive in the arena of social Catholicism, they had brought to it a sense of balance and comprehension of the times which were of more value than the theoretical discussions of some of their predecessors in other countries. The chief significance of *Rerum Novarum,* according to De Gasperi, was that the Church recognized its social obligations to mankind. Some of the hopes aroused by the encyclical had not been fulfilled, but the Holy See could not be expected to construct an entirely new economic order. Encyclicals were not intended to be detailed blueprints of concrete constructions; rather they were expositions of general principles.[9]

Beginning in 1933 and continuing until the fall of 1938, when the journal ceased publication, De Gasperi wrote a column in the Vatican bi-monthly *L'Illustrazione Vaticana,* which was edited by Giuseppe Dalla Torre and carried articles on religious, historical, and artistic matters. De Gasperi's column was entitled "La Quindicina Internazionale" and was written under the pen name of "Spectator." He discussed for the most part the activities of Catholic organizations and parties, relying heavily upon the Catholic press of England, France, Austria, Spain, and the United States. Among the American publications that De Gasperi apparently read regularly were *America* and *Commonweal.* Occasionally he referred to political and economic developments both in Italy and abroad. These references, often couched in veiled language, revealed a man still unreconciled with Fascism, a man still devoted to "Center" positions.

In surveying international politics and diplomacy at the outset of 1933, his outlook was optimistic: "When I think of international politics during the half-century before the war and compare them with those of our day, I find I am an optimist regarding the future of the human race, and I feel obliged to judge tolerantly the generation which today directs the political destinies of the world." He thought that the work of a statesman or a diplomat had become increasingly difficult, and as he pondered over the intricacies of modern diplomacy, he marveled at the wealth of information that had to be possessed by the modern statesman. The congresses of the nineteenth century and the meetings of the prewar ententes and alliances did not require nearly as much work as a postwar meeting at Geneva. At one time, a man was considered a success if he mastered European politics; now he had to be an expert on world politics, for "the war and the dynamism of our epoch have multiplied, complicated and universalized problems."[10] The events of 1933 were to dissipate his optimism.

De Gasperi sought to view controversial questions, namely, war debts, as impartially as possible. He pointed out that Americans believed their taxes were connected with war debts, and that the Kansas farmer was understandably vexed when he heard that European cities were being expanded, industrial plants were being enlarged, and new war machines were being constructed. Europeans, on the other hand, blamed their arms build-up on the failure of the United States to enter the League. The League policy of the United States had unfortunate repercussions on that of Great Britain, constraining her to seek evasion of Article 16.[11]

For the League of Nations De Gasperi had a profound admiration, although he was keenly aware of its deficiencies, both structural and moral. Although the League had failed in the Manchurian affair, De Gasperi felt that the very fact of League intervention, through the Lytton Commission, had been "morally significant." It was necessary for the League to act in order to prevent a bad example from setting a precedent.[12] De Gasperi also followed with interest the Pan-Europe movement. In commenting upon a Pan-European Congress held in Vienna on May 16, 1934, De Gasperi noted that the movement was fighting on two fronts: against extreme nationalism and against extreme internationalism. Pan-Europe was taking a middle position between these two extremes, and was aspiring to express organically the common spiritual heritage of European civilization.[13]

Developments in Germany filled him with consternation and gloom; particularly distressing to him was the dissolution of the Center Party, the party he had always admired for its nonconfessionalism, its advanced social welfare program, and its devotion to constitutional government. On the occasion of its dissolution in the summer of 1933, De Gasperi wrote at length on its origin, development, and services on behalf of the German nation. He said the Center Party had striven to rise above class and religious antagonism, preaching Christian solidarity and tempering liberty with authority. He predicted correctly: "The Center Party leaves a patrimony of experience and of thought that will survive the dissolution of its organizational form not only in the memory but also in the culture of German Catholics."[14]

Hitler's regime De Gasperi quickly characterized as dictatorial and totalitarian.[15] The cooperation of the Catholic political leader, Franz von Papen, in the work of eliminating democratic, parliamentary government aroused his strong disapproval.[16] In analyzing Hitler's victory in the plebiscite of November 1933 on the issue of German withdrawal from the League of Nations, De Gasperi ascribed it to the general indignation against the Treaty of Versailles and to the success of Nazi propaganda, which had asserted that there had been no real military defeat in 1918 and that the collapse of Germany had been brought about by Socialists and parliamentary Democrats.[17]

De Gasperi equated the ideology of Nazism with denial of Christian personalism. Nazism found justification for immoral deeds, such as the June Purge, in "reasons of state." "As far as we are concerned, we shall limit ourselves to saying that similar deeds have been extolled only in epochs in which has been lost a sense of human dignity and personality."[18] The fate of the German Catholics obviously distressed him, and he praised the resistance of German Catholics in the face of persecution and ostracism. The "battle" atmosphere left him with little room for optimism.[19] The Protestant churches were not, in his opinion, much better off, for Nazism postulated a religion that was essentially pre-Christian.[20]

As a former Austrian, De Gasperi was naturally interested in the country that was one of Hitler's main objectives. Looking at the small Danubian republic in 1933–1934, De Gasperi saw her as being in a state of suspension as far as parliamentary government was concerned. The Christian Socialists were forced to abandon the parliamentary system, at least temporarily, in order to strengthen the state against the inroads of Nazism. At the same time, they sought a solution of the "Center," that is, a government that was neither statist nor individualist, a government based on the force of laws and not on the law of force. Austria's regime of the Center was headed by a man who was "clever and energetic," Engelbert Dollfuss. De Gasperi regarded his tragic death in July 1934 as a great calamity.[21] Toward Austrian Socialism, with which he had a familiarity dating to the turn of the century, De Gasperi was totally lacking in sympathy. He accused Austrian Socialists of always having "one foot in parliament and another on the barricades," and of utilizing political power to "destroy the family and stifle the Faith."[22]

He watched with dismay the German efforts to take over Austria, and when the long-heralded *Anschluss* took place in March 1938, De Gasperi expressed the fear that the anti-Catholic campaign would spread to Austria. His fears were soon realized, and his columns chronicled in detail the attacks on Catholic institutions.[23]

French Catholicism was another subject of great interest to De Gasperi. Surveying the French nation as a whole, he divided it into the "fils de Voltaire" and the "fils des Croisés." However, the French Catholics of his day wished to avoid the errors of Boulangism, anti-Dreyfusism, and monarchial conservatism. The members of the *Parti démocrate populaire* believed in republicanism and democracy, a planned

The Years of Obscurity

economy (as opposed to state capitalism), and parliamentary reform.[24] These aims evidently met with De Gasperi's approval. Of the French Catholics he mentioned by name, he singled out Jacques Maritain for special praise. He quoted approvingly Maritain's assertion in *La Vie Intellectuelle* that it was time wasted to extol medieval Christianity; that the State should be pluralist, but with legislation in accordance with the moral law; and that the temporal order should be autonomous. De Gasperi saw a resemblance between the thought of Maritain and Toniolo insofar as both called for a repudiation of a regime based upon bourgeois humanism and insisted upon personal sanctity as a prerequisite for a new order.[25] De Gasperi equated the rightist leagues with which France was then plagued with the *fasci di combattimento*. Their ideology was based on the integral nationalism of Charles Maurras, the corporativism of La Tour du Pin, and the mystical and revolutionary syndicalism of Georges Sorel.[26]

De Gasperi's references to the Soviet Union are sparse, even though he asked if Bolshevism was not the "most ferocious adversary of Christianity, in fact, of every supernatural faith?"[27] He attributed the Soviet adoption of the Popular Front technique in 1935 to two factors: Stalin's fear of Germany and Japan, and the Communist failure to bring about a world revolution. To avoid losing their freedom to organize and develop as a political party, the Communists were resorting to the Popular Front. Nevertheless, commented De Gasperi, the mere adoption of the technique indicated a certain evolution, perhaps still remote, toward recovery of the Russian body politic. The fact that Communist parties were now defending national interests and upholding the established social order was bound to make them reconsider their own doctrinal positions. The promulgation of the Soviet constitution of 1936 and the adoption of legislation to strengthen the family gave encouragement to those who hoped that the Russian dictatorship would evolve slowly toward democracy. De Gasperi was not, however, unmindful of the fact that the supremacy of the Communist Party was in no way diminished by the new developments in the Soviet Union.[28]

In discussing Spanish affairs, De Gasperi pointed out that just as French Catholics could in conscience support the Republic, so too could Spanish Catholics back a republican regime. He quoted both papal and Spanish sources to indicate that there was no essential incompatibility between Catholicism and republicanism. But, said De Gasperi, the Spanish Republic should abandon the anticlerical tendencies that were so offensive to the conscience of the nation. What Spain needed was a government of the Center.[29] He saw the origins of the Spanish Civil

War in the failure of the Republic to respect religion, although the immediate outbreak of the war was the work of the army. He did not think that war was the only remedy for the troubles that had beset Spain, and he deplored the atrocities of the war.[30]

Turning his eyes to the United States, he commented upon the New Deal. He characterized it as an evolution rather than a revolution, and he quoted John A. Ryan on its compatibility with the principles laid down by the Papacy in *Quadragesimo Anno*. He saw Franklin D. Roosevelt as continuing in the footsteps of Wilson's "New Freedom." The new president was a "pragmatist," an experimenter, and De Gasperi obviously admired him for his willingness to try different techniques in an effort to bring the United States out of the throes of the depression.[31]

Mindful of his delicate position, De Gasperi had little to say concerning political developments in Italy. On corporativism, however, a subject on which he was an expert, he expressed his views, and not always with prudence. He considered Italian corporativism an "absolute novelty," first, because it embraced the entire nation and, secondly, because the Fascist Party was an essential part of every corporate organ. The corporations had not been set up in accordance with the principles of *Quadragesimo Anno*. The encyclical was concerned with the social, not the political order, and its directives were not to be identified with any political form or any particular constitution.[32] To show that Fascist corporativism was not the same as the corporativism expounded by nineteenth-century Catholic social thinkers or by the papal encyclicals, De Gasperi wrote three articles on corporativism.[33] The first two were concerned with the origins and development of modern corporativism and the third, the most important, was on post-First World War corporativism. In the latter he pointed out that in 1919 all except the proponents of class warfare spoke of a corporative system. As developed under Fascism, however, corporativism became tied to two things: one party and a totalitarian regime. According to Christian corporativism, corporations were natural societies, with social and economic functions that were subject to the laws of justice and charity.

De Gasperi suggested the following criteria in judging social movements: Does the movement harmonize with the supreme end of man? Does it respect and favor the free and responsible activity of the human personality? Does it correspond to the supreme evangelical laws of charity and justice? Are the relations between individual, family, and State consonant with the exigencies of the natural law and the precepts of the social encyclicals?[34] On the question of state intervention in the economic order, he took a Centrist position, accepting the need for limited state intervention. He wrote: "The golden line is in the middle; it is traced by natural law and taken note of in the papal encyclicals."[35] Analyzing the contemporary Christian social movement throughout the world, he saw it as having a positive character; it was not intended to solidify the status quo but rather to serve as an impetus to the substantial rectification of the existing social order.[36] The decline and failure of European Socialism afforded Catholics a superb opportunity to win over the working classes.

De Gasperi's comments on international developments, particularly those in which the Fascist regime was involved, were few and guarded. His remarks on the Ethiopian War, of which he privately disapproved, were largely quotations of foreign articles on the subject. Thus he cited an article from the *Reichspost* of Vienna which asserted that the blessing given by Italian clergymen to the soldiers going to Ethiopia was given to individuals and did not signify a judgment on the merits of the war. Another quotation came from an article by the Belgian jurist, Charles de Vischer, in the *Bulletin de l'Union belge pour la Societé des Nations*, in which the author maintained that while aggression with the aim of expansion was not justifiable, Italy possessed the right to protest against the political and economic order of the postwar world.[37] These were undoubtedly De Gasperi's sentiments as well.

With Conrad Henlein and his demands for the Sudeten Germans of Czechoslovakia De Gasperi showed little patience. If the German community of Czechoslovakia was entitled to full autonomy, then why not also the minorities in all countries, whether they be nationalities, creeds, or races. He condemned Henlein's postulates for the Sudeten Germans because they were based on the "right of race" which was an "egocentric concept" and did not flow from the essential equality of all men.[38]

De Gasperi showed equal impatience with the adoption of a racialist program in Italy. In the middle of July 1938, the Italian press published ten theses on race, formulated by a group of Italian professors and supported by the Ministry of Popular Culture. In his commentary on the theses, De Gasperi noted that they diverged from the Nazi concept of race in that there was no exaltation of any super-race and in the admission that present races were made up of diverse proportions of different races. Nevertheless, continued De Gasperi, the theses embodied the doctrine of racism, for thesis 7 stated that the Italians proclaimed themselves racists and thesis 9 excluded Jews from the Italian race. De Gasperi, pointing out that the Papacy had condemned racism, attributed the adoption of a racialist program to the strengthening of cultural and ideological ties between Italy and Germany. The fact that the German press acclaimed the racialist proclamation as a victory for Germany was, in De Gasperi's opinion, cause for alarm.[39]

One of De Gasperi's most significant articles of this period was a review of Benedetto Croce's *Storia d'Europa,* which he wrote under the pseudonym of V. Bianchi for *Studium* in 1932.[40] The review gave De Gasperi an opportunity to recall to Catholics the attitude of some of their co-religionists of the past century toward political liberty and human dignity. Croce had asserted that Catholicism was opposed to liberty. De Gasperi's answer was that with respect to political liberty the Catholics of the nineteenth century could be divided into two groups, the reactionary and the progressive, or the pessimistic and the optimistic. Cortes di Valdegamas would be an example of the first group, and Montalembert, Balbo, and Ozanam of the second. Many German and Belgian Catholics had also demonstrated their attachment to constitutional government and political liberty. Croce, asserted De Gasperi, had made his biggest mistake in designating as reactionary those social Christians who were inspired by *Rerum Novarum.* For Leo and his followers, the motive force of social reform was the autonomous association, not the State, and there was nothing reactionary about this concept. De Gasperi concluded his review by asking Croce a series of rhetorical questions, such as: (1) What had been the effect of the Hegelian concept of the State on European history? (2) What is the status of the individual according to the Hegelian view? (3) What happens to political liberty when, as Croce maintained in his *Frammenti d'etica,* the State wished to be a real Church, to have the cure of souls as well as of bodies?

Under the pen name of G. Fortis, a name he had used at the turn of the century, De Gasperi wrote in *Associazione Universitaria* for 1934 an appeal to youth, under the title of "Siate voi stessi! siate ottimisti" (Be yourselves; be optimists").[41] He praised Christian personalism, which steered a middle course between individualism on the one side and collectivism on the other, and he discerned a Christian spirit working as a leaven in society:

> We remain . . . optimistic. We could see the collapse of the present social order, knowing that the Church alone, surviving, would be able to save civilization. . . .
> We do not believe in cataclysm and apocalyptic visions; we believe and trust rather that even in the present social convulsions, as Balbo showed for the revolutions from '89 to 1848, the Christian leaven will work as a regenerative force and that the new ages will know new Christian progress.[42]

It must be remembered that the writings summarized in this chapter were not intended for any clandestine press; they were published in a country where Fascism was at the height of its power. Palmiro Togliatti, the head of the Italian Communist Party from 1944 until his death in 1964, wrote a book in 1958[43] in which he criticized De Gasperi for not using stronger language in denouncing Fascism—but the fact is that De Gasperi, unlike Togliatti, had not found safety abroad. It was necessary for De Gasperi to use guarded language, but nevertheless he was able to affirm certain essential truths, to place on guard those Catholics who were naive and disposed to compromise with Fascism. He thus kept alive the social Catholic traditions of political liberty and respect for civil rights.

During the mid- and late thirties, when the Fascist world appeared to have forgotten Alcide De Gasperi, some old *Popolari* friends began to frequent or telephone De Gasperi's home. Occasionally a representative of the anti-Fascist political refugees abroad would come to Rome, and De Gasperi would go to meet him.[44] Conversations among the former *Popolari* would become quite animated when important political events transpired, as, for example, the national plebiscite of March 25, 1934. The plebiscite was preceded by the plea of the head of the Diocesan Junta of Rome that every Catholic reinforce with his vote the "restorative work of the regime." During the election voters were given two papers, one with the word "si" and colored in green, white, and red, and one with the word "no" in plain paper. More than 95 per cent of the electorate went to the polls, and of these more than ten million votes were cast for the official list; only 15,000 voted "no." This must have been small consolation to the coterie that gathered at the De Gasperi residence on Via Bonifacio VIII.

In 1935 De Gasperi had to undergo an operation. Though minor in nature, he feared death and took the precaution of writing out his last will and testament. The words he used reveal a man proud of his obstinancy, proud of having "fought the good fight." Addressing himself to his wife, he wrote:

> If Providence wishes to close my earthly life before I have discharged my obligations as a father, I entrust to the Supreme Paternity of God my children, and I have absolute certainty that the Lord will assist you day by day in making them grow up to be good and courageous.
> Besides the relatives, I recommend them to the aid and support of those few but generous friends who during the period of the trials preserved their friendship for me. I cannot leave my daughters the

means of fortune, because I have had to renounce fortune in favor of loyalty to my principles. Soon they will be adults, and they will understand the world in which they live. They will then learn from you that their father fought and suffered for the ideals of human goodness and Christian democracy. Reading my letters of the past and some notes in my memoirs, they will learn to appreciate justice, Christian fraternity, and liberty.

I die with the knowledge of having fought the good fight and with the certainty that one day our principles will triumph.

In a postscript he added: "Inform Monsignor Tisserant of my death and ask him to transmit to His Holiness my thanks for all that he has been able to do for me. Let His Holiness know that I die with an immutable sense of attachment to the Holy See and with the conviction of having fought and worked for the defense of the essential principles of Christianity in public life and for the freedom of the Church."[45]

There was another side of De Gasperi: he could be the most lighthearted and gay person when in the company of his family and closest friends. He enjoyed playing with his daughters and taking them to Piazza Mazzini for pastry. Just before each Christmas he and Francesca delighted in preparing an elaborate creche which was concealed from the children until Christmas Eve. Bethlehem, the cave, the Holy Family, and the shepherds were all made of papier-maché and rested upon the precious volumes of De Gasperi's library.

Probably nowhere was De Gasperi happier than in his summer home in Sella di Valsugana. Each summer, when the Vatican Library closed for the annual summer vacation, the De Gasperi family journeyed northward to its refuge in the Dolomite Alps. Located about twelve kilometers from Borgo Valsugana, the house, known as Villa Romani and still the summer residence of the De Gasperi clan, is approached by a winding mountain road. Of typical Alpine architecture, the house stands alone, surrounded by snow-capped mountains, dark green forests, and fields of wild flowers.[46] De Gasperi knew the location of every mountain peak, every ravine, every stream of water. In the morning, he would go out alone into the forests to fill his lungs with the pure bracing air, but when he wanted to go on a hike of several hours' duration, he took with him his children and their friends. Followed by five or six youngsters ranging in age from ten to fifteen, he would move rapidly from one crag to another. To each level of the walls of Manazzo he gave a name: the level of the horses, the level of the sheep, the level of the bears. When they reached the top, De Gasperi would cup his hands, and filling them with water from the mountain stream, would offer a drink to his exhausted young comrades. In the evenings, especially on holidays, family, friends, and peasants would gather together to build a bonfire and sing mountain songs. House-painting was another of De Gasperi's pastimes. Each time summer arrived, the window shutters, garden benches, tables and chairs changed from red to green or from yellow to turquoise.[47]

Back in Rome a variety of tasks awaited De Gasperi. In addition to working at the library and writing anonymously, he endeavored to do his old friends such favors as were in his power. Thus he sought a teaching job in Rome for the daughter of an old friend from Trent; for the daughter of an ex-*Popolare* deputy, he sought a "recommendation" when she was about to undergo exams preparatory to graduating from a secondary school, even though he was doubtful of the value of such recommendations.[48]

The presence of De Gasperi in the Vatican was irksome to Mussolini, who tried to have him discharged, particularly during the 1931 crisis over Catholic Action. On April 8, 1931, Count Cesare Maria de Vecchi di Val Cismon, the Italian ambassador to the Holy See, made seven demands upon the Holy Father: (1) to moderate the Catholic press; (2) systematize the situation in the frontier dioceses; (3) to "take care that Catholic Action does not become, as it is becoming, a political party, but remains within the terms of the Concordat and abandons all syndicalist provocation;" (4) to praise Italy in the forthcoming commemoration of *Rerum Novarum*; (5) to constrain *L'Osservatore Romano* to use a "more Christian" polemical tone; (6) to send away from Rome various *Popolari* "ringleaders," especially De Gasperi, who was opposed to Fascism and whose continued presence in the Vatican "could only augment suspicions and misunderstandings"; and (7) to refrain from insisting publicly on "morality," "holy-day rest," and "nonfulfillment of the Concordat," for such expressions discredited the Italian government abroad. The Pope replied April 16. With reference to the third demand, he denied categorically that Catholic Action had become an enemy of the State, and he added that whoever was an enemy of Catholic Action was an enemy of the Pope. Concerning the sixth demand, requiring the dismissal of ex-*Popolari*, Piux XI said it would be mean and cowardly to dismiss them from Vatican service. Referring to De Gasperi in particular, the Holy Father said he did not regret and would never regret having given "an honest man and an honest father of a family a little of the bread" of which he had been deprived by Mussolini. As for anti-Fascist activity, the Pope expressed certainty that De Gasperi would do nothing "in the least censurable in this regard."

There followed a virtual war between Church and State. In May

Fascist Party members and students attacked the headquarters of Catholic Action organizations both in Rome and in the provinces. Hostile and vulgar comments were made regarding Pius XI. At the end of the month, Mussolini sent an order to all police stations to close down the offices of Catholic youth organizations, including those of the *Federazione universitaria cattolica italiana* (*FUCI*, Federation of Catholic University Students). Meanwhile, on May 15, the Pope had issued *Quadragesimo Anno*, which stated that the corporative system had an excessively bureaucratic and political character. On June 29 he issued the strongly worded *Non Abbiamo bisogno* in which Fascism was described as "an ideology which openly resolves itself into a true, a real pagan worship of the State."

The controversy continued until September 1931 when a compromise was reached. Under its terms, Catholic Action was declared essentially diocesan and dependent directly upon bishops, who would select the lay and ecclesiastical directors of the organizations. The prelates would not appoint those who had belonged to parties antagonistic to the regime, and Catholic Action would not concern itself with politics. Neither would Catholic Action attempt to form professional and syndical organizations; such professional organizations as were already existent were for strictly spiritual and religious ends. Finally, Catholic Action organizations were to refrain from athletic activities and confine themselves to educational and recreational activities that had purely religious ends.[49] The compromise was one that favored the Fascist State, giving it almost unlimited scope in winning the youth of Italy.

De Gasperi felt that the Church had unduly humiliated itself. In a meditative mood, he wrote: "For too long the precepts of dignity have been neglected. To get on one's knees is all very well but religious education should also teach one how to stand on one's feet. The attacks of the outlaws are violent, but whoever acts according to his own conscience has nothing to worry about. The evil becomes great when through insincere condescendence one loses one's self-respect."[50] The general attitude of subservience on the part of prelates distressed De Gasperi, who found their characterization of Mussolini as "a man of Providence" incomprehensible. The testimonials on behalf of Fascism increased during the tenth anniversary of the Fascist victory, and in his scrapbook De Gasperi pasted an article from *L'Osservatore Romano* under which he wrote: "I cried and suffered and wished I could still be in prison rather than witness such lack of conscience and cowardice."[51] To Don Giulio he exhorted: "Work, for it is the only way to alleviate the bitter-

The Years of Obscurity

ness of certain inexplicable spectacles."[52] At the time of the Ethiopian War he cut out and pasted in his scrapbook articles describing pastoral letters in support of the war.

When a friend made his peace with Fascism, he would write the friend's name in his diary with the significant notation, "tu quoque."[53] Concerning his own conduct, he harbored no regrets: ". . . to the past, I look with pride and to the future with serenity."[54] Perhaps De Gasperi was too severe on churchmen and on his former friends. The fact is that the Fascist government never succeeded in taking over the Catholic Action organizations, which operated in every commune, nourishing hopes and recalling to mind Christian social teaching. It is noteworthy that the Fascist hierarchy included hardly any Catholics coming from or adhering to Catholic Action, the Confraternity of St. Vincent de Paul, or any other religious organization. It included in its ranks almost no daily communicant.[55] Among the episodes of lay Catholic popular resistance during these years was the trial held in 1933 of members of a Guelf movement in Milan. The defendants were Piero Malvestiti, Gioachino Malavasi, Olviero Ortodossi, and Armando Rodolfi. Accused and found guilty of conspiring against Fascism and therefore "against the nation" they were sentenced to from three to five years of imprisonment.[56]

After the strengthening of ties between Italy and Germany and the adoption of a racialist program in Italy, the Church moved farther away from Fascism. The schism between State and Church paved the way for the rebirth of a Christian Democratic movement, to whose ranks came not only former *Popolari* but also university graduates, the lower clergy, and the organizations forming a part of Catholic Action.

In 1939, after the Second World War had begun, the Fascist regime once again took note of De Gasperi. Roberto Farinacci accused Giuseppe Dalla Torre of seeking Vatican citizenship for De Gasperi and of preparing the way for the return of Don Sturzo. De Gasperi's comment was ". . . I thought I was considered dead and instead they think me alive. Let us hope that this is a good sign that I shall live many more years in the tranquillity of my family."[57] The years from 1940 to 1942 were filled with sadness for De Gasperi. In April 1940, as Mussolini moved ever closer to entering the war on the side of Germany, De Gasperi wrote: ". . . for several days, contrary to my usual custom I see things darkly. May God be good to us."[58] De Gasperi's forebodings were justified; in June Italy entered the war as the ally of Hitler. The country was woefully unprepared for war, as everyone except Mussolini seems to have realized. De Gasperi would have been interested to know that on June 10 Ciano had written in his diary: "I am sad, very sad. The adventure begins. May God help Italy."[59]

In October 1940 De Gasperi's long-time friend and protector, Archbishop Endrici, died. To Don Giulio De Gasperi wrote in tribute: "I in particular have lost a fraternal friend who did not abandon me in the saddest moments and was a courageous witness for me before the authorities and the public."[60] "May the Lord repay him for the affection that he showed me in moments when many withdrew from me and did not recognize me."[61]

The staggering losses sustained by his country in 1940–1942 did not please De Gasperi, even though he had opposed entry into the war. Following their bungling invasion of Greece, in October 1940, the Italians had lost their East African Empire. Their German allies attempted to retrieve the situation in 1941, but in November and December the Italians suffered, in conjunction with the Germans, a crushing defeat in Africa. In ferocious desert warfare, the British Army drove back the Italo-German forces in eastern Libya, capturing huge numbers of troops. In January 1942, as the British toll of victories in Libya still mounted, De Gasperi observed: "It has been a long winter. For the first time I feel the attacks of age, and I become fearful concerning my age, because others, speaking of those in their sixties, frequently say 'he is finished; he is too old'. . . ." He then reminded himself that Galileo wrote *Dialogo dei due massimi sistemi del mondo* when he was sixty-eight years of age, and this was also Churchill's age.[62] No doubt these thoughts encouraged him to think that he could still serve his Church and country in spite of his advanced age.

CHAPTER VII

THE CLANDESTINE PERIOD

THE DAY AFTER ITALY ENTERED THE SECOND WORLD WAR, De Gasperi called to his home on Via Bonifacio VIII some former members of the *Partito Popolare* who were residing in Rome. He predicted that Italy would lose the war, because England would succeed in bringing the United States into it, and American entry would be decisive. With Italy's defeat on the field of battle, the Fascist regime would collapse, and consequently it was necessary to plan for the future.[1] During the next two years De Gasperi met regularly but cautiously with his anti-Fascist friends and discussed with them the organization and program of a revived Christian Democratic party.

The entry of students into such a party was of particular interest to De Gasperi, and the development of the *FUCI-movimento laureati* movements had encouraged belief that these groups would help provide the leadership for the new party. In 1925 the Federation of Italian Catholic University Students (*FUCI*) had been reorganized by Igino Righetti of Rimini and an ecclesiastical assistant, Monsignor Giovanni Battista Montini, the son of the Brescian *Popolare* Giorgio Montini.[2] As president of *FUCI*, Righetti, who never became a Fascist, sought to guide an intellectual elite in its Christian social and intellectual responsibilities. In 1932 he organized, outside of Catholic Action, the *movimento laureati* for Catholic university graduates; included in the movement were Catholic university graduates who were not Catholic Action members at all. A basic premise of the *movimento laureati* was that the culture of the Church must be brought in closer touch with contemporary society. The first local nuclei of the movement were established in 1934, and Righetti resigned from the presidency of *FUCI* to devote himself entirely to it. In January 1936 the first national congress of the movement took place. Obstacles to its expansion were both external and internal: the vigilant eye of Fascism was quick to find pretexts for hampering its activities, while within Catholic Action there were some who were antagonistic to the *movimento laureati*. Righetti died March 7, 1939, but the movement he founded remained in existence. In 1942 several of the *FUCI-movimento laureati* groups established ties with De Gasperi, who had always attached great importance to the role of university students in ideological movements, and both came into contact with two anti-Fascist Catholic formations in the North, the La Pira circle of Catholic Action in Florence and the Guelf movement in Lombardy. Subsequently all of these varied groups and movements were to fuse to form the Christian Democratic Party.

Late in July 1942 De Gasperi went to the Trentino to confer with Edoardo Clerici, Enrico Falck, Piero Malvestiti and other Milanese exponents of the Guelf movement. From the Trentino he traveled to Milan, where he took part in the organization of an executive commission of study and action. The commission included Giovanni Gronchi, Stefano Jacini, Malvestiti, Achille Grandi, and the sons of Filippo Meda. Malvestiti had the distinct impression that De Gasperi envisioned a great lay Catholic party of the Center, which would take in also men of Ivanoe Bonomi's persuasion.[3]

Meanwhile, other anti-Fascist parties were beginning to form or to revive. Thus Ferruccio Parri, Adolfo Tino, Ugo La Malfa, Luigi Salvatorelli and others were establishing the Party of Action; Giuseppe Romita, Bruno Buozzi, and Lelio Basso were reorganizing the Socialist Party; Giorgio Amendola and Celeste Negarville were constituting the Communist Party; and Bonomi, Marcello Soleri, Nicolò Carandini and Manlio Brosio were reviving the ranks of liberal democracy to bring forth the Liberal Party and the Labor Democratic Party. By the end of 1942, the leaders of the anti-Fascist parties were known to each other, and all were frequenting Bonomi's home in Piazza della Libertà in Rome.

The Christian Democrats held their meetings in the study of Giuseppe Spataro, which was located on Rome's noisy and well-populated Via Cola di Rienzo. In Spataro's study, a large room with yellow armchairs and sofa, the future leaders of the Christian Democratic Party had their first contacts with the exponents of the Socialist Party. From time to time the chief of police of Rome, who was friendly, would warn them that the location was under surveillance, and he would urge them to use caution. By reason of his experience, temperament, and

The Clandestine Period

character, De Gasperi was recognized by all as the logical head of the Christian political party that was in the process of being revived. Interestingly enough, in June 1944 Mussolini told a journalist at Salò that of all the survivors of the old democratic parties, De Gasperi was the man best suited to lead postwar Italy.[4] To the meetings on Cola di Rienzo came also the Labor Democrats, Bonomi and Meuccio Ruini, and the Communists, Giorgio Amendola and Mauro Scoccimarro. The gatherings at Cola di Rienzo and Piazza della Libertà laid the foundation for the formation of the multiparty anti-Fascist front and the Committee of National Liberation. On April 27, 1943, the Anti-Fascist United Freedom Front was formed, with Bonomi as its spokesman; the agreement was later put into writing and signed by Alessandro Casati for the Liberals, Giuseppe Romita for the Socialists, Meuccio Ruini for the Labor Democrats, De Gasperi for the Christian Democrats, and "an obscure Communist" for the Communists.[5] The pact pledged the parties to a political truce during the war and the period of reconstruction. Their common goal would be a democratic regime based upon the popular will.

In the period immediately before and after the fall of Mussolini, politically conscious Italian Catholics were much preoccupied with the role that they should play in the forthcoming New Order. Some took the position that no collaboration with organisms that contained Communists was possible. Others held that it was possible to "baptize Communism" and a group of these even formed a party of Catholic Communists, headed by Franco Rodano and Adriano Ossicini. Another faction doubted that it was opportune for Catholics to form a political party, alleging that such an attempt would result in a revival of anticlericalism; they preferred to have Catholics join the existing parties. But De Gasperi's position was that it was necessary for Catholics to form a political party of their own, and it was this point of view which won out.[6]

While the anti-Fascist bloc was in the process of formation, De Gasperi continued working at his Vatican post, making preparations for the celebration of the quadricentennial of the Council of Trent. To judge from his correspondence with his old friend Don Giulio in 1942–1943, the anniversary of the Council of Trent was his primary concern. On July 16, 1943, when the annual summer vacation began for the employees of the Vatican Library, De Gasperi took a "leave of absence," which turned out to be permanent. Three days later, he witnessed from the *Museo Lapidario Vaticano* the first aerial bombardment of Rome. He saw hundreds of planes circle the city and then drop their bombs on its periphery. Among the edifices hit was the Church of San Lorenzo fuori le Mure, in which he would be buried eleven years later. The same church contains the tomb of Pope Pius IX, under whom Italian Catholics had been excluded from political life. It was under De Gasperi that Italian Catholics were to achieve full insertion into the political life of the nation.

With the succession of Italian defeats abroad, the anti-Fascists were not the only ones to organize in anticipation of the future. Two other distinct groups emerged: dissident Fascists and royalist military leaders. Dissident Fascists, such as Galeazzo Ciano, Dino Grandi, and Giuseppe Bottai, all members of the Fascist Grand Council, hoped to eliminate Mussolini and to separate Italy from the disastrous alliance with Germany. They sought to attach themselves to the military men around the court who disapproved of the conduct of the war. The latter included General Vittorio Ambrosio, who was appointed chief of the High Command early in 1943 and who failed in his efforts to persuade Mussolini to break with Hitler.[7]

By the summer of 1943 the war was nearing a climax as far as Italy was concerned. At the beginning of June Bonomi had been received by Victor Emmanuel III, whom he urged to overthrow the Fascist regime, detach Italy from the German alliance, and end the war. The King had listened with interest but had not allowed a word to betray his intentions.[8] In July, after the invasion of Sicily by the Allies and the aerial bombardment of Rome, the King finally acted. On the night of July 24–25 the Grand Council met and called for the restoration of all powers to the King. The vote was 19 to 7, which the King interpreted as a vote of "no confidence" in Mussolini. On July 25 Mussolini was arrested as he left the royal residence. Marshal Pietro Badoglio became chief of state, heading a cabinet of technicians. On July 26 the new Italian government proclaimed martial law throughout Italy and decreed the dissolution of the Fascist Party. Fearing German reprisals if there ensued an open breach with Germany, Badoglio announced that the war would continue. In the meantime, he hoped to make approaches to the Allies in order to obtain better terms than unconditional surrender. His attempts to contact the Anglo-Americans were, however, impeded by the entry of German troops into Italy.

As early as the morning of July 25, a Sunday, rumors concerning the fall of Mussolini were circulating throughout Rome. De Gasperi immediately proceeded to the home of Alberto Bergamini (Liberal and former editor of *Il Giornale d'Italia*), where he discussed the meaning of the events that had transpired during the night with Gronchi, Bonomi, Casati, Ruini, Spataro, and Tommaso Della Torretta (Liberal). Bonomi recommended that they abstain from any government formed by the King because it would not be clearly anti-Fascist and it was not, moreover, prepared to end the war immediately. De Gasperi supported Bonomi's recommendation.[9] On this same day, July 25, 1943, De Gasperi and his associates formally adopted the name of *Democrazia Cristiana* for their party.[10]

The following morning, as De Gasperi crossed the almost deserted Piazza Venezia, he encountered a motor lorry carrying a group of young men. Waving the tricolor, they had attached a rope to the neck of a bronze bust of Mussolini, which was bobbing up and down on the pavement. There could now be no doubt about the finality of Mussolini's fall and the temper of the people.

At a meeting on August 2 in the study of Spataro, the anti-Fascist parties decided unanimously to urge the government to sever its alliance with Germany.[11] A week later Bonomi presented to Badoglio the members of the Central Committee of the anti-Fascist parties: Casati for the Liberals, De Gasperi for the Christian Democrats, Luigi Salvatorelli for the Party of Action, Bruno Buozzi for the Socialists, Giorgio Amendola for the Communists, and Meuccio Ruini for the Labor Democratic Party. These gave to Badoglio their August 2 resolution urging withdrawal from the war. De Gasperi wanted to discuss the international situation, but the marshal asked him to await the decision of the government, which would be made with full knowledge of all the elements of the situation.[12] At another meeting held in Spataro's study on August 11, the anti-Fascists discussed the attitude they should assume in the face of Badoglio's failure to liquidate Fascism more quickly and to break with Germany. Some favored a popular insurrection, but De Gasperi and Bonomi opposed this suggestion, stating that Italians should not be called upon to chase the Germans out of Italy until the Anglo-Americans were on the Italian mainland.[13] These two had to work hard to prevent their colleagues from breaking with Badoglio and to persuade them to maintain contacts with at least two ministers who enjoyed the esteem of anti-Fascists, Leonardo Severi and Leopoldo Piccardi.[14]

By the end of July the Italian government had already decided to negotiate with the Allies. General Giuseppe Castellano of the Italian High Command was sent to Lisbon, where on August 19 he met Major Walter Bedell Smith and Brigadier K.W.D. Strong of General Eisenhower's staff in the British Embassy. Smith read to Castellano the terms of the armistice, later to be called the Short Armistice. Article 12 compelled Italy to accept political, economic, and financial terms later to be defined. Smith gave Castellano an *aide-mémoire,* later to be known as the "Quebec Document," which was to become the basis of Italy's postarmistice foreign policy. It stated that the extent to which the terms of the armistice would be modified in favor of Italy would depend on the degree to which the Italian government and people aided the United Nations against Germany during the war. Whenever the Italian forces or Italians fought the Germans, they would be given all possible aid by the United Nations. With respect to the navy, Smith said that while he could put nothing in writing, he could say that the Italian flag would continue to fly over the ships. On September 3 Castellano signed the Short Armistice at Cassibile, Sicily. On the same day Smith gave Castellano a copy of the Long Armistice, whose initial clauses provided for the unconditional surrender of the Italian land, air, and sea forces. On September 8, as the Anglo-Americans landed at Salerno, Marshal Badoglio announced to Italy the armistice with the United Nations, and on the following day he fled from Rome with the royal family and the military leaders. The Italian troops were thrown into a state of confusion and disorganization by the sudden turn of events. Of an Italian army of sixty-one divisions in Italy, France, the Balkans and the islands, only seven, ill-equipped and demoralized, were left to the Allies.

On September 10 the royal entourage arrived in Brindisi, and on the following day Badoglio ordered the Italian troops to consider the Germans as enemies. His requests to the Allies for an alliance were repulsed, but Eisenhower recommended the status of co-belligerency to lend some prestige to the King, who was given four provinces to rule, Taranto, Lecce, Bari, and Brindisi. The King was asked to declare war on the Germans. The royal declaration came on October 13, and on the same day the Allies recognized Italy as a co-belligerent. While they recognized the royal government headed by Badoglio, the Allies emphasized the right of the Italian people to decide ultimately the institutional question. Co-belligerence did not give Italy allied status; Italy was still considered an enemy state. On September 29 Badoglio had signed the Long Armistice, protesting, however, the use of the term "unconditional surrender." Certain amendments were subsequently made by the American, British, and Soviet governments which eliminated the term "unconditional surrender," but the terms were said to have been accepted unconditionally by Marshal Badoglio. In return the Italian navy had to be surrendered, and this took place on November 17, 1943. The Long Armistice amendments were signed and backdated to November 9.[15] The armistice was to be executed by a Control Commission. Meanwhile, Mussolini had been rescued by the Germans from his prison atop Gran Sasso and had established a puppet regime at Salò.

On September 8, as the Anglo-American forces landed at Salerno, the Central Committee of the Christian Democratic Party was established, with De Gasperi as its president. On the following day, in a house on Via Adda, De Gasperi joined Bonomi, Pietro Nenni, Romita, Amendola, Ruini, La Malfa, Casati, and Sergio Fenoaltea to discuss the situation that had arisen from the Italian surrender and the precipitous flight from Rome of Badoglio and the King. Out of the discussions came the formation of the *Comitato centrale di liberazione nazionale* (*CLN*, Central Committee of National Liberation), composed of the representatives of the Christian Democratic, Socialist, Actionist, Labor Democratic, Communist, and Liberal parties and presided over by Bonomi. La Malfa wanted a declaration of principles, but De Gasperi characteristically expressed opposition to "useless words." Bonomi prepared a brief text to announce the formation of the *CLN*: "At the moment that Nazism seeks to restore in Rome and in Italy its Fascist ally, the anti-Fascist parties constitute themselves into the Committee of National Liberation and call upon all Italians to do battle and to resist and to reconquer for Italy the place that is due her by the consensus of the free nations."[16] Subsequently committees paralleling the Central Committee of National Liberation were established in the other provinces, the most important of which was the Central Committee of National Liberation of Upper Italy (*CLNAI*), with headquarters in Milan.

On September 11 and 12 the *CLN* met in the apartment of Carlo Antoni on Via del Gesù. Amendola and La Malfa proposed two declarations: one proclaimed the fall of the monarchy, which had abandoned the capital and the direction of the nation, and the other called for a popular insurrection against the Germans. De Gasperi and Bonomi again concurred: they said that while the monarchy could be deplored, it was in contact with the Allies, and a declaration concerning its fall could destroy one of the few cards that Italy could still play. In the end the participants approved a manifesto that would be launched once a vast popular action was under way.[17] While the *CLN* debated, Rome fell under Nazi control. To elude capture by the Nazis or pro-Nazi Italians, all the leaders of the anti-Fascist parties began to leave their homes to seek refuge with trusted friends or relatives.

On September 15 De Gasperi met Emilio Bonomelli, an old friend who was in charge of Castel Gandolfo, in the Church of St. Robert Bellarmine. Bonomelli took De Gasperi to Castel Gandolfo, where he gave him a small apartment in a secluded corner of the papal building. De Gasperi was delighted to discover that he would be under the protection of an ex-*carabiniere* who had been a friendly guard when he was a prisoner in the Ciancarelli Clinic. De Gasperi remained in this refuge until the beginning of December. Not too far away, in another inconspicuous corner was Giuseppe Bottai, Mussolini's former minister of education and civil commissioner in Greece.[18] Only on rare occasions did De Gasperi leave his hiding place and then it was to meet his colleagues or to search for a more centrally located haven. During De Gasperi's absence from the center of Rome, Gronchi substituted for him in the meetings of the *CLN*. At a meeting held October 16, Gronchi drew up, assisted by Scoccimarro, Nenni, La Malfa, Casati, Ruini, and Bonomi, an order of the day which stated that the spiritual unity required for the prosecution of the war of liberation could not be achieved under the aegis of the existing government and that an extraordinary government should be substituted which reflected the forces that had combated Fascism. This government should (1) assume all the constitutional powers of the state, (2) lead the war of liberation, and (3) convoke the people at the end of hostilities to decide the institutional question.[19]

In mid-November De Gasperi came out of his papal hideaway to attend a meeting of the *CLN* at the home of Monsignor Pietro Barbieri on Via Cernaia. He was accompanied by the president of *FUCI*, Giulio Andreotti, who met him in Piazza Santa Maria Maggiore. De Gasperi displayed considerable nervousness, and he talked about his arrest in 1927. No doubt he felt he was in far greater danger in 1943.[20]

When De Gasperi left Castel Gandolfo it was to take refuge in a new wing of the Lateran Seminary which, like Castel Gandolfo, possessed extraterritoriality under the terms of the Lateran Treaty. Here in the heart of Rome, he was closer to his colleagues, many of whom were already or were soon to be guests of the Lateran Seminary, such as Bonomi, Casati, Nenni, Ruini, Soleri, Bergamini, Giuseppe Saragat, and other noted anti-Fascists. In time about eight hundred persons enjoyed the hospitality of Monsignor Ronca, the Rector of the seminary. The refugees were divided into homogeneous groups (i.e., political, military, Jewish, and so forth) and were segregated from each other. Many of the guests took the names of the seminarians whose rooms they occupied. Thus De Gasperi became Alfonso Porta (today Alfonso Porta is pastor of the Church of San Vitale in Rome) and Nenni became Pietro Emiliani. Their rooms were in the following order: Saragat, Ruini, De Gasperi, Casati, Bonomi, and Nenni. On the premises were an oven, a slaughter house, and a mill, and food was never lacking. Don Palazzini was entrusted with the care of the political refugees, and he maintained contacts with their associates and relatives on the outside. From time to time Gronchi, Gonella, Longinotti, Scoccimarro, and Sergio Fenoaltea (secretary of the CLN) made visits to the seminary. De Gasperi frequently received his daughter Maria Romana or his wife. On Sundays Monsignor Ferrero di Cavallerleone said Mass, and De Gasperi served. Sometimes Nenni, who did not participate in the religious services, would turn up the volume of his radio, whereupon Bonomi would go out to ask him to lower it.[21]

With almost the entire CLN in the Lateran Seminary, it was possible to discuss political affairs, such as the composition and functions of the new extraordinary government and the role of the King.[22] Nenni thought in terms of a government made up substantially of the CLN, whereas De Gasperi and Bonomi favored one with a broader base. The governmental question, particularly as it related to the King, was complicated by the decision of the Liberals on the outside to demand the abdication of the King and his replacement by his son, so that at the future Constituent Assembly, they might defend a "cleansed monarchy."[23] On December 30, 1943, Enrico De Nicola, the famous Neapolitan jurist, proposed the Lieutenancy, under which the King was to delegate permanent power to a Lieutenant General of the Realm and retire from public life without abdicating. The crown prince would be the Lieutenant General. These developments were perplexing to the inmates of the seminary.

The enforced cohabitation at the seminary of men of diverse ideologies and backgrounds was a preparation for their subsequent political life in the nation. De Gasperi often engaged in conversations with Nenni, going over past ground to determine whether or not a less heated polemic between the *Popolari* and the Socialists might have prevented the victory of Fascism. The colloquies between the reserved Trentine and the exuberant Romagnuol became quite protracted and lively at times. De Gasperi concluded from these conversations that the Socialists and perhaps even the Communists were no longer so anxious to have their parties come to power.[24] Later, when De Gasperi and Nenni became political enemies, there remained the memories of the friendly debates in the Lateran Seminary, held in what seemed an oasis of security amid the military terror which then gripped Rome. Even at the seminary, however, there were moments of fear and tension. On January 31, 1944, for example, a patrol of drunken German soldiers became very noisy outside the gates of the Lateran. Fearing an invasion of the premises, the officials of the seminary advised their political guests to conceal themselves in a subterranean chamber. For more than an hour they remained seated on a pipe, surrounded by total darkness. De Gasperi prayed, while Nenni cursed good-naturedly in his native Romagnuol.[25]

On the outside, important political events were transpiring, knowledge of which reached the Lateran refugees through the radio and personal messengers. One of these events was the Congress of Bari, called by the delegates of the Committees of National Liberation in the South and held January 28–29, 1944. The first interregional meeting of the Christian Democratic Party took place simultaneously. During the previous month, the Central Committee, influenced by De Gasperi, had adopted a resolution stating that the institutional question should be deferred until the liberation of the country had been accomplished. At Bari, however, the Christian Democrats adopted a resolution which differed somewhat from that of the Central Committee: it stated that the party looked forward to the abdication of the King as a condition for the pacification of the country. The adoption of this resolution made it possible for the Christian Democrats to offer a compromise when a disagreement developed at the congress. Here the Communists, Socialists, and Actionists had presented a resolution stating that the presidency of the congress should be transformed into a revolutionary government that would replace the King. The majority of the delegates rejected this proposal and adopted instead a compromise Christian Democratic resolution, which declared that the condition of the country did not permit an immediate solution to the institutional question. However, a prerequisite for moral and material reconstruction was the immediate abdication of the King. An Executive Junta, composed of one representative from each of the parties, was constituted to obtain the royal abdication.[26]

After the Congress of Bari, the Central *CLN* entered a period of crisis owing to the intransigence of the Socialists, who asserted the moral and political incompatibility of the anti-Fascist parties with the monarchy, and therefore not only with Victor Emmanuel but also with any regency. They sought the creation of an extraordinary anti-Fascist government to which would be granted all the powers of parliament and the King. In view of the tenacity of the Socialist position, which was supported by the Actionists, Bonomi resigned on March 24, 1944, from the presidency of the *CLN*. De Gasperi endeavored to play a mediating role. He agreed with Bonomi that the matter of primary concern was the war of liberation, but he also felt that an attempt should be made to get the leftist parties to remain in collaboration with the other parties.[27]

The Clandestine Period

While the debate on the Crown continued, the long-time Italian Communist, Palmiro Togliatti, returned from Moscow. To the surprise and confusion of the Actionists, Socialists, and Communists, who had been asserting that they would be contaminated by contact with the monarchy, Togliatti expressed willingness to collaborate with the royal government, and he offered his services to Badoglio.[28] Thus Badoglio, who had moved from Brindisi to Salerno, could form in April 1944 a government of the six parties. The King refused to abdicate, but he agreed to the Lieutenancy for his son Umberto, and on April 6 the Executive Junta accepted Umberto. On April 22 the first *CLN* government was formed under Badoglio; it pledged that it would not try to upset the Lieutenancy until the people had made the final decision. The Christian Democrats were represented by Giulio Rodinò as minister without portfolio and Salvatore Aldisio as minister of the interior. Togliatti became minister without portfolio. With the resolution of the crisis within the *CLN*, Bonomi returned to its presidency.

In the meantime, De Gasperi had been forced to leave his Lateran refuge for another Vatican shelter, the headquarters of the *Propaganda Fide*; for on February 5, 1944, news had arrived at the Lateran that the Fascist police had invaded the Basilica of St. Paul and had arrested several Jews and generals. No longer was religious property safe from intrusion, and the Lateran officials advised their refugees to seek other havens.[29] With a hat drawn low over his face, De Gasperi went one afternoon to the central offices of the *Propaganda Fide* in the Piazza di Spagna. While he waited in a nearby bar, his wife entered the building to beg Cardinal Celso Costantini for permission for her husband to remain there for several days. In his memoirs Cardinal Costantini described the arrival of De Gasperi:

> De Gasperi came over, pale but calm. He told me that he had received a truly Christian treatment at the Latern Seminary. I was happy to be able to offer him hospitality in such turbulent times. He is a personal friend; he is not sought by the police, and is not subject to the draft. He is an employee of the Vatican but is considered a formidable adversary of Fascism. . . .
>
> He is a very noble figure both as a Christian and as a scholar. He is a man who has tempered with his own sufferings strength of character and he has paid with an iniquitous imprisonment the fault of having exercised free thought and of having refused to debase himself before Mussolini. . . .[30]

De Gasperi had remained at the *Propaganda Fide* headquarters until the liberation of Rome. Maria Romana went to see him almost every day, stuffing into the pockets of her overcoat the articles he had written for the clandestine Christian Democratic press or notes for members of the *CLN*. At times De Gasperi seemed oblivious of the fact that he was sixty-two years of age and in a dangerous situation. One morning he hid under the tiles of the sloping roof outside his attic room some confidential papers. A few days later, when he went to retrieve them, he discovered that they had disappeared. Seeing something white near the edge of the roof, he crawled out onto the roof, though it was broad daylight and the Piazza was crowded with passersby. The excursion turned out to have been in vain: when he returned to his room, he found that the paper was blank. His own papers had probably been carried away by the wind.[31]

On June 5, 1944, the Allies entered Rome, and only then was De Gasperi able to return to his home on Via Bonifacio VIII. On June 7 the Central Directory of the Christian Democratic Party held its first meeting in Rome. It was presided over by De Gasperi, who proposed that the religious authorities be requested to celebrate on June 24, a Mass for the 335 Italians slaughtered by the Germans in the Ardeatine Caves on March 24. He expressed the hope that the bodies would not be removed from the place of execution and that a memorial would be erected on the spot, which had already been consecrated by the blood of Christian martyrs.[32]

On June 10, with the other *CLN* leaders De Gasperi went to the Grand Hotel to meet with Marshal Badoglio, after which the latter went to the Lieutenant General and offered his resignation. Badoglio was succeeded as head of the government by Bonomi, whose ministers without portfolio were De Gasperi, Benedetto Croce, Carlo Sforza, Saragat, Ruini, Togliatti, and Alberto Cianca. Christian Democrats entrusted with portfolios were Gronchi as minister of industry, commerce, and labor, and Umberto Tupini as minister of justice. De Gasperi probably derived the most satisfaction from the governmental appointment, for it signalized his return to the political life which he had long considered his mission. On June 11, when he went to Castel Gandolfo to see his old friend Bonomelli, the latter noted that De Gasperi's normally cold grey eyes were shining with ill-concealed emotion.

General Mason Macfarlane, chief commissioner of the Allied Control Commission, approved the ministry on the condition that the armistice terms be accepted. Decree-Law 151, issued June 25, 1944, granted the ministry the power to issue decrees having the force of law in the name of the lieutenant general and provided for the convocation of a constituent assembly upon the liberation of the country. The premier was to take an oath of allegiance to the Crown, but the other ministers were not obligated to do so.

On July 15 the Allied Control Commission established itself in Rome; it was the organ through which relations between the United Nations and the Italian government were conducted. Originally the Allied Control Commission and the Allied Military Government were separate entities, the former under the supreme allied commander in Algiers and the latter under the theater commander in Italy. In a reorganization of the Control Commission in January 1944, the headquarters and general staffs of the two organizations were combined, becoming known as AMG/ACC in Italy. The AMG functioned in territory in the forward areas behind the Allied lines, while the ACC functioned in territories more remote from the front line and under the administration of the Italian government. The relationship of the Control Commission to the Italian government and administration was one of supervision rather than of direct administration, as in the case of the Allied Military Government.

By the time Rome was liberated and the *CLN* was granted official recognition through the formation of the Bonomi government, De Gasperi had prepared a platform for his party. During the clandestine period numerous study commissions had been established despite the dangers of the moment: the Constitutional Commission, presided over by Umberto Tupini; the Labor Union Commission under Grandi; the Economic Commission under Pietro Campilli; and the Commission for Industrial Questions under Gronchi. The coordinating center was Spataro's study. News concerning the party and its activities were carried in the clandestine journal, *Il Popolo,* which bore the same name as Donati's journal of the *Popolare* era and was directed by Guido Gonella. De Gasperi wrote for the paper under the pseudonym of "Demofilo."

By the autumn of 1943 the general lines of the program to be presented to the public had been delineated. The final text was prepared by De Gasperi, and under the title of *Idee ricostruttive della Democrazia Cristiana,* it circulated throughout Italy during the period of Nazi-Fascist domination.[33] The program drew its inspiration from the traditions of Popularism but it also looked toward the future and was designed to take care of the problems created by two decades of Fascist rule. This program must now be briefly summarized, for De Gasperi's enemies were to charge later that he failed to carry it out (particularly with regard to regional autonomy and social change) and that its reformist tone was merely an attempt to compete with the leftist parties for the allegiance of the masses.

The main thesis of the *Idee* was that the indispensable premise for the inviolable rights of the human person was political liberty. The future regime was to be a representative democracy, expressed by universal suffrage and founded upon an equality of rights and duties. The most important organ of the State would be parliament, which would consist of two chambers, one elected by universal suffrage, and the other by professional organizations in the regions.

The most effective guarantee for the maintenance of liberty would be the establishment of regions as autonomous entities, representing and administering local and professional interests. Regional autonomy would permit an adequate solution of the specific problems of the South and of the islands. The representative body of each region would be based primarily on the professional organizations.[34]

According to the *Idee*, the greatest social effort of the State would be directed toward the suppression of the proletariat. To attain this objective, it would be necessary to impose reforms upon industry, agriculture, and the tax system. In industry workers would participate in the profits, management, and capitalization of enterprises, although the specific form of such participation would vary according to the nature of the enterprise. The State was to eliminate the industrial and financial concentrations which were the artificial creations of economic imperialism, and it was to modify the laws which until then had favored the concentration of wealth and production in the hands of a few. For such monopolies as were in the nature of things, public control would be imposed, "not as a step toward a collective system in whose economic benefits we do not believe and which we consider harmful to liberty, but as a measure of defense against the formation of an industrial and financial feudalism which we consider equally dangerous for a free people."

In agriculture the objective of the new State would be the gradual transformation of the day laborers into tenant farmers and proprietors, or when technical reasons so required, into associates in the management of agricultural enterprises. An agrarian reform program, which would be entrusted to the regions, would limit the amount of land that could be held.

The *Idee* also stated that a better distribution of wealth could be achieved through a reform of the fiscal system. A graduated income tax would prevent any exorbitant concentration of wealth and should therefore be the pivot of any tax system. Tax reforms would be preceded by emergency measures, involving confiscation of surplus profits derived from the war or from the Fascist regime.

The *Idee* concluded by outlining principles for the postwar international order. It stated that the principle of national self-determination should be accepted by all peoples, but it added that nations should accept also limitations on their sovereignty in the interest of a wider solidarity. Organs of confederation, having continental and intercontinental ties, should be promoted. National societies should surrender the right to seek justice for themselves and should accept instead an international organization that had adequate means for resolving international disputes. The new community of nations should bring about the progressive and controlled disarmament of all nations, victorious and vanquished. It should take under its jurisdiction colonial territories, with a view to promoting the moral and self-governing progress of the peoples concerned.

In order to assure to nations the indispensable conditions of existence, there should be a more equitable distribution of raw materials. Liberty of emigration should be fostered, and autarchy and tariff protectionism should be gradually abolished. A financial organization, set up by the international community, should have the task of facilitating the stabilization of currencies. In the new postwar community of nations, the people of Italy, having been guiltless of any war of conquest, would expect full recognition of their independent status and integrity.

De Gasperi commented upon and amplified the *Idee* in three articles published in *Il Popolo* in the winter of 1943-1944 under the pseudonym of "Demofilo": "The Word of the Christian Democrats," "Our Christian Democracy and its Traditions," and "Our Movement and its Ideology."[35] Particularly interesting and instructive is De Gasperi's discussion of the limited and autonomous character of the party, contained in "The Word of the Christian Democrats." Unlike Giorgio La Pira, De Gasperi did not believe that a party should aim at integrating the social body with the Mystical Body. He saw the party solely as an instrument designed to function in the political sector of society, that is, in the State. He asserted:

> ... the party is an organism limited in character which need not act or innovate in every field, because it realizes that other organisms act at the same time and in the same space on diverse levels: outside and above is the religious society, that is, the Church with its spiritual and organizing forces (Catholic Action); below, there are scientific,

cultural, and economic societies with their own autonomy and their own rules. This is why, differing from those who see in the State the assumption, substitution and centralization of all faiths and all social forces, we do not present ourselves as the integral promoters of a universal regeneration but as the bearers of a specific political responsibility, inspired of course by our ideology but determined also by the circumstances in which it must be realized. And that is why, even when acknowledging our debt to the principles of civil renovation taught us by the social Catholic school and reaffirmed with luminous vigor in the pontifical message to the world at Christmas in 1942, we avoid ostentatious declarations. These would seem to place us on the same level of recent experiences or proclamations, which exploited Catholicism as an instrument of government, or would give us the air of boasting or pretending to have, on the terrain of politics, the officially delegated representation of all Italian Catholics.

We believe it legitimate to think that our conduct over so many years of public life . . . leaves no doubt that in future political actions we propose to give to God what is God's and to Caesar what is Caesar's.[36]

Thus De Gasperi clearly defined the competence of political parties. The Christian Democratic Party, while a party of believers, with an ideology of Christian inspiration, was not the only legitimate party for Catholics, nor was it an instrument for the achievement of the spiritual objectives of the Church. Three years later, in a speech at the Teatro Brancaccio, De Gasperi specifically denied having received any directive from the Vatican to found a party, and, equally significant, he denied that the Vatican would have had the right to issue any such directive.[37]

In this connection it should be noted that the mature De Gasperi had definitely turned away from some of the concepts of Italian social Catholicism. He had come to the conclusion that certain of Toniolo's ideas—such as corporatism and the goal of an integral Catholic reconquest of society—had become obsolete because times had changed.[38] The Fascist experience undoubtedly had had the effect of clarifying and sharpening De Gasperi's views on the limited and autonomous character of political parties and on the distinction that must prevail between the sphere of state action and that of ecclesiastical action.

CHAPTER VIII

RETURN TO POLITICAL LIFE

THE FIRST BONOMI GOVERNMENT, WHICH RE-ENTERED ROME on July 15, 1944, after spending a few weeks at Salerno, functioned amid great difficulties. For one thing, the war still had to be prosecuted, and Bonomi called upon the Allies to permit Italy to put a strong army into the field. The Allies, however, manifested great skepticism regarding the value of building up the Italian army.[1] Secondly, at the Palazzo dei Marescialli in Piazza Indipendenza, some of the ministers without portfolio acted in a manner which suggested that they considered themselves the rivals of Premier Bonomi, a development which De Gasperi found disconcerting.

During the summer of 1944 De Gasperi delivered his first public political speeches in almost twenty years. For many of the participants, the rallies were the first that they had ever attended. On July 23, 1944, at the Teatro Brancaccio, the first meeting of the Roman section of the Christian Democratic Party was held. De Gasperi, as the main speaker, assured his audience that while the armistice, the terms of which were still secret, was "a harsh instrument of war" there was nothing in it that compromised the future. He urged all Italians to put aside divisive issues and to cooperate in the work of reconstruction. The new constitution, he said, would be determined by popular consultation. The new State should emerge not from a sense of revenge against Mussolini but rather from the conviction that it was the best State possible. The establishment of such a State would require a period of preparation and reflection.

In his references to Russia De Gasperi was quite conciliatory. He stated that cooperation between Russia and the West would produce a new and better world. Russia was to be commended for seeking a fusion of races: "This effort, this attempt at the unification of the human race is Christian; it is eminently universal in a Catholic sense. Also Christian is the attempt to minimize the differences between social classes . . ., to elevate manual labor." At the same time, he pointed to the totalitarian character of the Communist regime, a character which was inimical to liberty. Of special interest are the words which he addressed to Togliatti:

> Colleague Togliatti, we have appreciated, as it deserved, your declaration of respect for the Catholic Faith of the majority of the Italian people, and we hope that the entire party will draw the practical consequences of your declaration. The mutual tolerance in the forms of civil living which you propose and which we willingly accept constitutes, as opposed to the past, a notable advance, which may make us meet more often on the hard road that we must traverse for the redemption of the Italian people. But up there on the incline—and with the eyes of Faith I seem to see His luminous figure—walks another Proletarian, also Jewish, like Marx; two thousand years ago, He established the International based on equality, universal fraternity, the Fatherhood of God. He aroused ardent love, untold heroism, and sacrifices to the point of immolation. But the man inclined to evil resists Him; he is avaricious (*mammona iniquitatis*), proud (*superbia vitae*), and bloodthirsty. On the eve of the war, the voice of the pope resounded in vain. Well, it is necessary to take to the road once again, to follow that Divine Figure. Has not each one of you already encountered that Proletarian, Christ, with His kind look, during the days of pain and tragedy in the shelters, in the prisons, or in the darkness of the catacombs?[2]

The speech reflected the situation of the moment, when England and the United States regarded the Soviet Union as a gallant ally and within Italy there was Christian Democratic and Communist collaboration on more than one level. Not only were Christian Democrats cooperating with the Communists in the partisan war against the Germans but they were serving in the same cabinet with the Communists. In an article for the *New York Times*, Don Luigi Sturzo wrote: "The complete governmental cooperation between the Christian Democratic Party and the Communist is a political cooperation made necessary to fight the German army and the Fascist puppet government and to reorganize civil and economic life in the liberated provinces with the help of the Allied Military Government. It represents a full expression of the people's will emerging from chaos to life." Concerning cooperation after the liberation, he said: "I do not know how much cooperation between the Communists and the five other parties in the government will be possible," adding, however, "if the present declarations of the Communist chief in Italy in favor of small property, of the democratic system of religious tolerance are accepted by the whole party and approved by Moscow, the way for a new step in the collaboration of all parties will still be open."[3] It was during these same days that the Municipal Junta of Rome went in a body to the Vatican to pay their homage to Pope Pius XII; included in the Junta were two Communists.[4]

Among the urgent problems that confronted De Gasperi as head of the Christian Democratic Party were the achievement of syndical unity and the amplification of the party's organs and program. During the clandestine period, after the Corporate State of Fascism had collapsed, trade union organizers among the Christian Democrats, the Socialists, and the Communists had revived the pre-Fascist trade unions, especially in the South. On June 14, 1944, the Socialist Confederation of Labor and the Catholic ("White") Italian Confederation of Laborers came together in the Pact of Rome to form the *Confederazione Generale Italiana del Lavoro* as the major confederation of workers. The objectives of the organization, as stated in the Pact of Rome, were to defend the interests of labor more effectively and to assist in the country's economic reconstruction. The confederation subsequently sought to revive the various national federations of workers by trades and also the regional associations. Syndical unity was to prove impossible in view of the divergent political groups within labor, but in the immediate postwar period, the goal of trade union reconstruction was sufficient to hold the groups together.[5] De Gasperi favored syndical unity.

In the late summer of 1944 De Gasperi was occupied with the formation of party sections in the territories being liberated in central Italy. In August 1944 the provinces of Rome, Frosinone, and Latina passed from Allied administration to that of the Italian government. Meanwhile on July 29–30 De Gasperi attended an interregional party convention held at Naples. Those present included the members of the party's Directing Commission, the Central Executive Junta, and the Christian Democrats in the government.[6] De Gasperi's talk, in which he elaborated upon the methods and objectives of the party, was applauded at length and was summarized in the programmatic declaration voted at the conclusion of the convention. The language is strikingly reminiscent of hundreds of speeches De Gasperi had made since his Austrian years. Moral regeneration, reform, the method of liberty, centrism, respect for law and order: these had long been Degasperian themes.

> The Christian Democratic Party responds to two irrepressible exigencies of Italian political life. The first . . . is essentially a moral problem; without a recovery of moral consciousness on the part of all classes of the Italian people, material and civil reconstruction is impossible. . . .
> The second exigency is the politico-social revolution that is being accomplished and that we desire for reasons of justice. . . . In the boldest reforms and in every governmental directive, Christian Democracy responds to that exigency with the strongest obligation to defend liberty of conscience and of institutions and to uphold the method of freedom in civil competition. We invoke and accept in full the decisions of universal suffrage, but we shall no longer allow the destinies of the nation to be determined by plutocratic cliques or Jacobin conventicles, nor compromised by party squadrons or market insurrections.
> We are a party of *order and law;* we are doing a work of discipline in the entire country, and for the sake of the solidarity of the anti-Fascist parties, we are sacrificing many particular programs. *Nevertheless, let no one delude himself; if tomorrow the law were to be threatened and violated, and tyrannical and dictatorial desires were to be hinted at . . ., we would not allow ourselves to be surprised as the country was surprised in 1922. To the menace that comes from the Right or from the Left, we shall offer all the resistance, active and passive, of which the people will be capable.*[7]

At the conclusion of the convention, the first National Council of the party was elected; it included De Gasperi, Andreotti, Spataro, and Antonio Segni. The Council elected De Gasperi as secretary general of the party and Scelba as vice-secretary. It also set up a Directory, made up of De Gasperi, Scelba, Aldisio, Cassiani, Achille Grandi, Spataro, Gonella, and Restagno. It confirmed Gonella in the editorship of the party organ, *Il Popolo.*

On September 9–11, 1944, the National Council convened in Rome and adopted resolutions which called for the confiscation of landed estates above a prescribed size and the distribution of the expropriated property among those lacking land or possessing an insufficient amount of it.[8] During this meeting De Gasperi discussed at length the institutional question and sought to defend himself against the charge, made by some members of his party, of "institutional agnosticism." He said: "It is not true that we belong to the agnostics, the disoriented . . ., we belong to those who do the right thing at the right time, and we favor the maximum concentration of all the forces which are sincerely democratic around a program of political liberty and social justice."[9]

While the Council was in session, a significant exchange of letters took place between De Gasperi and Togliatti. Syndical unity having been achieved, at least on paper, Togliatti was ready for a pact of political unity with the Christian Democrats, and De Gasperi's affirmations on labor unity gave reason to suppose that he might consider a political accord with the Communists. On August 31 he had issued a statement on the revival of trade unionism which reiterated the interest of the party in labor unity; at the same time it also pointed out that the basis for such unity was respect for the moral and religious conscience of the workers and the nonpolitical character of the syndical organizations.[10] On September 9 Togliatti sent De Gasperi a letter in which, after affirming the "absolute respect" of the Communist Party for the religion of the Italian people and its desire for "fraternal collaboration with all the democratic and anti-Fascist Italian forces," he said: "In particular we wish and hope that it may be possible to come to a concrete political accord with your party, for the purpose of creating, on the basis of a program of struggle against the reactionary forces which have already brought Italy to ruin and of profound political and social renovation, a block of popular forces which may guarantee the triumph and stability of a democratic and progressive regime. . . ."[11] In his reply of September 12, De Gasperi said that the "basic premise of every collaboration present or future is the creation and safeguarding of a climate of liberty and self-discipline." He pointed out that only the day before he had heard of four Christian Democratic meetings in Lazio being broken up by Communists. "This is absolutely intolerable and inexcusable, particularly if one realizes that there is always the possibility of debate. If this system aims to prevent us from expressing our thought, even though it differs from your ideology, which is antithetical to ours, how could one hide its gravity. And if this were to become epidemic and to be applied on a large scale, by what moral right could we condemn the intolerant spirit of the Fascist one-party system which through its notorious Sunday riots went forward to the March on Rome and tyranny . . . ?" He concluded his letter by telling "dear Togliatti" that while he himself might be willing to respect the right of the Christian Democratic Party to free expression, the actions of his colleagues on the periphery nourished "fear and diffidence."[12]

As a member of Bonomi's government, De Gasperi shared the premier's concern regarding the implications of the partisan movement and the execution of the purge. Both require a few words of explanation. The partisan movement behind German lines consisted of two categories: military men who had gone underground after their units had disintegrated and groups under party leadership. Relations between the groups under political leaders and the representatives of the regular army were strained. The Allied military leaders were also suspicious of the partisans; they had a repugnance for irregulars, and they disliked the leftist orientation of much of the partisan movement. Nevertheless, in the autumn of 1943 an agreement was reached between the Allies and the representatives of the Partisan Military Junta of Central Italy, according to which the Allies would provide arms to political bands and the latter would furnish information to the Allies and also help Allied prisoners to escape. As the bands expanded during the succeeding months, so did their objectives. They wanted to form large armies, with a unified command, for the war against the Germans. Both the Allies and the Italian government feared that they would try to establish a separate government.

The central control organ for the resistance movement in the North was the Committee of National Liberation of Upper Italy (*CLNAI*), which represented five parties (there was no Labor Democratic Party in the North). To coordinate the military efforts of the partisans, the *CLNAI* established on June 9, 1944, a supreme headquarters of the Volunteers of Liberty Corps. The Allies sent General Raffaele Cadorna to lead the Corps; the vice-commanders were Luigi Longo, a Communist, and Ferruccio Parri, an Actionist. On August 30 the *CLNAI* issued a circular stating that it represented the Italian government and that it would exercise the powers of government; it authorized the regional and provincial Committees of National Liberation to do likewise. Not until December 26, however, did the Bonomi government agree to recognize the *CLNAI* as its representative in occupied Italy. At its request, the Allies permitted the admission of partisan groups as units into the Italian army, and these participated in the great spring drive of 1945.[13]

The over-all military importance of the partisans has been a matter of controversy; they did tie down a number of German divisions in the North, and their achievements helped to restore morale. But socially they injected bitterness into life, they encouraged disrespect for the law, and they accentuated the class struggle.[14] In a speech which De Gasperi delivered in Trent in 1951, he acknowledged the contribution made by the partisans to the liberation of Italy, but he deplored the fratricidal conflict that had accompanied partisan warfare. This aspect of the war had represented the "great crime of Cain."[15]

The purge was another issue that added bitterness and vindictiveness to the Italian scene. Amplifying the norms that had emanated from the Badoglio government, the Bonomi ministry established a High Commission for Sanctions against Fascism. The commission was subdivided into a penal section for the punishment of those guilty of crimes, and an administrative section for the purge of governmental offices, the liquidation of property belonging to Fascist organizations, and the penalization of those who had derived profits from the Fascist regime. It was a heavy, cumbersome machinery, whose operation often worked injustices. Carlo Sforza headed the purge machinery, assisted by Mauro Scoccimarro. Alleging that the top grades of the administration were still filled with men who had been Fascists, they proceeded to dismiss these men from the government. Meanwhile, on the local level, Communists were not above using the purge machinery to entrench themselves or to even up old scores.

Sforza and Scoccimarro were supported by the parties of the Left, but the other parties pointed out that many of the officials who were now being dismissed from the administration had risen through merit, not through subservience to Fascism. This was De Gasperi's point of view. De Gasperi opposed a rigid enforcement of the purge also because he did not wish to carry into the future the rancor and hatred of the past, particularly in view of the fact that the nation as a whole had supported the Fascist dictatorship. He did not think that those who had been guilty of crimes should go unpunished, nor did he think that ex-Fascists had a right to consider themselves on the same par as those who had suffered exile or at least privations for twenty years. However, once crimes had been punished, the past should be forgotten.[16] The purge, in short, was not to become a festering sore in the body politic. De Gasperi's post-Second World War views on the purge were similar, in substance, to those he had held in 1919, when Trentine "Patriots" clamored for the punishment of those who had been pro-Austrian or not sufficiently pro-Italian during the war.

The purge, which was one of the few things that the Italian government could undertake on its own, free of Allied interference, was mainly responsible for the ministerial crisis that erupted in the autumn of 1944. At the beginning of November, the Liberal, Marcello Soleri, minister of the treasury, and the nonparty man, Admiral Raffaele De Courten, minister of the navy, resigned in protest against the purge policies of Scoccimarro. On November 26 Bonomi went to the Quirinale to present the resignation of his government to the Lieutenant General. He had expected to be asked to form a new one, again based on the *CLN*, and was surprised to learn that the Lieutenant General had begun "consultations." In other words, the monopoly hitherto exercised by the central CLN was now being contested.

The six parties, and particularly the Action and Socialist Parties, proposed Carlo Sforza as premier or at least as minister of foreign affairs. The choice of Sforza for either post was, however, vetoed by Churchill, who accused the Count of not having maintained his pledge, given prior to repatriation, not to work against the monarchy and Badoglio. The veto startled public opinion, illustrating as it did the dependent character of the Italian government. On November 28 De Gasperi, together with Alberto Cianca (Actionist), and Saragat, went to see the English ambassador, Sir Noel Charles, who merely confirmed the veto.

The evening before, an interesting event had taken place: Togliatti had invited to his office Nenni and De Gasperi and had proposed to them the formation of a government made up of the three mass parties and presided over by De Gasperi. The latter had replied that since the candidature of Bonomi was still alive, it did not seem proper to him to place another name in the running, much less his own. Nenni, for his part, was dubious about placing a practicing Catholic at the head of the government; this would be a novelty in Italian politics. Togliatti later denied having made such a proposal.[17]

The crisis dragged on for several days, partly because of the unwillingness of the Socialists to accept Bonomi as premier and partly because of the isolationist attitude of the Action Party after the veto of Sforza. After a brief Ruini candidature, the Lieutenant General asked Bonomi to form a new government. De Gasperi convened in his office the representatives of the six parties and urged unity upon them. The response of the Actionists and Socialists was negative. At the Piazza del Gesù, at the headquarters of the Christian Democratic Party, there was talk of a government *a tre*—Christian Democrats, Liberals, and Labor Democrats—should the attempt to reconstitute a Bonomi ministry fail. Togliatti, however, was willing to support Bonomi, and on December 12 a new Bonomi ministry was formed; it was *quattro*, with Christian Democrats, Liberals, Labor Democrats, and Communists. Vice-premiers were Rodinò and Togliatti. Manlio Brosio became minister without portfolio. Bonomi retained the Ministry of the Interior and of African Affairs. De Gasperi became minister of foreign affairs; his undersecretaries were the Communist, Eugenio Reale (later named ambassador to Warsaw and replaced by Celeste Negarville), and the Liberal, Renato Morelli. Scoccimarro became minister of Occupied Italy, aided by the Liberal, Medici Tornaquinci. The question whether or not the government should have the confidence of the CLN had thus been decided in favor of the *CLN*. Nenni, as well as the Actionists, retired from the government in expectation of the "vento del Nord."

In December 1944 De Gasperi, as minister of foreign affairs, entered upon the most responsible governmental position he had ever held. As early as September 1944, the Italian government had been invited to appoint direct representatives to Washington and London, and the Allied Control Commission had been renamed the Allied Commission. In anticipation of the full recovery of sovereignty, De Gasperi attempted to bring his country back into the international community. He resumed or expanded diplomatic relations de jure or de facto with such countries as France, Austria, Canada, Hungary, Czechoslovakia, the Union of South Africa, Egypt, China, India, Iran, and the Philippines. He also sought to interest the heads of the United Nations in a reexamination of the whole Italian question. On January 22, 1945, he announced that about a million Italians were participating in the war against Germany; these included combat forces actually on the battle line, service troops in southern Italy, and former prisoners of war doing various war jobs for Britain and the United States. The figure did not include the partisans.[18] This was probably De Gasperi's answer to Churchill, who in a speech in the House of Commons a few days previously had asserted that Britain did not "need Italy as a partner."[19] The statement has caused much consternation and discouragement in Italy.

On February 8 De Gasperi sent a note to the Big Three, requesting the transformation of Italy's co-belligerent status into that of an ally. The request was rejected, but by the end of the month, Allied controls over Italy were relaxed. On February 25, Harold Macmillan, chief of the Allied Commission, visited Bonomi and De Gasperi and presented a memorandum, the so-called Macmillan Memorandum, which contained provisions favorable to Italy. Thus the controls imposed by the armistice were limited to the war zone and for military purposes, and the Allied veto on government acts and appointments was abolished. Peripheral Allied organs were to be withdrawn from the first day of April. The memorandum represented Italy's partial recovery of juridical sovereignty.

Two of De Gasperi's immediate preoccupations were how to relieve the critical food shortage and how to secure the release of all Italian prisoners of war. The food problem was seriously embarrassing the government. De Gasperi met Harry Hopkins at the end of January to brief him on Italy's urgent need for wheat, and he asked support for the Italian Mission which had gone to the United States to discuss the matter. Simultaneously he entered into negotiations with Argentina, which soon made available 100,000 tons of grain. To obtain the release of Italian prisoners, particularly those detained in the Balkans, he sought the intervention not only of the Allied governments but also of UNRRA and the International Red Cross.

When plans were announced for the convocation of a conference at San Francisco to write the definitive Charter of the United Nations, De Gasperi wrote to the Allies to request that Italy be invited to attend the conference. The Allies declined to do so, and on the day that the conference began, De Gasperi sent to the conference a note protesting the exclusion of Italy and pointing out that Italian air, naval, and land forces had contributed to the victory of the United Nations.

The liberation of northern Italy while the San Francisco Conference was getting under way necessitated a re-examination of the composition and program of the Bonomi government, in view of the more radical temper of the North. In this area, as in other parts of Italy, the Christian Democratic Party had a strong organization, but it was farther to the Left than its branches in central and southern Italy. It was represented in the *CLNAI* by Achille Marazza, who personally favored drastic reform measures. Aware of the revolutionary spirit of the North, De Gasperi sent an appeal to all northern Italians to avoid "factious convulsions and Jacobin improvisations."[20]

With the permission of the Allies, a delegation representing the *CLNAI* flew to Rome early in May. It was composed of two Socialists, Morandi and Pertini, two Communists, Sereni and Bosi, two Christian Democrats, Marazza and Bodrero, one Actionist, Valiani, and two Liberals, Arpesani and Vocchiero. On May 10 the Socialist Party called a meeting at the Teatro Brancaccio. Sandro Pertini gave a speech which shocked public opinion: he said that if the Lieutenant General were to go to the North, he would receive a treatment *alla Piazzale Loreto* (the place where Mussolini's corpse was exposed). Nenni, on the other hand, gave a talk characterized by moderation, so much so that it was immediately characterized as "presidential" (i.e., worthy of a premier).

While the Socialists were meeting at the Brancaccio, the Christian Democrats published an order of the day which called upon the government to uphold the democratic method in the solution of the problems of public life. It also demanded the disarmament of all formations and the suppression of every expression of violence, whether individual or collective. It asked that preparations for a Constituent Assembly be hastened "as the only method of achieving a democratic order in the

State." De Gasperi's attitude was that no expansion of the powers of committees of national liberation was necessary; such committees had already fulfilled their function. Political elections were now the only method of restoring representative democracy.

That same evening, in a meeting of the party representatives, Nenni gave an explanation of his discourse, proposing without hesitation a Socialist (i.e., himself) as premier. The Liberals offered no objections, having been assured the Portfolio of the Interior. Scelba, however, substituting for De Gasperi who was ill, entered a strong dissent. He said that if it was necessary to find a replacement for Bonomi, it would be desirable to seek a person who would be above parties. If a party man was desired instead, he questioned the wisdom of seeking him among the Socialists, particularly in view of relations with the Allies. But, concluded Scelba, the first order of business was establishing better relations with the North; then it would be time to select the personnel of the government.

On May 17, with the consent of the Allies, a group of ministers and of party representatives, including De Gasperi, went to the North. The atmosphere in Milan was extremely tense. Communist banners flew over factories and many public buildings. The *CLNAI* liberally interpreted the powers delegated to it by the Rome government, and the general attitude of the northern leaders was that the Roman politicians were too old to conduct a thorough purge and to carry out the necessary reforms. On May 23 De Gasperi spoke to a meeting of the members of the Christian Democratic provincial committees of the North, and he sought to allay some of these fears. He said that Christian Democracy had no fear of reform, even radical reform, because this represented a constructive step, not subversion or anarchy. He emphasized, however, the importance of educating the people in expressing their opinion and in taking part in the democratic process, and he defined the principal immediate problems as (1) reconstruction to avert national famine, and (2) the safeguarding of liberty "from those residues of Fascism which have been deposited in the spirit and which have exterior forms which visibly recall the methods and systems of the past regime." This last remark was directed against the extreme Left.

On the following day, a meeting was held at 51 Via Cadore between the representatives of the Rome government and those of the *CLNAI*. The meeting had two parts. The first was concerned with the elaboration of the programmatic resolution drawn up by De Gasperi and Nenni. The resolution requested the Allies to transform the armistice into a pact of friendship and collaboration, to allow all Italy to come within the jurisdiction of the national government within the shortest time possible, and to establish over the contested frontier zones a provisional and impartial administration. It also stated that the parties would provide for elections to the Constituent Assembly as soon as possible. In the meantime, the government would hold administrative elections. The local *CLN*'s would be recognized as consultative organs of the local authority. This declaration amounted in effect to a dismantling of the *CLN* apparatus and the failure of Nenni's and Togliatti's program as summed up in the slogan "all power to the *CLN*." The resolution reiterated the need for a new government.

The second part of the conference was opened by Nenni, who once again proposed a Socialist as premier. Amendola and Valiani warmly endorsed his proposal. It was now two o'clock in the morning. In spite of the hour, De Gasperi vigorously objected, affirming that a Socialist premier would be viewed diffidently by the Allies and would, moreover, run counter to the orientation of the majority of the Italian people. The Socialists had a unity pact with the Communists, and this would accentuate the lack of balance that a Nenni premiership would represent. He expressed himself as being favorable to the premiership of a man who would be above parties, but if no accord could be reached on a nonparty man, then Christian Democracy was best qualified to assume the direction of the government. After elections no objection could be raised to a Socialist premier if the Socialists were to win them, but in the meantime a Catholic country could not have as its head the representative of a party that was ideologically materialistic. It was being asserted that the government should represent the forces of labor and of the partisans, and Christian Democracy fulfilled these prerequisites. The net effect of De Gasperi's talk was to block a Nenni premiership.[21] At the end of the meeting, one Actionist said: "This man will govern us for the next five years."[22]

The demands of the northern politicians for quick and drastic reforms were not the only matter on De Gasperi's mind during the spring of 1945. As minister of foreign affairs, his primary concern was the peace treaty, and, more immediately, the status of Trieste. On May 1, 1945, when the German garrison at Trieste surrendered to an Australian general, Yugoslavia attempted to establish a right to the city by sending in armed partisans. The action was a violation of an accord signed by Tito in July 1944 and confirmed in February 1945, stating that Yugoslav troops were not to pass a line to the west of Fiume and that all Istria was to be placed under Allied occupation. De Gasperi immediately wired Washington and London, protesting that the movement of Yugoslav troops beyond the eastern frontier and into Trieste was unjustifiable militarily, politically, and morally. On May 3 the Italian government, in hailing the victory of the Allies over Germany, adopted a resolution which stated that the eastern frontier question should remain unprejudiced until peace had been established and until constitutional organs elected by the two peoples could decide upon their respective rights. On May 13 De Gasperi instructed the Italian ambassador to England, Nicolo Carandini, to go to the Foreign Office to ask that every decision concerning frontiers be deferred until the peace negotiations. The ambassador was also to point out that a reign of terror was in progress in the Yugoslav-occupied territories. Four thousand persons had disappeared from Gorizia.

On May 14 the Allies sent a note to Yugoslavia to demand the immediate retirement of troops from the zone of Anglo-American military occupation in northeastern Italy, including Trieste. De Gasperi warned that if Tito continued to hold Trieste, the result would be a "strong nationalistic and reactionary government in Italy."[23] On May 17 Marshal Tito decided to withdraw from part of the territory his troops had occupied, but not from Trieste. On May 23 the Allied representatives, meeting at Caserta, categorically demanded of Marshal Tito the evacuation of the city, requesting him to withdraw his troops to the east of the Isonzo (Morgan Line). Subsequently an accord was reached at Belgrade between Tito and Marshal Alexander whereby Yugoslav troops were withdrawn from Trieste.[24]

The question of the premiership and the composition of the new government remained unresolved. On June 7 De Gasperi wrote a letter to Nenni proposing a Christian Democratic premiership and a Socialist vice-premiership which would be endowed with effective powers, particularly with respect to the Constituent Assembly. Nenni's answer was negative, for the Socialists still aimed at the premiership. On June 8 Bonomi convoked the ministry, which had been practically nonoperative for two months, and four days later he submitted his resignation. Nenni then went to the Quirinale for "consultations." Since the Christian Democrats and the Socialists were deadlocked, Ferruccio Parri, the noted partisan commander in North Italy and the head of the Party of Action, was invited to Rome. On June 15 De Gasperi had a two-hour talk with Parri, whom he considered a moderate. The reciprocal impressions were good, and on June 20 a new government was formed with Parri as premier and minister of the interior. Brosio and Nenni became vice-premiers. De Gasperi stayed on as minister of foreign affairs. Togliatti went to the Ministry of Justice, Jacini to the War Ministry,

Gronchi to the Ministry of Industry, Scelba to the Post Office, and Gaetano Barbareschi (Socialist) to the Ministry of Labor. In place of the Ministry of Occupied Italy there was created that of "Postwar Assistance" under the Actionist, Emilio Lussu. Another new ministry was that of food, which was entrusted to the Labor Democrat, Enrico Mole, a friend of De Gasperi's since Aventine days. There was also created a High Commissariat for Hygiene and Sanitation, entrusted to a Liberal, Professor Gino Bergami. Twenty-four undersecretaries represented equally the six parties of the *CLN*.

The convocation of a Constituent Assembly and reconstruction were the immediate fundamental tasks of the new government. One of the first acts of Parri's government was to bring into existence a *Consulta Nazionale* to advise on legislative and administrative matters.[25] There was some dissension within the ministry regarding the qualifications for "consultors." De Gasperi did not favor the exclusion of certain ex-parliamentarians, but he was overruled. Another area of discord concerned elections. The leftist parties wanted the first election to be a referendum on the institutional and constitutional question. De Gasperi, supported by the Labor Democratic and Liberal parties, was of the opinion that the electorate needed some preliminary instruction in electoral procedures and hence favored the holding of less crucial elections, such as communal elections, as a first step in electoral education.

On July 31, in Piazza Borghese in Rome, the first national meeting of the Christian Democratic Party took place. The participants included the members of the National Council and the secretaries from all the provincial branches. Enrico Mattei was present, together with Christian Democratic partisans. Diverse personalities and ideological orientations were represented, but it was De Gasperi who was in command. He said that after the unification of the country, the party should adopt an organization which would enable it to capture the great masses of the people. He denounced, however, the prevailing revolutionary spirit, affirming determination to prevent the sudden proclamation of a new State. At the end of the conference, the National Council adopted a resolution stating that at the national party congress the party would take a stand on the institutional question. Before the congress convened, the party would conduct an inquiry among all the members to ascertain their preference.[26]

Meanwhile, the Allies were discussing among themselves the terms of the peace treaty for Italy. To break the isolation in which Palazzo Chigi found itself, De Gasperi wrote on August 22 a long and conciliatory letter to American Secretary of State James F. Byrnes. Concerning

Trieste, he declared that Italy was prepared to accept the Wilson Line of 1919 as a basis of negotiation with Yugoslavia. Fiume and Zara should be granted autonomy through special statutes, while Pola and Cattaro should be demilitarized, subject to the creation of a completely independent Albania. For Alto Adige, the new government of Italy planned regional autonomy under a statute similar to that of the Valle d'Aosta. Concerning the unexpected French demand for a rectification of the Alpine frontier, the Italian government was not adverse to compromise, especially if achieved by direct negotiation. With respect to the colonial problem, he said that Italy valued her African colonies as a source of absorption for her surplus workers. In principle there was no incompatibility between the interests of Italian workers and "trust" administration under the United Nations, but in practice the collective method would not correspond to the "peculiar necessities of the Italian colonies." Without depriving Italy of her rights in the Cyrenaica plateau, rights acquired by labor, it should be possible to satisfy strategic exigencies on the North African coast by creating special military, air, and naval bases in Tobruk and Marmarica. On the eastern coast, it would be possible to give the Kingdom of Ethiopia an outlet to the sea. Finally, he stated the willingness of the Italian government to entrust to Greece the Dodecanese Islands.[27]

In September, upon very short notice, De Gasperi was invited to attend the meeting of the Council of Foreign Ministers in London to expound the Italian point of view on the Italo-Yugoslav frontier. On September 16 De Gasperi landed at Finchley, a military airport to the north of London; he thus became the first Italian official to enter England after the war. The atmosphere was frigid, and De Gasperi was not spared the humiliation of having to go through customs. When asked how long he intended to remain in England, he snapped: "The shortest time possible." He was accompanied to Lancaster House for the discussions by Carandini and a few technical experts. Speaking to the foreign ministers of the Big Five (Byrnes for the United States, Ernest Bevin for England, Georges Bidault for France, Wang Shih-Chieh for China, and Vyacheslav Molotov for the USSR), De Gasperi indicated what territorial sacrifices Italy was willing to make in the interest of a just European order. His proposals were essentially those contained in the August 22 letter to Byrnes. With each of the five ministers, De Gasperi spoke briefly and informally, expounding the Italian point of view. To Molotov he said: "We represent two countries of workers. We must resolve the same problems of want. . . . On this plane we can establish collaboration between our peoples."

After a week of discussions at Lancaster House, De Gasperi visited the Italian prisoner of war camp located near London. As he approached the prisoners, some walked away; others frigidly stared at him. Unacquainted with De Gasperi's background, these men saw in him only the symbol of the country responsible for their sufferings. Undaunted by their reaction, De Gasperi ascended a small platform to speak to them. His audience was amazed to hear a lackluster voice, a voice that had none of the eloquence of the voice that had accompanied their departure for the front. Perhaps for that reason the ex-soldiers listened more attentively as De Gasperi described the efforts he was making to obtain their swift repatriation. He also told them that the new democratic Italy anxiously awaited their return, for the enormous task of reconstruction could not be carried to completion without them. At the end of his talk De Gasperi was rewarded by hearing warm applause. From all sides the men crowded around him, begging him to take personal messages to their families in Italy. These were probably the happiest moments of the London visit.[28]

On his way back to Italy, De Gasperi stopped off in France to see General De Gaulle and to receive assurances that France would not support the cession of the Brenner Pass to Austria.[29] On September 29 De Gasperi gave a report on his London and Paris missions to the *Consulta Nazionale*, which gave him an ovation in recognition of his apparent success. In fact, after his return to Rome, his stature grew almost hourly, and he gained greatly in the esteem of his countrymen. There was a general sense of indignation when the Foreign Ministry confirmed on October 3 that an unidentified would-be assassin had taken a shot at De Gasperi as he was en route to the Consultative Assembly. No one had been hurt, but the glass of his car had been shattered.[30]

Meanwhile, the Parri ministry, in spite of its good will and talented personnel, was failing to make any substantial progress in solving Italy's domestic problems. Apart from Parri's own lack of knowledge of public administration, pressures from the leftist parties prevented him from returning industry to private control, and pressures from the Right prevented the pursuit of drastic reforms. The result was that the government stood virtually still. In the country at large disorder and violence prevailed, with irregular formations terrorizing cities and villages. In Sicily the barracks of the *carabinieri* were assaulted by bandits. The artificial ministerial peace was finally broken by the Liberals, who withdrew from the government, charging Parri with having failed to restore law and order (November 21).

On November 24 Parri called together a meeting of his ministers and in an effort to avoid resigning he announced that he would appeal to the *Consulta*. De Gasperi's reply was that the resignation of the government should have followed automatically upon the withdrawal of the Liberals, for the Parri mandate had been based on a coalition of the six parties. An appeal to the *Consulta* was inopportune and useless and would only delay the solution of the crisis. The premier could, if he wished, present himself to the *CLN*. As for the Christian Democratic Party, it did not necessarily desire decisions and solutions *a sei* at any cost; rather it sought a deep examination of the whole political situation. After this meeting Parri went to the Quirinale where he submitted his resignation.

Later that same day, Parri called a meeting of the *CLN* in the Viminale. It was attended by Italian and foreign journalists, and the air was charged with electricity. From the northern partisans who were present came threats of defending by force the spirit of the revolution. In his talk to the assembled gathering, Parri said that even a slight movement to the Right or to the Left would be sufficient to bring about a civil war and attempts to reinstate Fascism. He hinted that a *coup d'etat* was being prepared by the Liberals and the Christian Democrats. As the foreign press representatives hastened to report to their papers Parri's sensational accusation, De Gasperi, pale and visibly shaken by the charge, jumped to his feet and said:

> Not so much as the secretary of a party having a wide base in the country but as the minister of foreign affairs, I am gravely concerned. The premier has given an evaluation of the circumstances that led to the crisis; that was his right. However, I am concerned, since the foreign press is here, lest our foreign colleagues give to some affirmations of the premier a literal meaning that would go beyond his intentions. Responding in a dialectical form to the truly ruthless attacks, to which he has been subjected from some quarters, Parri thought that he could speak of a supposed *coup d'etat* which Christian Democracy would attempt with its attitude of these days. I would not want foreign countries to think that Christian Democrats had acted against democracy. Our only intention is to defend in Italy the democratic method.... In my party there is only the firm intention not to delay in any manner the installation of democracy and to defend it against everyone, whether of the Right or of the Left....[31]

The ministerial crisis lasted two weeks, during which various pre-Fascist politicians, such as Orlando, Nitti, and De Nicola, were considered and rejected. Through a process of elimination, the candidacy of De Gasperi was proposed and found acceptable. Most of the meetings during this two-week period had been held at night, much to the mystification of journalists. It was later disclosed that De Gasperi was responsible for the late meetings. A neighboring woman insisted on playing the radio and phonograph at all hours of the night, and De Gasperi had been losing so much sleep he had decided he might as well be attending meetings. The same woman had once denounced De Gasperi to Mussolini as "anti-Fascist."

As soon as De Gasperi was charged by the Lieutenant General with the formation of a cabinet, he called for the cooperation of all parties. For a time the Liberals refused to enter his ministry, for they wanted to add ministers from outside the *CLN*, and they objected, moreover, to giving the Ministry of the Interior to a Socialist, as seemed likely. Finally, after De Gasperi suffered a fainting spell (which some termed a fake) and after he wrote to the Liberals affirming the necessity of abolishing all exceptional measures and offices as quickly as possible, they agreed to enter his government.[32]

On December 10, 1945, the first De Gasperi cabinet was sworn in at the Quirinale. A power failure caused the royal residence to be without electricity, and consequently the ceremony was conducted in the soft glow of slender candles against a backdrop of rich tapestries. De Gasperi may have seen some symbolism in the restoration of electricity in the last minute of the ritual.

In conclusion it might be useful to summarize the lessons learned by De Gasperi during the long and often painful apprenticeship that preceded his assumption in December 1945 of the highest political post in the Italian government.

In the realm of domestic affairs, the need for accepting a pluralistic society was the most important lesson that the school of experience inculcated in De Gasperi. In his mature years, as he looked back upon history and upon the vicissitudes of his own lifetime, he could perceive little value in restoring the homogeneous society of the Middle Ages. He did not think that such restoration was even possible, for society, as he saw it, was in a state of evolution, with each age possessing its own dynamism.

Acceptance of a pluralistic society required the rejection of any integralist solution to the problems of the day, particularly when such integralism was to be achieved through the instrumentality of a political party. In 1943 De Gasperi unequivocally stated that a political party was limited in its composition and competence and could not be the promoter of a universal palingenesis; rather it was the bearer of a specific political responsibility. Both the circumstances of the age and the party's ideology determined the nature of the responsibility.

Another lesson was the necessity of upholding the autonomy of the party. Even in his Trentine days, he was of the opinion that in nonreligious and nonpolitico-ecclesiastical affairs, the party was responsible to no external force for its actions. During the mid-1920's failure to insist upon the autonomy of the *Partito Popolare* had made this party susceptible to ecclesiastical pressure, and the *Popolari* had been sacrificed for the sake of settling the Roman Question. In establishing the Christian Democratic Party, De Gasperi was careful not to seek any mandate from the Vatican, for he did not believe that the Vatican was empowered to grant such a mandate.

But if De Gasperi was a firm believer in the independence of political parties, he did not at the same time exclude influences upon public policy that came from the Christian patrimony. The party man, he believed, remained linked with his spiritual mother, the Church, and consequently his public as well as his private actions were bound to be affected by his Christian conscience. De Gasperi's own convictions were inseparable from his Christian heritage, even though his religion was essentially a private matter. Profoundly spiritual in the inner depths of his being, he had an instinctive aversion for people who say their prayers on street corners, who boast of their orthodoxy and religious intransigence.

The value, even if only moral, of collaborating with other parties in the achievement of common goals was another lesson learned by De Gasperi during the long apprenticeship. In his Trentine period, he would have been willing to cooperate with Socialist and Liberal leaders in working for an Italian university and a larger measure of self-government for the Trentino. During the Fascist period, he was prepared to form an alliance with the Socialists in order to prevent Fascism from consolidating itself, and he joined the anti-Fascist parties in the Aventine Secession as a moral protest against the policies of Mussolini. During the clandestine period of the Second World War, he cooperated with all anti-Fascists, including Communists and Socialists, in helping to rid Italy of Nazi-Fascist domination. When he formed his first ministry he hoped for the sincere collaboration of the leftist parties. Long before Pope John XXIII wrote *Pacem in Terris*, De Gasperi was acting on the assumption that cooperation was possible and even desirable between people of differing ideologies "in doing whatever is naturally good or conducive to good."

De Gasperi's long years of experience in politics gave him a practical knowledge of men and of the factors that consciously or unconsciously motivate their actions. He learned to accept men as they are, not as they seemed to be or wished to be. It was this knowledge of human psychology—a knowledge acquired at the cost of much personal suffering and humiliation—that was at the base of his realism. By the time his own political career was over, his *abilità* in politics would be compared with that of Cavour and Giolitti.

From his initial entry into public life, De Gasperi had discovered that democracy has a social as well as a political content, that a truly democratic order presupposes concern for social justice. The *Idee* of 1943 were not for De Gasperi propaganda but conviction. Throughout his life, beginning with his student days, he had an affinity for the disinherited. When social justice was at stake, he never preached resignation.

In foreign affairs, De Gasperi the European was also in gestation from the early years of the twentieth century. He fought against chauvinistic nationalism, against the "religione della patria," and on the eve of the First World War, he deplored the fact that Christian parties had lost their sense of internationalism. During the early 1920's he sought the formation of a Christian International that would promote peace and fraternal cooperation. In the *Idee* he urged nations to accept a limitation of sovereignty in the interest of a wider solidarity. That he would become an architect of Europe's unity in the post-Second World War period was inevitable.

From the point of view of methodology, if there is one refrain that runs through all of De Gasperi's writings and speeches from his Austrian years to the end of the Second World War, it is the "method of liberty." All problems, whether political, social, or economic, were to be approached in an orderly fashion, through set constitutional procedures, without resort to *coups d'etat*, riots, mass parades, or "Jacobin conventicles." De Gasperi was a reformer by nature, but his reformism was of the legal, evolutionary variety; it was totally devoid of either demagoguery or doctrinarism. His penchant for constitutionalism and for gradualness stemmed from his balanced temperament. Abhorring radicalism, whether of the Right or of the Left, he was a man of the Center, though at times (as in 1943) he could veer close to Center-Left positions.

Willingness to compromise on nonmoral matters was another De Gasperi characteristic acquired during the long apprenticeship. Ever since his years in Austrian politics, he rejected the formula of "all or nothing." He believed that if a goal could not be attained in its entirety immediately, then it was preferable to accept a partial realization than to turn aside from it completely. One should accept whatever was within the realm of the possible. When the Hapsburg government offered the Fiemme-Bolzano railroad, De Gasperi accepted it because nothing else was possible at the time. *Possibilismo*, then, was part of his ideology.

Surveying De Gasperi's forty years' apprenticeship, one is struck by the recurrence of certain themes—the need for adaptation, the method of liberty, the wisdom of Center positions, the advisability of avoiding a doctrinaire approach to men and politics. Experience seemed to offer confirmation of the essential validity of his philosophy of life. Only in the rejection of integralism and corporativism as understood by Toniolo and in the crystallization of his views on the autonomy of political parties is there any real change in mental attitudes.

To summarize: in December 1945, Alcide De Gasperi was both by training and temperament more qualified than any other Italian to launch Italy on her career as a democratic republic and as a faithful ally of the Free World.

NOTES

NOTES FOR CHAPTER I

1. The best general work on the geography, history, and culture of this area is Giuseppe Morandini's *Trentino-Alto Adige* (Turin, 1962), which is Vol. III in the series *Le Regioni d'Italia,* ed. Roberto Almagia, 18 vols. (Turin, 1960 -). For a history only, see Antonio Zieger, *Storia del Trentino e dell'Alto Adige* (Trent, 1926).
2. Pre-First World War statistics for the Trentino are from: Great Britain, Foreign Office, Handbook No. 33, *Trentino and Alto Adige* (London, 1920).
3. The name is still common in the Trentino, where it is spelled as one word. When Alcide Degasperi entered the *Reichsrat* in 1911, the name was erroneously listed as "de Gasperi." After the union of the Trentino with Italy, administrative acts spelled the name as "De Gasperi."
4. Full length biographies of De Gasperi have been written in Italian by his daughter and former associates: Maria Romana Catti De Gasperi, *De Gasperi, uomo solo* (Milan, 1964); Giulio Andreotti, *De Gasperi e il suo tempo* (Milan, 1956); Igino Giordani, *Alcide De Gasperi* (Milan, 1955). For an anthology of De Gasperi's writings between 1902 and 1915, including his speeches in the Austrian Parliament, see Alcide De Gasperi, *I Cattolici trentini sotto l'Austria,* ed. Gabriele De Rosa, 2 vols., in *Politica e Storia. Raccolta di studi e testi,* ed. Gabriele De Rosa, Vols. 9 and 10 (Rome, 1964).
5. Andreotti, *op. cit.,* p. 15.
6. *La Voce Cattolica,* Aug. 27, 29, Sept. 1, 1896. For the origins of this paper, see Antonio Zieger, *Stampa cattolica trentina (1848-1926)* (Trent, 1960), Chap. IV.
7. Andreotti, *op. cit.,* p. 14. On the cooperative movement, the best work is Ildebrando Moschetti, *Le Forze economiche del Trentino* (Milan, 1918).
8. *La Voce Cattolica,* Aug. 18-19, 1898.

9. *Ibid.*, Aug. 9-10, 10-11, 1899.
10. De Gasperi's reminiscences in *ibid.*, Sept. 3, 1904. For the origins of the *AUCT*, see also *AUCT, 50 AUCT* (Trent, 1946), pp. 5-10.
11. Andreotti, *op. cit.*, p. 16.
12. *Ibid.*, p. 23.
13. See letter to his brother Mario, quoted in Catti, *op. cit.*, pp. 28-29.
14. For his attitude toward Catholicism between 1902 and 1908, see especially *La Voce Cattolica*, Sept. 1-2, 1902; *Fede e Lavoro*, Oct. 17, 1902; *Il Trentino*, Nov. 24, 1906, June 1, 1907, Sept. 5, 1908.
15. *Il Trentino*, Dec. 31, 1910.
16. *La Voce Cattolica*, Sept. 21-22, 1901.
17. *Ibid.*, April 1-2, 1902.
18. *Ibid.*, Sept. 1-2, 1902. *Fede e Lavoro* (Sept. 5, 1902) described the speech as being "inspired by that modernity which is so pleasing."
19. Zieger, *Stampa cattolica trentina*, pp. 139-141.
20. *La Voce Cattolica*, Nov. 10, 1902.
21. *Ibid.*, July 18, 1903.
22. *Ibid.*, Feb. 16, 1903; Aug. 17, 1904.
23. *Fede e Lavoro*, Oct. 2, 1903.
24. *Ibid.*, Oct. 9, 1903.
25. *La Voce Cattolica*, July 2, 1903.
26. *Ibid.*, Sept. 10, 1903.
27. *Ibid.*, Jan. 29, 1904.
28. *Ibid.*, March 17, 1904.
29. *Ibid.*, Oct. 20, 1904.
30. Andreotti, *op. cit.*, p. 30.
31. The fracas is described, with variations, in *ibid.*, pp. 30-31; Catti, *op. cit.*, p. 31; *La Voce Cattolica*, Jan. 11, 1905.
32. *Ibid.*, Nov. 26-27, Dec. 27-28, 1901, Jan. 2-3, Sept. 1-2, 1902; Modesto Demattè, *Alcide Degasperi all'alba del XX secolo* (Trent, 1962), pp. 61-85.
33. *Fede e Lavoro*, Sept. 1, 1905.
34. *Ibid.*, Sept. 22, 1905.
35. Vigilio Zanolini, *Il Vescovo di Trento e il governo austriaco durante la guerra europea* (Trent, 1934), pp. 16-25.

NOTES FOR CHAPTER II

1. *Fede e Lavoro*, Aug. 25, 1905.
2. On universal suffrage, *La Voce Cattolica*, Oct. 11, Nov. 6, 7, 1905, Jan. 22, 24, 27, Feb. 6, 1906; on compulsory voting, *Il Trentino*, May 15, Oct. 9, 1906.
3. *La Voce Cattolica*, Dec. 13, 1905. The *Unione* was composed of the representatives of all Catholic economic and cultural organizations.
4. *Il Trentino*, March 17, 1906.
5. *Ibid.*, May 15, 1906.
6. *Ibid.*, Jan. 3, 1907.
7. *Ibid.*, Jan. 8, 1907.
8. *Ibid.*, Jan. 28, 1907.

Notes

9. *Ibid.*, Feb. 7, 1907.
10. *Ibid.*, March 1, 1907.
11. *Ibid.*, March 4, 1907. Andreotti, *op. cit.*, p. 44, has alleged cordiality between De Gasperi and Battisti. The columns of their respective papers do not lend much support to this allegation, although De Gasperi undoubtedly respected Battisti.
12. *Il Trentino,* March 30, 1907.
13. *Ibid.*, April 2, 8, 24, 1907.
14. The franchise reform of 1906-1907 allotted parliamentary seats according to the following key:

Italians	1 for 38,000 people
Germans	" " 40,000 "
Rumanians	" " 46,000 "
Slovenes	" " 50,000 "
Poles	" " 52,000 "
Croats	" " 55,000 "
Czechs	" " 55,000 "
Ruthenians	" " 102,000 "

    Robert A. Kann, *The Habsburg Empire* (New York, 1957), p. 212, note 47. For the national distribution of seats in proportion to the national population figures, see *ibid.*, p. 223.
15. *Il Trentino,* July 3, 1907.
16. Quoted in Giulio Andreotti, *De Gasperi e il suo tempo* (Milan, 1955), p. 38.
17. Congress is described in *Il Trentino,* Aug. 26 to Sept. 7, 1907.
18. *Ibid.*, Sept. 11, 1907.
19. *Ibid.*, July 21, 1908.
20. *Ibid.*, Sept. 23, 1907.
21. *Ibid.*, Oct. 9, 1907.
22. *Ibid.*, Sept. 19, 1907.
23. *Ibid.*, Dec. 17, 1907.
24. *Ibid.*, Nov. 2, 1907.
25. *Ibid.*, March 31, 1908.
26. Antonio Zieger, *Stampa cattolica trentina (1848-1926)* (Trent, 1960), p. 165; Antonio Zieger, *La Stampa cattolica trentina fra il 1913 e il 1919* (Rome, 1963), p. 7.
27. *L'Avvenire del Lavoratore,* Jan. 29, 1909.
28. *Il Popolo,* Feb. 18, 1909.
29. See his letter to his friend Torquato Nanni in Benito Mussolini, *Opera Omnia,* edd. Edoardo and Duilio Susmel, 36 vols. (Florence, 1951-1963), II, 263-264.
30. *L'Avennire del Lavoratore,* March 11, 1909; *Il Trentino,* March 9, 1909. The two versions differ somewhat. For this episode see also F. Olasz, *Benito Mussolini a Trento 1909* (Milan, 1958); Richard A. Webster, "Il primo incontro tra Mussolini e De Gasperi," *Il Mulino,* VII (1958), 51-55.
31. Mussolini, *Opera Omnia,* II, 2.
32. *Il Popolo,* May 29, 1909.
33. *Ibid.*, July 14, 1909.
34. *Il Trentino,* April 22, 1909.

35. According to a statute adopted in 1851 and revised in 1888, the electors were divided into three Corps, depending on taxes paid. There were 60 electors in the First Corps; 600 in the Second; and 2,000 in the Third. Each elected only 12 councilors. More than 2,500 citizens remained deprived of the franchise. De Gasperi represented the Prince Bishop of Trent and as such was elected by the First Corps of electors.
36. *Verbali del Consiglio comunale 1910* (Trent, 1911), pp. 29-44.
37. *Verbali del Consiglio comunale 1911-1912* (Trent, 1912), pp. 164-173, 187-196.
38. *Il Trentino*, Feb. 21, 1910.
39. *Ibid.*, July 19, 1909.
40. *Ibid.*, Nov. 16, 1910.
41. For his views on the Triple Alliance, *ibid.*, May 5, 7, 1909; on the Italo-Turk War, *ibid.*, Nov. 4, Dec. 1, 1911, Oct. 22, 1912.
42. *Ibid.*, May 12, 1911.
43. Andreotti, *op. cit.*, p. 46.
44. *Ibid.*, p. 47. De Gasperi's activities in the Austrian Parliament are described by Gino Valori in *Degasperi al parlamento austriaco 1911-1918* (Florence, 1953). The book must be used with caution; Valori selects his facts to sustain a thesis, namely, that De Gasperi's primary loyalty was to the Hapsburg monarchy, not to the Italian nationality.
45. *Il Trentino*, July 24, 1911.
46. *Il Popolo*, July 29, 1911.
47. *Il Trentino*, Oct. 14, 1911. To prevent the "American meat trust" from exploiting the meat shortage in Austria-Hungary, the *Popolari* voted for the importation of frozen meat from Argentina. *Ibid.*, April 9, 1912.
48. *Ibid.*, Oct. 26, 1911.
49. Andreotti, *op. cit.*, pp. 51-55.
50. *Il Trentino*, Feb. 14, July 9, 1913.
51. *Ibid.*, Feb. 25, 1913.
52. Described in *Il Trentino*, Sept. 15, 27, 1913.
53. *Ibid.*, May 8, 1913.
54. *Verbali del Consiglio comunale 1914-15* (Trent, 1915), p. 16.
55. *Ibid.*, Jan. 3, 1914.
56. *Ibid.*, April 21, 1914. Elections to the Diet were by the same colleges that elected the members of the *Reichsrat*, each college electing three deputies.
57. *Ibid.*, May 30, June 13, 1914.

NOTES FOR CHAPTER III

1. *Il Trentino*, Aug. 6, 1914.
2. *Ibid.*, Aug. 13, 1914.
3. *Ibid.*, Oct. 17, 1914.
4. For the De Gasperi-Macchio conversation, see Franz Conrad von Hoetzendorff, *Aus Miener Dienstzeit*, 5 vols. (Vienna, 1921-1925), V, 112-113; Italian translation in Giulio Andreotti, *De Gasperi e il suo tempo* (Milan, 1955), pp. 57-58, fn. 1.

Notes

5. "Brevi Cenni sulle condizioni politiche e morali del Trentino," Nov. 30, 1914, Archivio Centrale dello Stato, Rome (hereafter cited as ACS), Carte Sonnino, Busta 1, Fascicolo 4, Trento e Trieste.
6. Bollati [Italian ambassador in Berlin] to Cabinet, Tel. No. 1309, Sept. 15, 1914, ACS, Carte Salandra, Scatola 1, Fascicolo 3.
7. Andreotti, *op. cit.*, pp. 61-62.
8. *Il Trentino*, Nov. 19, 1914.
9. *Ibid.*, Nov. 24, 1914.
10. On Italian Catholicism and the war, see Filippo Meda, *I Cattolici italiani nella guerra* (Milan, 1928); Ernesto Vercesi, *Il Vaticano, l'Italia e la guerra* (Milan, 1925); Ernesto Vercesi, *Il Movimento cattolico in Italia, 1870-1922* (Florence, 1923), Chap. XVI.
11. Luigi Sturzo, *Politics and Morality* (London, 1938), p. 109.
12. Cf. Andreotti, *op. cit.*, p. 64; Maria Romana Catti, *De Gasperi, uomo solo* (Milan, 1964), pp. 72-73. According to Modesto Dematté, *Alcide Degasperi all'alba del XX secolo* (Trent, 1962), p. 119, De Gasperi had been requested by Bishop Endrici to sound out Sonnino on the ecclesiastical arrangements that would prevail in the Trentino in the event of Italian annexation.
13. Ministero dell'Interno (hereafter cited as Min. Int.) to Prefect of Rome, March 25, 1915, ACS, Direzione Generale di Pubblica Sicurezza, Ufficio Riservato (hereafter cited as PS, UR), (1911-1915), 1915, Busta 96, Fascicolo 216 (III).
14. *Ibid.* References to De Gasperi in the reports to Sonnino were also hostile. See note 5.
15. Quoted in Guido Miglioli, *Con Roma e con Mosca* (Milan, 1946), p. 16.
16. Bertini to Director General PS, June 6, 1915, ACS, PS, UR (1911-1915), 1915, Busta 113, Fascicolo 260. The movements of Pope Benedict were carefully scrutinized by the police. A report of Oct. 30, 1915, describes a walk taken by the Pontiff in the Vatican gardens, complete with a diagram!
17. Ambassador of Italy to Sidney Sonnino, April 18, 1916, ACS, Min. Int., PS, Affari Generali e Riservati (hereafter cited as AGR) (1914-1926), 1918, Pacco 49, K 2. "K 2" was the government's classification for subversive movements and parties.
18. Gino Marzani, Alcide De Gasperi et al., *Il Martirio del Trentino* (hereafter cited as *Il Martirio*) (Milan, 1919), p. 91.
19. Antonio Zieger, *La Stampa cattolica trentina fra il 1913 e il 1919* (Rome, 1963), p. 11.
20. Enrolling in the Italian army, Battisti was captured by the Austrians on July 10, 1916, and was hanged July 12 in the courtyard of the Castello del Buon Consiglio in Trent. Italian Socialist literature refers to him as "the martyr."
21. *Il Martirio*, p. 92.
22. *Ibid.*
23. On the composition and functions of the committees, see Dematté, *op. cit.*, pp. 146-149, 248-249.
24. For the work of the committee, *Bolletino del Segretariato per Richiamati e Profughi*, 1915-1918; *Il Martirio*, p. 95.

25. One possible source of income at this time was the severance pay he received from the Bishop when *Il Trentino* suspended publication.
26. For internal conditions in 1916, see Wolf von Schierbrand, *Austria-Hungary; the Polyglot Empire* (New York, 1917).
27. Z. A. B. Zeman, *The Break-up of the Habsburg Empire, 1914-1918* (London, 1961), pp. 111-112.
28. On the role of the *Popolari* in this parliament, see Guido De Gentili, *La Deputazione trentina al parlamento di Vienna durante la guerra* (Trent, 1920). There were now eight deputies from the Trentino: seven *Popolari* (Conci, De Carli, De Gasperi, Delugan, De Gentili, Grandi, and Tonelli), and one Liberal, Valeriano Malfatti.
29. De Gentili, *op. cit.*, pp. 13-18.
30. *Ibid.*, pp. 36-37.
31. *Stenographische Protokolle über die Sitzungen des Hauses der Abgeordneten des österreichischen Reichsrates* (hereafter cited as *Stenographische Protokolle*), Session XXII, Sept. 28, 1917, pp. 1325-1329. Quotation from p. 1329.
32. On De Gasperi's role in the Wagna incident, see *Bolletino del Segretariato per Richiamati e Profughi*, Oct. 20, 1917.
33. Pastoral letter in De Gentili, *op. cit.*, pp. 226-229.
34. *Stenographische Protokolle,* Oct. 4, 1918, pp. 4427-4431.
35. *Ibid.*, Oct. 11, 1918, p. 4626.
36. De Gentili, *op. cit.*, pp. 312-319.
37. *Stenographische Protokolle*, Oct. 25, 1918, pp. 4680-4681.

NOTES FOR CHAPTER IV

1. On the origins and development of the Catholic movement in Italy, see Fausto Fonzi, *I Cattolici e la società italiana dopo l'unità* (Rome, 1960); Richard A. Webster, *The Cross and the Fasces* (Stanford, 1960); Giuseppe Dalla Torre, *I Cattolici e la vita pubblica italiana (1866-1920)* (Vatican City, 1944); Gabriele De Rosa, *Storia politica dell'azione cattolica in Italia*, 2 vols. (Bari, 1953-1954); Francesco Magri, *L'Azione cattolica in Italia* (Milan, 1953); Ernesto Vercesi, *Il Movimento cattolico in Italia 1870-1922* (Florence, 1923).
2. Giorgio Tupini, *I Democratici cristiani* (Milan, 1954), Appendix I, pp. 326-328; Michael P. Fogarty, *Christian Democracy in Western Europe, 1820-1953* (Notre Dame, 1957), pp. 319-320.
3. For the life and thought of Toniolo, see F. Vistalli, *Giuseppe Toniolo* (Rome, 1954).
4. Webster, *op. cit.*, pp. 11-12.
5. Fonzi, *op. cit.*, p. 102.
6. A. William Salomone, *Italian Democracy in the Making* (Philadelphia, 1945), pp. 38-40.
7. Webster, *op. cit.*, pp. 16-20.
8. Italian Socialism first asserted itself as a working-class party in 1882; in 1892 the first Italian Socialist party was founded, known as the Italian Workers' Party. In 1893 it took the name of Italian Socialist Party.

Notes

9. Mario Einaudi and François Goguel, *Christian Democracy in Italy and France* (Notre Dame, 1952), pp. 5-6.
10. Tupini, *op. cit.*, Appendix II, pp. 328-330.
11. *Il Programma del Partito Popolare Italiano. Come non è e come dovrebbe essere* (Milan, 1919).
12. *Il Nuovo Trentino*, April 10, 1919.
13. *Ibid.*, April 12, 1919.
14. Antonio Zieger, *Stampa cattolica trentina (1848-1926)* (Trent, 1960), p. 188.
15. "Relazione sull'opera svolta dal Governatorato di Trento dal 20 dicembre 1918 al 10 febraio 1919," Archivio Centrale dello Stato, Rome (hereafter cited as ACS), Carte Luigi Credaro, Busta 30.
16. "Relazione sull'attività dal Governatorato di Trento dal 1 maggio al 31 luglio 1919," *ibid.*
17. De Gentili, De Gasperi and Conci to Credaro, Sept. 17, 1919, ACS, Carte Credaro, Busta 34.
18. Endrici to Credaro, Dec. 2, 1920, ACS, Carte Credaro, Busta 32.
19. Credaro to Nitti, Oct. 11, 1919, ACS, Carte Credaro, Busta 31.
20. *Il Nuovo Trentino*, April 25, 1919.
21. *Ibid.*, May 1, 1919.
22. *Ibid.*, May 10, 1919.
23. Vercesi, *op. cit.*, p. 186.
24. *Il Nuovo Trentino*, June 16, 1919. On the deliberations of the congress, see Gabriele De Rosa, *Storia del Partito Popolare* (Bari, 1958), Chap. II; P.P.I., *La Vita del Partito Popolare Italiano nei suoi tre primi congressi* (hereafter cited as *Partito Popolare . . . tre primi congressi*) (Rome, 1923), pp. 9-18.
25. De Rosa, *Storia del Partito Popolare*, p. 79.
26. *Il Nuovo Trentino*, Oct. 14, 1919.
27. *Ibid.*, Aug. 22, 1919.
28. *Ibid.*, July 17, 1919; July 28, 1919.
29. *Il Nuovo Trentino*, Oct. 28, 1919.
30. *Ibid.*, Jan. 17, 31, 1920.
31. On the Congress of Naples, De Rosa, *Storia del Partito Popolare*, pp. 115-126; *Partito Popolare . . . tre primi congressi*, pp. 19-37; Secondo Congresso del P.P.I., ACS, Ministero dell'Interno (hereafter cited as Min. Int.), Direzione Generale di Pubblica Sicurezza (hereafter cited as PS), Affari Generali e Riservati (hereafter cited as AGR) (1914-1926), 1920, Pacco 80, K2, Napoli.
32. *Il Nuovo Trentino*, April 22, 1920.
33. *Ibid.*, July 7, 9, 1920.
34. *Atti parlamentari, Camera dei deputati*, XXVI Legislatura, Discussione 1, June 24, 1921, pp. 206-210.
35. *Ibid.*, XXVI Legislatura, Discussione 1, June 24, 1921, p. 208; July 26, 1921, pp. 728-729.
36. *Ibid.*, XXVI Legislatura, Discussione 1, July 26, 1921, p. 730.
37. *Ibid.*, XXVI Legislatura, Discussione 2, Aug. 3, 1921, p. 1161.
38. De Rosa, *Storia del Partito Popolare*, p. 185.
39. On Fascist activity in Trent, letter of Credaro to Giolitti, April 22, 1921, ACS, Min. Int., PS, AGR, (1914-1926), 1921, Pacco 86, G1, Trento.

40. On the legislative work of the *Popolari*, see Giulio De Rossi, *Il Partito Popolare Italiano nella XXVI Legislatura* (Rome, 1923).
41. *Atti parlamentari, Camera dei deputati*, XXVI Legislatura, Discussione 3, Dec. 19, 1921, pp. 2703-2708.
42. Igino Giordani, *La Politica estera del Partito Popolare Italiano* (Rome, 1924); Giorgio Gualerzi, *La Politica estera dei Popolari* (Rome, 1959). For efforts to construct a Christian International in the mid-1920's, see Giuseppe Rossini, "I Tentativi per un'Internazionale Popolare," *Civitas*, N.S. XI (1960), I, 123-132.
43. *Il Corriere d'Italia*, Oct. 14, 18, 1921; *Il Nuovo Trentino*, Oct. 7, 14, 1921.
44. For the Congress of Venice, see De Rosa, *Storia del Partito Popolare*, pp. 204-209; *Il Partito Popolare . . . tre primi congressi*, pp. 38-63.
45. *Il Partito Popolare . . . tre primi congressi*, pp. 52-53.
46. The "veto" of Giolitti has often been described as a Sturzian veto. As De Rosa points out, however, it was Sturzian only insofar as it was *Popolare*. De Rosa effectively disposes of another myth concerning this famous veto, namely, that the *Popolari* opposed Giolitti because of a proposed tax reform which would have been distasteful to ecclesiastical authorities. De Rosa, *Storia del Partito Popolare*, pp. 194-195.
47. *Il Nuovo Trentino*, Feb. 25, 1922.
48. *Ibid.*, Feb. 16, 1922.
49. *Ibid.*, July 1, 1922.
50. *Atti parlamentari, Camera dei deputati*, XXVI Legislatura, Discussione 4, Feb. 17, 1922, p. 3018.
51. *Il Nuovo Trentino*, June 3, 1922.
52. Quoted in Maria Romana Catti, *De Gasperi uomo solo* (Milan, 1964), pp. 81-82.
53. For general accounts, see De Rosa, *Storia del Partito Popolare*, pp. 217-298; Giuseppe Petrocchi, *Collaborazionismo e ricostruzione popolare* (Rome, 1923), pp. 186-254.
54. *Atti parlamentari, Camera dei deputati*, XXVI Legislatura, Discussione 8, July 15, 1922, pp. 8195-8198.
55. *Ibid.*, XXVI Legislatura, Discussione 8, July 19, 1922, p. 8265.
56. Luigi Sturzo, *Popolarismo e Fascismo* (Turin, 1924), p. 61; Stefano Jacini, *Storia del Partito Popolare Italiano* (Milan, 1951), p. 133.
57. Sturzo, *op. cit.*, p. 65.
58. Mussolini later said that he had to occupy Trent to prevent it from threatening his strategy. Benito Mussolini, *My Autobiography*, trans. Richard Washburn Child (New York, 1928), p. 170.
59. Jacini, *op. cit.*, Documento IX, pp. 300-303.
60. Quoted in Catti, *op. cit.*, p. 89.
61. *Il Nuovo Trentino*, Oct. 16, 1922.
62. Einaudi and Goguel, *op. cit.*, p. 22.

NOTES FOR CHAPTER V

1. Gabriele De Rosa, "Vita ed opere del Principe Rufo Ruffo della Scaletta," *Rassegna di politica e di storia*, N. 63, VI (Jan. 1960), 23.

2. Quoted in Stefano Jacini, *Storia del Partito Popolare Italiano* (Milan, 1951), pp. 148-149.
3. *Ibid.*, p. 167.
4. In a speech in the Chamber of Deputies in July 1923 De Gasperi said that the *Popolari* had entered Mussolini's government in the hope of bringing Fascism to the path of constitutionalism: *Atti parlamentari, Camera dei deputati*, XXVI Legislatura, Discussione 11, July 15, 1923, p. 10676.
5. *Il Nuovo Trentino*, Nov. 6, 1922.
6. *Ibid.*, Nov. 3, 1922.
7. *Atti parlamentari, Camera dei deputati*, XXVI Legislatura, Discussione 9, Nov. 16, 1922, pp. 8390-8391.
8. *Ibid.*, Nov. 17, 1922, pp. 8443-8445; *Il Nuovo Trentino*, Nov. 21, 1922.
9. Gabriele De Rosa, *Storia del Partito Popolare* (Bari, 1958), pp. 325-345.
10. Bertini to Ministero dell'Interno, March 24, 1923, Protoc. 8836, Archivio Centrale dello Stato, Rome, Ministero dell'Interno, Direzione Generale di Pubblica Sicurezza, Affari Generali e Riservati (hereafter cited as ACS, Min. Int., PS, AGR) (1914-1926), 1923, Pacco 70, K2.
11. The order of the day bore the signatures of Cesare Nava, Egilberto Martire, Giacinto Paradisi-Miconi, Giulio Sansonetti, and Dell'Arno de Rossi. De Rosa, *Storia del Partito Popolare*, p. 347.
12. For a summary of the proceedings at the congress, see *ibid.*, Chap. IX. For De Gasperi's report and order of the day, *Il Nuovo Trentino*, April 13, 1923.
13. ACS, Min. Int., PS, AGR, (1914-1926), 1923, Pacco 70, K2. The papers of Michele Bianchi, the Secretary General of the Fascist Party, also testify to the anti-Fascist activities of the *Popolari*: ACS, Carte Bianchi, Busta 2, Fascicolo 15.
14. De Gasperi and Romani to Mussolini, Aug. 16, 1923, Protoc. 22892, ACS, Min. Int., PS, AGR, (1914-1926), 1923, Pacco 70 K2; Guadagnini to De Bono, Aug. 19, 1923, Protoc. 22037, *ibid.*
15. Jacini, *op. cit.*, pp. 115-116. See also Pietro Scoppola, *Dal Neoguelfismo alla Democrazia Cristiana* (Rome, 1957), pp. 143-145.
16. Richard A. Webster, *The Cross and the Fasces* (Stanford, 1960), pp. 82-83.
17. *Il Nuovo Trentino*, June 28, 1923. See also issues of June 19 and 26.
18. De Rosa, *Storia del Partito Popolare*, pp. 395-402; Giulio Andreotti, *De Gasperi e il suo tempo* (Milan, 1956), p. 108.
19. *Atti parlamentari, Camera dei deputati*, XXVI Legislatura, Discussione 11, July 15, 1923, pp. 10677, 10679.
20. Webster, *op. cit.*, p. 89.
21. *Il Popolo* (Rome), March 29, 1924.
22. *Il Nuovo Trentino*, Jan. 29, 1924.
23. *Ibid.*, Feb. 12, 1924.
24. *Ibid.*, March 3, 1924.
25. *Ibid.*, March 30, 1924.
26. *Ibid.*, April 3, 1924.
27. *Ibid.*, March 22, 1924.
28. Those elected were Bertone, Buratti, and Marconcini for Piedmont; Cappa and Boggiano Pico for Liguria; Mauri, Grandi, Bresciani, Longi-

notti, Merizzi, Baranzini, Jacini, and Montini for Lombardy; De Gasperi, Brenci, Galla, Capra, Merlin, Carbonari, Guarienti, Uberti, Fantoni, and Gilardoni for the Venezias; Micheli, Milani, Corini and Braschi for Emilia; Gronchi and Martini for Tuscany; Tupini for the Marches; Cingolani and Di Fausto for Lazio and Umbria; Rodinò and Bosco Lucarelli for Campania; Anile for Calabria; Aldisio, La Rosa, and Termini for Sicily; Delitalia for Sardinia.

29. De Rosa, "Vita ed opere del Principe Rufo Ruffo della Scaletta," p. 28.
30. Min. Int. to Prefect of Trent, May 14, 1924, Protoc. 10983, ACS, Min. Int., PS, AGR, (1914-1926), 1924, Pacco 98, G1.
31. Guadagnini to Min. Int., Memorandum on "Situazione politica a Trento," Nov. 3, 1924, Protoc. 29379, *ibid.*
32. Guadagnini to Min. Int., May 17, 1924, Protoc. 12126, *ibid.*; Richard to Min. Int., Sept. 5, 1924, Protoc. 22478, *ibid.*
33. *Il Nuovo Trentino*, June 3, 1924.
34. *Atti parlamentari, Camera dei deputati*, XXVII Legislatura, Discussione 1, June 7, 1924, p. 254, and June 12, 1924, p. 298.
35. *Il Popolo* (Rome), June 14, 1924.
36. For the government's reaction to the Matteotti affair, ACS, Min. Int., PS, AGR, (1914-1926), 1924, Pacco 65, C1.
37. Charles Delzell, *Mussolini's Enemies* (Princeton, 1961), pp. 15-16.
38. Min. Int. Memorandum, April 3, 1925, ACS, Min. Int., PS, AGR, (1914-1926), 1925, Pacco 108, K2.
39. *Il Popolo* (Rome), July 1, 1924.
40. *Il Nuovo Trentino*, July 8, 1924.
41. *Ibid.*, July 18, 1924.
42. *Ibid.*
43. "La Parte dei cattolici nelle presenti lotte dei partiti politici in Italia," *Civiltà Cattolica*, LXXV (1924), III, 297-306.
44. *L'Osservatore Romano*, Sept. 10, 1924.
45. Daniel Binchy, *Church and State in Fascist Italy* (London, 1941), p. 158.
46. *Il Nuovo Trentino*, Oct. 16, 1924.
47. *Ibid.*, Nov. 12, 1924.
48. *Il Popolo d'Italia*, Oct. 12, 1924.
49. *Ibid.*, Oct. 24, 26, 1924.
50. *Ibid.*, Nov. 12, 23, 25, 26, 1924.
51. *Ibid.*, Nov. 22, 1924.
52. *Ibid.*, Dec. 17, 18, 25, 1924.
53. *Il Nuovo Trentino*, Nov. 8, 11, 18, Dec. 23, 1924.
54. Rome, 1953, reprint from 1925 ed. The pamphlet contained quotations from Austrian papers and authorities in criticism of *Il Trentino*, the *Unione politica popolare*, and Alcide De Gasperi. Included were also excerpts from De Gasperi's speeches in the Austrian Parliament in denunciation of Hapsburg policies or officials.
55. Guadagnini to Min. Int., June 1, 1925, Protoc. 21516, ACS, Min. Int., PS, Casellario Politico Centrale, Busta 55, Fascicolo 2, No. 6775 (hereafter cited as CPC).
56. *Il Nuovo Trentino*, Jan. 9, 1925.

Notes

57. *Ibid.*, Jan. 27, 1925. The Jan. 28 issue was forbidden to publish the order of the day adopted by the National Council. By February 10, 1925, nine issues of the paper had been confiscated.
58. *Ibid.*, Feb. 24, 1925.
59. *La Rivoluzione Liberale* (Turin), May 31, 1925.
60. Andreotti, *op. cit.*, p. 113; *Il Nuovo Trentino*, June 12, 1925.
61. For the fifth National Congress, see *ibid.*, June 30, 1925; De Rosa, *Storia del Partito Popolare*, pp. 492-500.
62. *La Rivoluzione Liberale*, July 5, 1925.
63. *Il Nuovo Trentino*, Nov. 10, 1925.
64. De Rosa, *Storia del Partito Popolare*, p. 504. A "pentarchy," composed of Adelmo Alberti, Stefano Jacini, G. B. Migliori, Prince Rufo Ruffo, and Dino Secco Suardo replaced the directory of the party.
65. Photostat.
66. Questura of Rome to Min. Int., March 22, 1926, Protoc. 13271, March 31, 1926, Protoc. 14383, April 7, 16, 24, 27, 1926, ACS, Min. Int., PS, CPC.
67. Questura of Rome to Min. Int., May 30, 1926, Protoc. 23347, *ibid.*
68. Questura of Rome to Min. Int., June 14, 1926, Protoc. 26887, *ibid.*; Guadagnini to Min. Int., June 15, 1926, Protoc. 27755, *ibid.*
69. Prefect of Rome to Min. Int., Oct. (n.d.), 1926, Protoc. 51444, ACS, Min. Int., PS, AGR, (1914-1926), Pacco 87, C2.
70. Mussolini to Prefects of the Kingdom, Aug. 20, 1926, Protoc. 36013, *ibid.*, 1926, Pacco 85, C2.
71. Antonio Zieger, *Stampa cattolica trentina (1848-1926)* (Trent, 1960), pp. 220-222. Don Giulio Delugan managed to save the back files of *Il Nuovo Trentino* and other Catholic newspapers by taking them to the Jesuit church of St. Francis Xavier, where they were concealed in the bell tower (interview with Monsignor Giulio Delugan).
72. For the Vicenza incident, Lucciardi to Min. Int., Nov. 6, 1926, ACS, Min. Int., PS, CPC; Andreotti, *op. cit.*, pp. 116-117; Maria Romana Catti, *De Gasperi uomo solo* (Milan, 1964), pp. 104-111.
73. Copy, dated November 12, 1926, in the possession of Monsignor Giulio Delugan.
74. *Atti parlamentari, Camera dei deputati*, XXVII Legislatura, Discussione 7, Nov. 9, 1926, p. 6389.
75. The party was dissolved province by province by the decrees of individual prefects. De Rosa, *Storia del Partito Popolare*, p. 504.
76. Min. Int. to Prefects of the Kingdom, Feb. 15, 1927, Protoc. 30933, ACS, Min. Int., PS, AGR, (1927-1933), 1927, Pacco 108.
77. For De Gasperi's movements from Nov. 1926 to March 11, 1927: Statement of De Gasperi in Regina Coeli prison, March 19, 1927, ACS, Min. Int., PS, CPC; Questura of Rome to Min. Int., April 15, 1927, Protoc. 09359, *ibid.*; Andreotti, *op. cit.*, pp. 118-119.
78. Andreotti, *op. cit.*, p. 119.
79. Min. Int. to Prefects of Milan and Trent and to those on land and sea frontiers, Jan. 11, 1927, Protoc. 0872, ACS, Min. Int., PS, CPC.
80. Bocchini to Prefects of Ancona, Florence, Pisa, Bologna, Tel. No. 9258, March 11, 1927, *ibid.*; Bocchini to Prefect of Zara, Tel. No. 9275, March

11, 1927, *ibid.*; Bocchini to Prefect of Fiume, Tel. No. 9269, March 11, 1927, *ibid.*; Bocchini to Prefects of Venice and Trieste, Tel. No. 9276, March 11, 1927, *ibid.*
81. Bocchini to Prefects of the Kingdom, Tel. No. 9283, March 11, 1927, *ibid.*
82. Statement of De Gasperi, Questura of Florence, March 11, 1927, *ibid.*; statement of Strazzuso, Bacialli, and Mancini, Questura of Florence, March 11, 1927, *ibid.*; Regard to Min. Int., Tel. No. 13072 (4), March 12, 1927, Protoc. 05993, *ibid.*; Prefecture of Florence to Min. Int., March 12, 1927, Protoc. 06095, *ibid.* At Trent baggage sent from Orvieto was detained on the assumption that it belonged to De Gasperi. A minor diplomatic incident ensued when it developed that the baggage belonged to Joseph Stein, a German judge who had spent a month in Italy. Bevilacqua to Min. Int., Tel. No. 14210 (4), March 12, 1927, *ibid.*
83. Mussolini to Bocchini, n. d., *ibid.*
84. Bocchini to Prefects of the Kingdom, Tel. No. 9286, March 12, 1927, *ibid.*; Bocchini to Prefects of the Kingdom, Tel. No. 9394, March 12, 1927, *ibid.*
85. I should like to express my appreciation to Dr. Salvatore Corsaro, a director of Regina Coeli prison, for a tour of the section of the prison where De Gasperi was held in 1927. Located along the Tiber, this prison was constructed between 1881 and 1891 on property confiscated from a religious order (hence its rather incongruous name). The front of the building is made of huge blocks of grey stone and orange-colored masonry. As one enters the prison section, there is a rotunda which serves as a chapel on Sundays and holydays, unchanged since the days of De Gasperi except for the color of the walls. It was here that Pope John XXIII greeted the inmates in his famous visit of 1958.
86. Regard to Min. Int., March 13, 1927, Protoc. 06226, ACS, Min. Int., PS, CPC; Prefect of Florence to Min. Int., Memorandum No. 3831, March 13, 1927, enclosing statement of Pietro Romani, March 13, 1927, *ibid.*
87. Bocchini to Prefects of the Kingdom, Tel. No. 9447, March 13, 1927, *ibid.*
88. Min. Int. Memorandum, March 22, 1927, Protoc. 06531, *ibid.*
89. Min. Int. Memorandum, March 15, 1927, *ibid.*
90. Min. Int. Memorandum, March 15, 1927, Protoc. 06095 R, *ibid.*
91. PS Borgo Valsugana to Min. Int., March 16, 1927, *ibid.*
92. Augusto De Gasperi was in a *pensione* in Milan at the time, apparently unaware of the arrest of his brother. Upon his return to Trent on March 24, he was arrested. After the authorities had satisfied themselves that he was not implicated in his brother's clandestine departure from Rome, he was released. Vaccari to Min. Int., Tel. No. 16103, March 24, 1927, Protoc. 07028, *ibid.*; Bocchini to Vaccari, Tel. No. 10942, March 25, 1927, *ibid.*

Another Romani brother, Carlo, a textile merchant who resided in Rumania, learned of his sister's arrest while visiting his mother in Borgo Valsugana and immediately went to Rome. Although he was questioned by the Questura of Rome, he was not arrested. Statement of Carlo Romani, March 18, 1927, *ibid.*; Minute 374 of Min. Int., March 20, 1927, *ibid.*
93. Statement of Pietro Romani, March 18, 1927, Regina Coeli, *ibid.*; Angelucci to Min. Int., March 22, 1927, *ibid.*

94. De Gasperi said that after the incident at Vicenza, he had gone to Milan for the dual purpose of eluding personal threats and of finding work, having had to abandon *Il Nuovo Trentino*. He had remained in Milan until the last ten days of November, when he went to Rome, remaining in that city until March 10. His time in Rome had been spent mostly in studies of a historical nature. He could not give the names of the families that had been his hosts in Milan and in Rome because he did not wish them to be harrassed by the authorities. He had assumed the name of De Rossi casually, when introduced to a stranger in Rome, and he had retained it to elude detection. Toward the end of January he had gone to live in the room of his brother-in-law Pietro Romani, and Francesca had joined him in the early days of February. He had sought Touring Club membership cards to have some identification when looking for a place to stay or while working for a large company. The summons to appear in court had been prepared by a friend as a joke, in order to keep him in Rome a little longer, and he had had the "levity" to retain it instead of tearing it up.

The trip to Trieste would have been for a dual purpose: one was the recuperation of his wife, who had not been well, and the other was to ascertain job possibilities in that city. He did not know how long he would have remained in Trieste; it would have depended on local circumstances. If he did not find work there, it was his intention to go to Milan or Turin, but not without first going to Borgo to see his family. The map of Venezia Giulia found among his belongings was for the purpose of undertaking excursions in that area. The map of Fiume was an old one, having been drawn up before the boundaries between Italy and Yugoslavia had been delimited. He had had no intention of going to Fiume or of attempting clandestine expatriation. Statement of De Gasperi in Regina Coeli prison, March 19, 1927, *ibid*.

95. Memorandum for Chief of Police, March 20, 1927, *ibid*.
96. Mussolini to PS, "Very Urgent," March 20, 1927, *ibid*.
97. Bocchini to Minister of the Interior, March 28, 1927, Protoc. 07402, *ibid*.
98. Marginal note dated April 1, 1927, on Bocchini's communication of March 28, 1927, *ibid*.
99. Alcide De Gasperi, *Lettere dalla prigione*, ed. Francesca De Gasperi (Milan, 1955), pp. 14-15. Hereafter cited as "Lettere."
100. *Ibid.*, p. 30.
101. Bocchini to Min. Int., Memorandum 08321, April 10, 1927, for cabinet of His Excellency the Minister, ACS, Min. Int., PS, CPC; Questura of Rome to Min. Int., April 23, 1927, Protoc. 09877, *ibid.*; Questura of Rome to Min. Int., April 28, 1927, Protoc. 010537, *ibid*.
102. Questura of Rome to Min. Int., No. 8913, May 28, 1927, *ibid*.
103. *Lettere*, pp. 38-39.
104. Filippo Meda, *Avanti la Ecc. Corte d'Appello di Roma. Motivi aggiunti nell'interesse del Dott. Comm. Alcide De Gasperi* (Rome, n. d.); Questura of Rome to Min. Int., July 22, 1927, ACS, Min. Int., PS, CPC.
105. Min. Int. Memorandum, May 30, 1928, Protoc. 012622, *ibid*.
106. *Lettere*, p. 66.
107. *Ibid.*, p. 68.
108. *Ibid.*, pp. 73-74.

109. *Ibid.*, p. 75.
110. *Ibid.*, p. 76.
111. *Ibid.*, pp. 113-114.
112. G. Jaspar, "Un Maestro del corporativismo italiano," *Rivista internazionale di scienze sociali e discipline ausiliarie*, XXXVII, N. S. 1 (Jan. 1928), 3-28 (this article appears under the title of "Un Maestro del corporativismo cristiano" in Alcide De Gasperi, *I Cattolici dall'opposizione al governo* [Bari, 1955], pp. 123-153); G. Jaspar, "Le Direttive politico-religiose del 'Centro' germanico (1871-1928)," *Rivista internazionale di scienze sociali e discipline ausiliarie*, XXXVII, N. S. 2 (Aug. 1928), 181-196; XXVII, N. S. 3 (Nov. 1928), 97-132; XXXVIII, N. S. 1 (Feb.-March 1929), 146-156 (this article appears in De Gasperi, *I Cattolici dall'opposizione al governo*, under the title of "Il 'Centro' germanico," pp. 215-293).
113. Jan. 7, 1928, *Lettere*, pp. 103-104.
114. *Ibid.*, p. 156.
115. *Ibid.*, p. 165; Angelucci to Min. Int., July 11, 1928, Protoc. 015813, ACS, Min. Int., PS, CPC; Angelucci to Min. Int., PS, July 16, 1928, Protoc. 016453, *ibid*. According to the records in Regina Coeli prison, De Gasperi remained "at the disposition of the Questura, to be shadowed by the agents of the Questura."
116. Catti, *op. cit.*, p. 122. Cf. Giorgio Pini and Duilio Susmel, *Mussolini, l'uomo e l'opera*, 4 vols. (Florence, 1953-1955), III, 95.
117. Photostat of letter of De Gasperi to Director General of PS, Aug. 1, 1928, Protoc. 017811, ACS, Min. Int., PS, CPC; Bocchini to Prefect of Trent, Tel. No. 26135, Aug. 5, 1928, *ibid.*; Bocchini to Prefect of Trent, Tel. No. 27744, Aug. 19, 1928, *ibid.*
118. De Gasperi to Director General of PS, Sept. 27, 1928, *ibid.*
119. Bocchini to Questor of Rome, Oct. 8, 1928, *ibid.* When an agent reported that De Gasperi had angrily threatened suicide if the surveillance continued, Mussolini ordered a "less ostentatious" surveillance. Min. Int. Memorandum, Oct. 10, 1928, Protoc. 022075, *ibid.*
120. De Gasperi to Don Giulio Delugan, n. d. (photostat). Contents indicate that letter was written in the autumn of 1928.
121. *Ibid.*
122. De Gasperi to Don Simone Weber, letter of Jan. 20, 1929. For a more detailed analysis of De Gasperi's views on the Lateran Pacts, see my article "Alcide De Gasperi and the Lateran Pacts," *The Catholic Historical Review*, XLIX (1964), 532-539.
123. De Gasperi to Don Simone Weber, letter of Feb. 12, 1929.
124. De Gasperi to Don Simone Weber, letter of Feb. 26, 1929.
125. *L'Osservatore Romano*, March 13, 1929.
126. Letter to Don Giulio Delugan, March 15, 1929 (photostat).
127. For speech, see Benito Mussolini, *Opera Omnia*, XXIV, 43-90.

NOTES FOR CHAPTER VI

1. Letter of De Gasperi to Don Giulio Delugan, March 28, 1929 (photostat).
2. Letter of De Gasperi to Don Giulio Delugan, Dec. 23, 1929 (photostat).

Notes

3. Lucia, born in 1925, had been left with her grandparents in Borgo Valsugana. The other De Gasperi children were Maria Romana, born 1923; Cecilia, born 1930; and Paola, born 1933.
4. Interview with Nello Vian, secretary of the Biblioteca Apostolica Vaticana.
5. Testimony of D. Levi della Vida in *Il Popolo* (Milan), Aug. 29, 1954, pp. 92-93. This was a special commemorative issue.
6. The exposition was described by De Gasperi in *La Stampa cattolica nel mondo. Risultati ed insegnamenti della stampa cattolica nella Città del Vaticano* (Milan, 1939).
7. Quoted in Maria Romana Catti, *De Gasperi uomo solo* (Milan, 1964), p. 166.
8. Testimony of Cardinal G. Anselmo Albareda in *Concretezza*, Aug. 16, 1964, p. 10. This was a special commemorative issue.
9. Mario Zanatta, *I Tempi e gli uomini che prepararono la "Rerum Novarum"* (Milan, 1931). Reprinted in De Gasperi, *I Cattolici dall'opposizione al governo*, pp. 3-122. De Gasperi was very pleased with the reception that this book received: letter to Don Giulio Delugan, June 24, 1932.
10. *L'Illustrazione Vaticana*, Jan. 1-15, 1933, p. 9.
11. *Ibid.*
12. *Ibid.*, Jan. 16-31, 1933, pp. 55-56; Feb. 1-15, 1933, pp. 97-98; June 1-15, 1933, p. 413; Nov. 1-15, 1933, p. 851.
13. *Ibid.*, June 1-15, 1934, pp. 493-494.
14. *Ibid.*, July 16-31, 1933, pp. 555-556.
15. *Ibid.*, Jan. 16-31, 1933, p. 55; July 1-15, 1933, p. 494.
16. *Ibid.*, Jan. 16-31, 1933, p. 55.
17. *Ibid.*, Nov. 16-30, 1933, p. 904.
18. *Ibid.*, July 16-31, 1934, p. 626.
19. *Ibid.*, Dec. 16-30, 1933, p. 987; April 16-30, 1934, p. 360; Aug. 1-15, 1934, p. 666; March 16-31, 1935, pp. 293-294; April 16-30, 1935, p. 414; Aug. 1-15, 1935, pp. 819-820; June 1-15, 1937, p. 527.
20. *Ibid.*, Nov. 1-15, 1934, p. 941.
21. *Ibid.*, May 1-15, 1933, p. 329; July 1-15, 1933, p. 494; Oct. 1-15, 1933, p. 765; Jan. 1-15, 1934, p. 38; June 1-15, 1934, p. 493; Aug. 16-31, 1934, pp. 716-717.
22. *Ibid.*, March 1-15, 1934, p. 217.
23. *Ibid.*, March 16-31, 1938, p. 232; Sept. 16-30, 1938, p. 755; Oct. 1-15, 1938, p. 800; Oct. 16-31, 1938, p. 843.
24. *Ibid.*, Aug. 1-15, 1934, p. 667.
25. *Ibid.*, Feb. 16-28, 1935, pp. 179-180.
26. *Ibid.*, March 1-15, 1935, p. 235. While De Gasperi had no use for *Action Française*, he regarded the *Croix de Feu* more sympathetically, asserting that its nationalism avoided racism and included cooperation in the work of restoring peace to Europe, *ibid.*, pp. 235-236.
27. *Ibid.*, Sept. 1-15, 1935, p. 932.
28. *Ibid.*, March 1-15, 1936, p. 203; June 1-15, 1936, p. 507; July 16-31, 1936, p. 655.
29. *Ibid.*, Jan. 16-31, 1933, p. 56; May 16-31, 1933, p. 374; July 1-15, 1933, p. 495; Nov. 1-15, 1933, pp. 851-852; Dec. 16-31, 1933, pp. 987-988; Jan. 1-15, 1934, p. 38.

30. *Ibid.*, Aug. 16-31, 1936, p. 751; Sept. 1-15, 1936, p. 799; Sept. 16-30, 1936, p. 848.
31. *Ibid.*, Aug. 16-31, 1933, pp. 641-642; May 16-31, 1934, p. 447.
32. *Ibid.*, June 1-15, 1934, p. 493; May 1-15, 1935, p. 488; Aug. 16-31, 1935, p. 877; April 1-15, 1936, p. 316.
33. These articles, written under the pen name of "Rerum Scriptor," are in *ibid.*, Dec. 16-31, 1933, pp. 985-986; Jan. 1-15, 1934, pp. 27-28; March 1-15, 1934, pp. 191-192. A fourth article on this subject, intended for the magazine *Vita e Pensiero*, was not published. All four may be found in De Gasperi, *I Cattolici dall'opposizione al governo*, pp. 155-191.
34. *L'Illustrazione Vaticana*, Sept. 16-30, 1933, p. 726.
35. *Ibid.*, Aug. 16-31, 1933, p. 642.
36. *Ibid.*, Aug. 16-31, 1936, p. 751.
37. *Ibid.*, Nov. 1-15, 1935, p. 1157; Feb. 16-29, 1936, p. 158.
38. *Ibid.*, May 1-15, 1938, p. 359.
39. *Ibid.*, Aug. 16-31, 1938, p. 667.
40. Reprinted in De Gasperi, *I Cattolici dall'opposizione al governo*, pp. 513-530.
41. Reprinted in *ibid.*, pp. 470-475.
42. *Ibid.*, pp. 474-475.
43. Palmiro Togliatti, *L'Opera di De Gasperi* (Florence, 1958), pp. 61-74.
44. Most of the political exiles had gone to France, where in 1927 the Anti-Fascist Concentration was established, under the leadership of Pietro Nenni's Maximalist Socialists. In 1929 Italian exiles founded the "Justice and Liberty Movement" to fuse the principles of Liberalism and revisionary Socialism. Delzell, *op. cit.*, pp. 56-57.
45. Alcide De Gasperi, "Spiritual Testament," Sept. 4, 1935, *Lettere dalla prigione*, ed. Francesca De Gasperi (Milan, 1955), pp. 9-10.
46. When viewed by this author in 1963 the house was a cream-colored stucco structure of two stories, with a tile roof, green shutters, and a wooden balcony (decorated by De Gasperi) on the south side. From the outside the house appears small, but appearances are deceptive; within are seven bedrooms.
47. Catti, *op. cit.*, pp. 168-170.
48. Letters of De Gasperi to Don Giulio Delugan, June 21, 1932, Jan. 8, 1933, June 21, 1936.
49. The conflict over Catholic Action in 1931 is best described in Angelo Martini, *Studi sulla questione romana e la conciliazione* (Rome, 1963), pp. 136-173. See also Giuseppe Dalla Torre, *Azione cattolica e fascismo* (Rome, 1945); A. C. Jemolo, *Chiesa e stato in Italia negli ultimi cento anni* (Turin, 1952), pp. 659-666. For the Pope's references to De Gasperi, see Martini, *op. cit.*, pp. 139, 145.
50. Quoted in Catti, *op. cit.*, p. 152.
51. Quoted in *ibid.*, p. 155.
52. Letter of De Gasperi to Don Giulio Delugan, April 23, 1932.
53. Catti, *op. cit.*, p. 155.
54. Letter of De Gasperi to Don Giulio Delugan, Dec. 2, 1932 (photostat).
55. Jemolo, *op. cit.*, p. 679.
56. Malvestiti, a bank accountant, had begun his secret movement against the Fascist regime in 1928. The movement resembled the intransigent

Christian democracy of the early part of the twentieth century. See Piero Malvestiti, *Parte Guelfa in Europa* (Milan, 1945); Tupini, *op. cit.*, pp. 45-46; Webster, *op. cit.*, pp. 148-152.
57. Quoted in Catti, *op. cit.*, p. 173.
58. Card of De Gasperi to Don Giulio Delugan, April 22, 1940.
59. Galeazzo Ciano, *The Ciano Diaries*, ed. Hugh Gibson (Garden City, 1947), p. 264.
60. Letter of De Gasperi to Don Giulio Delugan, Oct. 29, 1940 (photostat).
61. Letter of De Gasperi to Don Giulio Delugan, Nov. 21, 1940 (photostat).
62. Quoted in Catti, *op. cit.*, p. 176.

NOTES FOR CHAPTER VII

1. Interview with Mario Scelba, who was present at this meeting.
2. In June 1963 Monsignor G. B. Montini, then Cardinal and Archbishop of Milan, was elected pope, taking the name of Paul VI. On *FUCI* and the *movimento laureati*, see Augusto Baroni, *Igino Righetti* (Rome, 1948); Francesco Magri, *L'Azione cattolica in Italia*, 2 vols. (Milan, 1953); Richard A. Webster, *The Cross and the Fasces* (Stanford, 1960), pp. 137-143.
3. Aldo Spinardi, ed., *Testimonianze su De Gasperi* (Turin, 1956), p. 81.
4. Giulio Andreotti, *De Gasperi e il suo tempo* (Milan, 1956), p. 133, fn.
5. Ivanoe Bonomi, *Diario di un anno* (Milan, 1947), p. xxiv.
6. Giorgio Tupini, *I Democratici cristiani* (Milan, 1954), pp. 48-49.
7. Norman Kogan, *Italy and the Allies* (Cambridge, Mass., 1956), pp. 13-14.
8. Bonomi, *op. cit.*, pp. 3-7.
9. *Ibid.*, pp. 29-35.
10. Demofilo, *Tradizione e "ideologia" della Democrazia Cristiana*, Quaderni della Democrazia Cristiana, No. 2 (Rome, n. d.), p. 14.
11. Bonomi, *op. cit.*, p. 53.
12. *Ibid.*, pp. 55-56.
13. *Ibid.*, pp. 71-72.
14. Andreotti, *op. cit.*, p. 137.
15. Kogan, *op. cit.*, pp. 32-49.
16. *Ibid.*, p. 100.
17. Tupini, *op. cit.*, p. 62.
18. Emilio Bonomelli, *Concretezza*, Aug. 16, 1964, p. 16.
19. Bonomi, *op. cit.*, pp. 120-124.
20. *Ibid.*, p. 131; Andreotti, *op. cit.*, p. 141.
21. *Ibid.*, pp. 139-141.
22. Bonomi, *op. cit.*, pp. 135-136.
23. *Ibid.*, p. 139.
24. *Ibid.*, pp. 136-137.
25. *Ibid.*, pp. 144-145; Meuccio Ruini, *Profili di storia. Rievocazioni—Studi—Ricordi* (Milan, 1961), p. 248.
26. Franco Salvi *et al.*, edd., *Atti e documenti della Democrazia Cristiana 1943-1959* (hereafter cited as *Atti e documenti*) (Rome, 1959), pp. 23-24; Tupini, *op. cit.*, p. 66; Charles Delzell, *Mussolini's Enemies* (Princeton, 1961), pp. 331-333.
27. Bonomi, *op. cit.*, p. 162.

28. *Ibid.*, pp. 174-176.
29. *Ibid.*, pp. 146-147.
30. Quoted in Maria Romana Catti, *De Gasperi uomo solo* (Milan, 1964), p. 184.
31. *Ibid.*, p. 186.
32. *Atti e documenti*, p. 29.
33. *Ibid.*, pp. 1-12; Tupini, *op. cit.*, Appendix 3, pp. 330-338.
34. Mario Scelba has told me that he is the author of the passages on regional autonomy and the representation of professional interests.
35. Reprinted in De Gasperi, *I Cattolici dall'opposizione al governo*, pp. 477-530.
36. *Ibid.*, pp. 487-488.
37. Alcide De Gasperi, *Discorsi politici*, ed. Tommaso Bozza, 2 vols. (Rome, 1956), I, 111.
38. De Gasperi, *I Cattolici dall'opposizione al governo*, p. 493; preface (written by De Gasperi) to Giuseppe Toniolo, *Democrazia Cristiana. Concetti e indirizzi*, 2 vols. (Città del Vaticano, 1949). In this preface De Gasperi acknowledges the fascination he felt for Toniolo's ideas during his youth.

NOTES FOR CHAPTER VIII

1. In August 1944 Churchill announced that the Italian army would be allowed an increase in effectiveness, with the enlarged army consisting of six combat groups totaling 45,000 men. The Italian army was trained by the British and integrated into the British Eighth Army. In the spring of 1945 five combat groups participated in the last great drive in northern Italy. To the end, however, the Italian government resented the Allied refusal to let it make a more substantial contribution to the war effort. Norman Kogan, *Italy and the Allies* (Cambridge, Mass., 1956), pp. 72-73.
2. Alcide De Gasperi, *La Democrazia Cristiana e il momento politico* (Rome, 1944), pp. 10-31; quotation on pp. 30-31. Also in Alcide De Gasperi, *Discorsi politici*, I, 1-20; quotation on pp. 19-20.
3. *New York Times*, July 15, 1944.
4. *Ibid.*, July 13, 1944.
5. Shepherd B. Clough, *The Economic History of Modern Italy* (New York, 1964), pp. 353-354.
6. Within the Central Committee of the party, a Directing Commission had been formed, presided over by De Gasperi, with Spataro as secretary during the clandestine period. On June 21, 1944, after the liberation of Rome and the nomination of Spataro as undersecretary of press and information, the Directing Commission set up a Central Executive Junta, whose members were De Gasperi, Spataro, Chiri, Gonella, Pastore, Restagno, Scelba, and Giorgio Tupini. Giorgio Tupini, *I Democratici cristiani* (Milan, 1954), p. 83.
7. Quoted in *ibid.*, pp. 84-85.
8. *Ibid.*, pp. 338-340.
9. Quoted in *ibid.*, p. 87.

Notes

10. *Atti e documenti*, pp. 54-57.
11. *Ibid.*, pp. 58-59.
12. *Ibid.*, pp. 59-61. Togliatti was not discouraged. At a convention of the Communist Party in Rome in April 1945, Togliatti characterized De Gasperi as "an honest worker" and "one with whom we can cooperate today." *New York Times*, April 9, 1945. In 1958 Togliatti charged that clerical pressure was responsible for De Gasperi's refusal to form a political accord in 1944. Palmiro Togliatti, *L'Opera di De Gasperi* (Florence, 1958), pp. 93-94.
13. Kogan, *op. cit.*, pp. 101-109. See also Charles Delzell, *Mussolini's Enemies* (Princeton, 1961), Chap. VII. Most Catholic partisans served in the non-political groups which were often fragments of the old army and whose exclusive purpose was war against the Germans and their Fascist supporters. Except in Tuscany the Christian Democrats did not have any party troops of their own until late in the war. By the end of the war, about 65,000 Christian Democrats were serving under Enrico Mattei. Catholic resistance took forms other than military: Church property was used for clandestine meetings, and many parish priests concealed refugees, recruited partisan fighters, and furnished aid and comfort to the Resistance. See Richard A. Webster, *The Cross and the Fasces* (Stanford, 1960), Chap. XIII.
14. Denis Mack Smith, *Italy, a Modern History* (Ann Arbor, 1959), p. 493.
15. De Gasperi, *Discorsi politici*, II, 32.
16. For De Gasperi's views on the purge and on anti-Fascism, see Giulio Andreotti, *De Gasperi e il suo tempo* (Milan, 1956), pp. 146-147; De Gasperi, *I Cattolici dall'opposizione al governo*, pp. 504-505.
17. Andreotti, *op. cit.*, pp. 148-149.
18. *New York Times*, Jan. 23, 1945.
19. *Il Popolo* (Rome), Jan. 19, 1945.
20. Quoted in Tupini, *op. cit.*, p. 105.
21. For the May conferences, *ibid.*, pp. 106-112; Andreotti, *op. cit.*, pp. 153-155; Leo Valiani, *Dall'Antifascismo alla resistenza* (Milan, 1953), pp. 172-174; Leo Valiani, *L'Avvento di De Gasperi* (Turin, 1949), pp. 21-24.
22. *Ibid.*, p. 24.
23. *New York Times*, May 15, 1945.
24. Paolo Canali (Adstans), *Alcide De Gasperi nella politica estera italiana* (Milan, 1953), pp. 17-23.
25. In March 1945 the Bonomi government had pledged to bring this *Consulta* into being. It was to act as an interim parliament and to make preparations for the Constituent Assembly. The *Consulta* held its first meeting on September 25, 1945. It consisted of 429 members, nominated by the government on the basis of lists prepared by the various parties, trade unions, and professional associations.
26. Tupini, *op. cit.*, pp. 115-117.
27. Canali, *op. cit.*, pp. 29-31; United States Department of State, *United States and Italy, 1936-1946*, Publication 2669, European Series 17 (Washington, 1946), pp. 165-170.
28. For the London Conference, Canali, *op. cit.*, pp. 32-37; article by Nicolò Carandini in *Concretezza*, Aug. 16, 1964, pp. 22-23.

172 The Long Apprenticeship

29. *New York Times*, Sept. 30, 1945.
30. *Ibid.*, Oct. 4, 1945.
31. Andreotti, *op. cit.*, pp. 167-168; *New York Times*, Nov. 25, 1945.
32. Tupini, *op. cit.*, pp. 121-126; *New York Times*, Dec. 1-10, 1945. The ministry was composed of Alcide De Gasperi as premier and minister of foreign affairs; Nenni (Socialist) as vice-premier and minister for the constituent assembly; Lussu (Actionist) as minister for the *Consulta Nazionale;* Romita (Socialist) as minister of the interior; Togliatti (Communist) as minister of grace and justice; Scoccimarro (Communist) as minister of finance; Corbino (Liberal) as minister of the treasury; Brosio (Liberal) as minister of war; De Courten (nonparty) as minister of the navy; Cevolotto (Labor Democrat) as minister of aeronautics; Mole (Labor Democrat) as minister of public instruction; Cattani (Liberal) as minister of public works; Gullo (Communist) as minister of agriculture and forests; Lombardi (Actionist) as minister of transports; Scelba (Christian Democrat) as minister of the Post Office; La Malfa (Actionist) as minister of reconstruction; Gasparotto (Labor Democrat) as minister of postwar assistance; Barbareschi (Socialist) as minister of labor and social security; and Gronchi (Christian Democrat) as minister of industry.

BIBLIOGRAPHY

MANUSCRIPT SOURCES

Carte Michele Bianchi, Busta 2. Archivio Centrale dello Stato (Rome). Hereafter abbreviated as ACS.
Carte Luigi Credaro, Buste 30-34. ACS.
Carte Giovanni Giolitti, Busta 5. ACS.
Carte Antonio Salandra, Scatole 1, 2, 5, 8. ACS.
Carte Sidney Sonnino, Busta 1. ACS.
Letters of Alcide De Gasperi to Don Giulio Delugan, 1926-1954. Monsignor Delugan has given most of the originals to the De Gasperi family. He has, however, retained photostatic copies.
Letters of Alcide De Gasperi to Don Simone Weber, 1929. Originals held by the De Gasperi family.
Ministero dell'Interno. Direzione Generale della Pubblica Sicurezza. Casellario Politico Centrale, Busta 55. ACS.
Ministero dell'Interno. Direzione Generale della Pubblica Sicurezza. Divisione Affari Generali e Riservati (1914-1926), (1927-1933). ACS. I examined all papers relating to the *Partito Popolare Italiano*, anti-Fascism, and De Gasperi.
Ministero dell'Interno. Direzione Generale di Pubblica Sicurezza. Ufficio Riservato (1911-1915), Buste 96, 113. ACS.
Records of Regina Coeli Prison. Regina Coeli, Rome.

PARLIAMENTARY SOURCES

Atti parlamentari. Camera dei deputati. Sessioni 1921-1926. Rome, 1921-1926.
Stenographische Protokolle über die Sitzungen des Hauses der Abgeordneten des Österreichischen Reichsrates, 1917-1918. Vienna, 1917-1918.

Verbali del Consiglio comunale di Trento, 1910-1915. Trent, 1911-1915.

BOOKS, ARTICLES, AND PAMPHLETS

Andreotti, Giulio. *De Gasperi e il suo tempo. Trento-Vienna-Roma.* Milan, 1956.
Artieri, Giovanni. *Tre Ritratti politici e quattro attentati.* Rome, 1953.
AUCT. 50 AUCT. Trent, 1946.
Badoglio, Pietro. *L'Italia nella seconda guerra mondiale.* Milan, 1946.
Baroni, Augusto. *Igino Righetti.* Rome, 1948.
Battaglia, Roberto. *The Story of the Italian Resistance,* trans. and ed. P. D. Cummins. London, 1957.
Battisti, Ernesta. *Italianità di Degasperi. Lettera aperta all'on. Meda.* Florence, 1957.
Belotti, Giuseppe. *Statura di De Gasperi.* Bergamo, 1954.
Benedetti, Dante. *De Gasperi politico e statista.* Rome, 1949.
Binchy, Daniel A. *Church and State in Fascist Italy.* New York, 1941.
Boggiani, Tommaso. *L'Azione cattolica e il Partito Popolare Italiano.* Genoa, 1920.
Bonomi, Ivanoe. *Diario di un anno.* Milan, 1947.
Canali, Paolo (Adstans). *Alcide De Gasperi nella politica estera italiana 1944-1953.* Milan, 1953.
Candeloro, Giorgio. *Il Movimento cattolico in Italia.* Rome, 1961.
Carrillo, Elisa A. "Alcide De Gasperi and the Lateran Pacts," *The Catholic Historical Review,* XLIX (1964), 532-539.
Catalano, Franco. *Storia del C.L.N.A.I.* Bari, 1956.
Catti De Gasperi, Maria Romana. *De Gasperi uomo solo.* Milan, 1964. (Published by Mondadori; author has granted permission for quotations from this book.)
Cavazzoni, Leone. *Stefano Cavazzoni.* Milan, 1955.
Ciano, Galeazzo. *The Ciano Diaries, 1939-1943,* ed. Hugh Gibson. Garden City, 1947.
Cingolani, Mario. *Alcide De Gasperi.* Rome, 1955.
Clough, Shepard B. *The Economic History of Modern Italy.* New York, 1964.
Conrad, Franz von Hoetzendorff. *Aus Meiner Dienstzeit 1906-1918.* 5 vols. Vienna, 1921-1925.
Crankshaw, Edward. *The Fall of the House of Habsburg.* New York, 1963.
Crialesi, V. and A. V. Rossi. *De Gasperi.* Rome, 1946.
Croce, Benedetto. *Quando l'Italia era tagliata in due.* Bari, 1948.
Dalla Torre, Giuseppe. *Azione cattolica e fascismo.* Rome, 1945.
———. *I Cattolici e la vita pubblica.* Rome, 1962.
De Gasperi, Alcide. *Le Basi morali della democrazia.* Rome, 1948.
———. *I Cattolici dall'opposizione al governo.* Bari, 1955.
———. *I Cattolici trentini sotto l'Austria,* ed. Gabriele De Rosa. 2 vols. Politica e Storia. Raccolta di studi e testi, ed. Gabriele De Rosa, Vols. 9-10. Rome, 1964.
———. *La Democrazia Cristiana e il momento politico.* Rome, 1944.
——— (Jaspar, G.). "Le Direttive politico-religiose del 'Centro' germanico

(1871-1928)," *Rivista internazionale di scienze sociali e discipline ausiliarie*, XXXVII, N. S. 2 (Aug. 1928), 181-196; XXXVII, N. S. 3 (Nov. 1928), 97-132; XXXVIII, N. S. 1 (Feb.-March 1929), 146-156.
———. *Discorsi politici*, ed. Tommaso Bozza. 2 vols. Rome, 1956.
———. *Il Discorso di Fiuggi*. Rome, 1949.
———. *Lettere dalla prigione 1927-1928*, ed. Francesca De Gasperi. Milan, 1955. (Published by Mondadori; editor has granted permission for quotations from this book.)
——— (Jaspar, G.). "Un Maestro del corporativismo italiano," *Rivista internazionale di scienze sociali e discipline ausiliarie*, XXXVII, N. S. 1 (Jan. 1928), 3-28.
———. *Premesse della ricostruzione*. Milan, 1946.
——— (Bianchi, V.). "Ripensando la 'Storia d'Europa,'" *Studium*, XXVIII (1932), 248-261.
——— (Jaspar, G.). "Il Segreto dei Gesuiti," *Vita e Pensiero*, XXII, N. S. (1931), 514-518.
———. *La Stampa cattolica nel mondo. Risultati ed insegnamenti della stampa cattolica nella Città del Vaticano*. Milan, 1939.
———. *Studi ed appelli della lunga vigilia*. Rocca San Casciano, 1953. Content of this book is included in *I Cattolici dall'opposizione al governo*.
——— (Zanatta, Mario). *I Tempi e gli uomini che prepararono la "Rerum Novarum."* Milan, 1931.
——— (Demofilo). *Tradizione e "Ideologia" della Democrazia Cristiana*. Quaderni della Democrazia Cristiana, No. 2. Rome, n. d.
Delzell, Charles. *Mussolini's Enemies*. Princeton, 1961.
Demattè, Modesto. *Alcide Degasperi all'alba del XX secolo*. Trent, 1962.
Donati, Giuseppe. *Scritti politici*. 2 vols. Rome, 1956.
Einaudi, Mario and François Goguel. *Christian Democracy in Italy and France*. Notre Dame, 1952.
Erzberger, Matthias. *Erlebnisse im Weltkrieg*. Berlin, 1920.
Fermi, Laura. *Mussolini*. Chicago, 1961.
Ferrari, Francesco. *L'Azione cattolica e "il regime."* Florence, 1957.
Fogarty, Michael P. *Christian Democracy in Western Europe 1820-1953*. Notre Dame, 1957.
Fonzi, Fausto. "I Cattolici e l'Italia moderna," *Itinerari*, Dec. 1956, pp. 603-624.
———. *I Cattolici e la società italiana dopo l'unità*. Rome, 2nd. ed., 1960.
———. "Il Giudizio sul risorgimento di un cattolica antifascista." *I Cattolici e il Risorgimento*. Istituto Luigi Sturzo. Rome, 1963. This is an article on Francesco Ferrari.
Galati, Vito. *La Democrazia cristiana*. Milan, 1958.
Gallarati Scotti, Tommaso. *Interpretazioni e memorie*. Milan, 1960.
Garosci, A. *et al*. *Il Secondo Risorgimento*. Rome, 1955.
Gemelli, Agostino and Francesco Olgiati. *Il Programma del Partito Popolare Italiano. Come non è e come dovrebbe essere*. Milan, 1919.
Giordani, Igino. *Alcide De Gasperi*. Milan, 1955.
———. *La Politica estera del Partito Popolare Italiano*. Rome, 1924.
———. *La Verità storica e una campagna di denigrazione*. Rome, 1953.
Great Britain, Foreign Office. *Trentino and Alto Adige* (Foreign Office Handbook No. 33). London, 1920.

Grindrod, Muriel. *The Rebuilding of Italy.* New York, 1955.
Gualerzi, Giorgio. *La Politica estera dei Popolari.* Rome, 1959.
De Gentili, Guido. *La Deputazione trentina al parlamento di Vienna durante la guerra.* Trent, 1920.
De Rosa, Gabriele. "L'Attività parlamentare del Meda nel periodo giolittiano," *Civitas,* N.S. IX (1958), 79-90.
———. *Filippo Meda e l'età liberale.* Florence, 1959.
———. *Giolitti e il fascismo in alcune sue lettere inedite. Politica e Storia. Raccolta di studi e testi,* ed. Gabriele De Rosa, Vol. 4. Rome, 1957.
———. *Rufo Ruffo della Scaletta e Luigi Sturzo. Politica e Storia. Raccolta di studi e testi,* ed. Gabriele De Rosa, Vol. 7. Rome, 1961.
———. *Storia del Partito Popolare.* Bari, 1958.
———. *Storia politica dell'azione cattolica in Italia.* 2 vols. Bari, 1953-1954.
———. "Vita ed opere del Principe Rufo Ruffo della Scaletta," *Rassegna di politica e di storia,* VI (Jan. 1960), 23-31; VI (Feb. 1960), 28-32.
De Rossi, Giulio. *Il Partito Popolare Italiano.* Rome, 1919.
———. *Il Partito Popolare Italiano dalle origini al congresso di Napoli.* Rome, 1920.
———. *Il Partito Popolare nella XXVI legislatura.* Rome, 1923.
Del Bo, Dino. *I Cattolici italiani di fronte al socialismo.* Rome, 1956.
Del Giudice, Vincenzo and Antonio Renier. *I Massimi problemi del Partito Popolare innanzi al congresso nazionale di Napoli, 8-10 aprile, 1920.* Place and date of publication not given.
Delugan, Giulio. *Alcide Degasperi nei ricordi di un amico.* Trent, 1954.
Guariglia, Raffaele. *Ricordi 1922-1946.* Naples, 1950.
Howard, Edith Pratt. *Il Partito Popolare Italiano.* Florence, 1957.
Intersimone, Giuseppe. *Scritti ed discorsi di Alcide De Gasperi.* Rome, 1963.
Jacini, Stefano. *I Popolari.* Milan, 1923.
———. *Storia del Partito Popolare Italiana.* Milan, 1951.
Jemolo, A. C. *Chiesa e stato in Italia negli ultimi cento anni.* Turin, 1952.
Kann, Robert A. *The Habsburg Empire.* New York, 1957.
———. *The Multinational Empire.* 2 vols. New York, 1964.
Kirkpatrick, Ivone. *Mussolini. A Study in Power.* New York, 1964.
Kogan, Norman. *Italy and the Allies.* Cambridge, Mass., 1956.
La Pira, Giorgio. *La nostra Vocazione sociale.* Rome, 1945.
Leone, Giovanni. *Testimonianze.* Milan, 1963.
Lombardini, Gabriele. *De Gasperi e i cattolici.* Milan, 1962.
Magri, Francesco. *L'Azione cattolica in Italia.* Milan, 1953.
———. *La Democrazia Cristiana in Italia.* 2 vols. Milan, 1954-1955.
———. *Dal Movimento sindacale cristiano al sindacalismo democratico.* Milan, 1957.
Malvestiti, Piero. *La Lotta politica in Italia.* Milan, 1948.
———. *Parte guelfa in Europa.* Milan, 1945.
Martini, Angelo. *Studi sulla questione romana e la conciliazione.* Rome, 1963.
Marzani, Gino and Alcide De Gasperi et al. *Il Martirio del Trentino.* Milan, 1919.
Meda, Filippo. *Avanti la Ecc. Corte d'appello di Roma. Motivi aggiunti nell'interesse del Dott. Comm. Alcide De Gasperi.* Rome, n. d.
———. *I Cattolici italiani nella guerra.* Milan, 1928.

Miglioli, Guido. *Con Roma e con Mosca*. Milan, 1945.
Monelli, Paolo. *Roma 1943*. Rome, 1945.
Montanelli, Indro. *Padri della patria*. Milan, 1949.
Morandini, Giuseppe. *Trentino-Alto Adige. Le Regioni d'Italia*, ed. Roberto Almagia, Vol. III. 18 vols. Turin, 1960 -.
Moschetti, Ildebrando. *Forze economiche del Trentino*. Milan, 1918.
Mussolini, Benito. *My Autobiography*, trans. Richard Washburn Child. New York, 1928.
———. *Opera Omnia*, edd. Edoardo and Duilio Susmel. 36 vols. Florence, 1951-1963.
Nenni, Pietro. *Storia di quattro anni*. Turin, 2nd. ed., 1946.
Olasz, F. *Benito Mussolini a Trento*. Milan, 1958.
Pacelli, Francesco. *Diario della Conciliazione*. Città del Vaticano, 1959.
P. P. I. *La Vita del Partito Popolare Italiano nei suoi tre primi congressi*. Rome, 1923.
Petrocchi, Giuseppe. *Collaborazionismo e ricostruzione popolare*. Rome, 1923.
———. *De Gasperi*. Rome, 1946.
Pini, Giorgio and Duilio Susmel. *Mussolini l'uomo e l'opera*. 4 vols. Florence, 1953-1955.
Pratesi, Piero. "Due Storie del Partito Popolare e la questione dell'autonomia," *Civitas*, N.S. IX (1958), 91-102.
Rossi, Cesare. *Personaggi di ieri e di oggi*. Milan, 1960.
Rossini, Giuseppe. "I Tentativi per un Internazionale Popolare," *Civitas*, N.S. XI (1960), 123-132.
Ruini, Meuccio. *Profili di storia. Rievocazioni—Studi—Ricordi*. Milan, 1961.
Salomone, A. William. *Italian Democracy in the Making*. Philadelphia, 1945.
Salvatorelli, Luigi and Giovanni Mira. *Storia d'Italia nel periodo fascista*. Turin, 1956.
Salvemini, Gaetano. *Il Partito Popolare e la questione romana*. Florence, 1922.
Salvi, Franco *et al.*, edd. *Atti e documenti della Democrazia Cristiana 1943-1959*. Rome, 1959.
Sarfatti, Margherita. *Life of Benito Mussolini*. London, 1926.
Schierbrand, Wolf von. *Austria-Hungary: The Polyglot Empire*. New York, 1917.
Scoppola, Pietro. *Dal Neoguelfismo alla Democrazia Cristiana*. Rome, 1957.
Smith, Denis Mack. *Italy. A Modern History*. Ann Arbor, 1959.
Spadolini, Giovanni. *Giolitti e i cattolici (1901-1914)*. Florence, 2nd ed., 1960.
Spinardi, Aldo, ed. *Testimonianze su De Gasperi*. Turin, 1956.
Staderini, Gino. *De Gasperi visto da un socialista*. San Giovanni Valdarno, 1954.
Sturzo, Luigi. *Politics and Morality*. London, 1938.
———. *Popolarismo e Fascismo*. Turin, 1924.
Taylor, A. J. *The Habsburg Monarchy 1809-1918*. London, new ed., 1949.
Thayer, John A. *Italy and the Great War. Politics and Culture, 1870-1915*. Madison, 1964.
Togliatti, Palmiro. *L'Opera di De Gasperi*. Florence, 1958.
Toniolo, Giuseppe. *Democrazia Cristiana. Concetti e indirizzi*. 2 vols. Città del Vaticano, 1949.
Tupini, Giorgio. *I Democratici cristiani. Cronache di dieci anni*. Milan, 1954.

United States, Dept. of State. *United States and Italy, 1936-1945.* Publication 2669, European Series 17. Washington, D. C., 1946.
Valeri, Nino. *Da Giolitti a Mussolini.* Florence, 1956.
Valiani, Leo. *Dall'Antifascismo alla resistenza.* Milan, 1959.
———. *L'Avvento di De Gasperi.* Turin, 1949.
———. *Tutte le strade conducono a Roma.* Florence, 1947.
Valori, Gino. *Degasperi al parlamento austriaco 1911-1918.* Florence, 1953.
Vercesi, Ernesto. *Il Movimento cattolico in Italia 1870-1922.* Florence, 1923.
———. *Il Vaticano, l'Italia e la guerra.* Milan, 1925.
Verucci, Guido. "Recenti studi sul movimento cattolico in Italia," *Rivista Storica Italiana,* LXVII (1955), 425-448, 529-554.
Vian, Nello. "Ritratto morale di Alcide De Gasperi," *Studium,* LII (1956), 225-243.
Vistalli, F. *Giuseppe Toniolo.* Rome, 1954.
Webster, Richard A. *The Cross and the Fasces.* Stanford, 1960.
———. "Il primo incontro tra Mussolini e De Gasperi," *Il Mulino,* VII (1958), 51-55.
Zanolini, Vigilio. *Il Vescovo di Trento e il governo austriaco durante la guerra europea.* Trent, 1934.
Zeman, Z. A. B. *The Break-up of the Habsburg Empire 1914-1918.* New York, 1961.
Zieger, Antonio. *La Democrazia Cristiana nel Trentino.* Rome, 1956.
———. *Stampa cattolica trentina (1848-1926).* Trent, 1960.
———. *Stampa cattolica trentina fra il 1913 e il 1919.* Rome, 1963.
———. *Storia del Trentino e dell'Alto Adige.* Trent, 1926.

NEWSPAPERS AND PERIODICALS

L'Avvenire del Lavoratore, 1909.
Bolletino del Segretariato per Richiamati e Profughi, 1915-1918.
La Civiltà Cattolica, 1924-1926, 1931.
Concretezza, Aug. 1964.
Il Corriere d'Italia, 1921-1922.
Fede e Lavoro, 1902-1905.
L'Illustrazione Vaticana, 1930-1938.
New York Times, 1943-1945.
Il Nuovo Trentino, 1919-1926.
L'Osservatore Romano, 1924, 1929, 1932, 1938.
Il Popolo (Rome), 1923-1925; 1943-1945.
Il Popolo (Trent), 1906-1914.
Il Popolo d'Italia (Milan), 1924-1926.
Risveglio Austriaco, 1916-1918.
La Rivoluzione Liberale, 1924-1925.
Studium, 1943-1945.
Il Trentino, 1906-1915.
Vita e Pensiero, 1931-1933.
La Voce Cattolica, 1896-1905.

INDEX

Acerbo project, 71-72
Adenauer, Konrad, 60
Albareda Cardinal Anselmo, 101
Albertorio, Don Davide, 5
Aldisio, Salvatore, 125, 162*n*
Alexander, Field Marshal Harold R., 143
Allied Control Commission, 127, 139
Allies (Anglo-Americans, Second World War), 118-121, 126-127, 131, 136, 139, 140, 141, 142, 143, 144-145
Alto Adige, 1, 145
L'Alto Adige, 4, 18, 35
Ambrosio, General Vittorio, 118
Amendola, Giorgio, 116, 119, 121, 142
Amendola, Giovanni, 72, 73, 82
America, 102
Andreotti, Giulio, 122, 134
Anti-Fascist United Freedom Front, 117
Antoni, Carlo, 121
Arcari, Paolo, 5
Associazione Femminile Tridentina, 24
Associazione Universitaria, 108
Associazione universitaria cattolica trentina (AUCT): Caldonazzo meeting, 11; Cles meeting, 5; foundation, 5; Mezzocorona meeting, 8; and Mussolini, 71; Pergine meeting, 5; Trent meeting, 9
Austria-Hungary: administration of South Tirol, 1; Italian university issue, 12-13, 26; treatment of Trentino during First World War, 35-37, 42-43
Avancini, Augusto, 18

Aventine Secession, 76, 78, 79, 82
L'Avvenire del Lavoratore, 22

Bacialli, Ettore, 86
Baden, Max von, 41
Badoglio, Pietro, 118, 119, 120, 121, 126, 137
Balbo, Cesare, 108
Bank of Rome, 73
Baranzini, Arturo, 84, 162*n*
Barbareschi, Gaetano, 144, 172*n*
Barbieri, Pietro, 122
Bari, Congress of, 124
Basso, Lelio, 116
Battisti, Cesare, 4, 5, 18, 26, 35, 58, 94, 155*n*, 157*n*
Beck, Max Vladimir, 36
Benedict XV (Pope, 1914-1922), 32-33, 50
Bergami, Gino, 144
Bergamini, Alberto, 118, 122
Bevin, Ernest, 145
Bianco, Francesco, 59
Bidault, Georges, 145
Bocchini, Arturo, 86, 87, 88, 94
Bolzano: *see* Alto Adige
Bonomelli, Emilio, 121, 126
Bonomelli, Bishop Geremia, 46
Bonomi, Ivanoe, 57, 62, 64, 72, 101, 116, 117, 118, 119; and *CLN*, 121, 122, 124, 125, 126, 138, 143; and *CLNAI*, 140, 141; Second World War governments, 126-127, 131, 135-143
Bottai, Giuseppe, 118, 122

Brauns, Heinrich, 60
Brenci, Gino, 81
Il Brennero, 75
Brest-Litovsk, Treaty of, 41
Brosio, Manlio, 116, 172*n*
Brupbacher, Fritz, 100
Bülow, Prince Bernard, 32
Buozzi, Bruno, 116, 119
Burian, Count Stephen, 43
Byrnes, James F., 144, 145

CLN: see Central Committees of National Liberation
CLNAI: see Central Committee of National Liberation of Upper Italy
Cadorna, General Luigi, 40
Cadorna, General Raffaele, 136
Calboli, Marquis Paolucci de', 44
Campilli, Pietro, 127
Carandini, Nicolo, 116, 143, 145
Carpaneda, Signora, 84
Casati, Alessandro, 117, 119, 121, 122
Castellano, General Giuseppe, 119
Catholic Action (Italy), 33, 50, 96, 111-112, 116. For beginnings, see Christian Democracy (Italy)
Catholic movement (Italy): see Christian Democracy (Italy)
Catholic movement (Trentino, Austria-Hungary), socio-economic activity, 4, 22
Catholics (Italy), voting before First World War, 47-48
Cavazzoni, Stefano, 50, 57, 64, 67, 69, 72
Center Party (Germany), 19, 60, 85, 92, 103
Central Committee of National Liberation (*CLN*), 117, 122, 123, 126, 127, 137, 138, 139, 142, 147; composition, 121; and institutional question, 124-125
Central Committee of National Liberation of Upper Italy (*CLNAI*), 121, 136, 140, 141
Central Powers, First World War, 31, 37, 43
Centro Nazionale Italiano, 72
Charles, Sir Noel, 138
Christian Democracy (Italy): origins and development, 5, 45-49; Program of 1899, 46
Christian Democracy (Trentino, Austria-Hungary), 3-4

Christian Democratic Party, 131, 138; Bari Congress, 124; formation, 115-117, 119; Naples convention, 133-134; first National Council, 134; first national meeting, 144; organization, 134, 170*n*; partisans, 171*n*; platform of 1943, 127-130; Rome meeting, 126; and syndical unity, 133
Christian Socialists (Austria-Hungary), 4, 7, 32
Churchill, Winston S., 138, 139
Cianca, Alberto, 126, 138
Ciano, Galeazzo, 114, 118
Ciccolini, Giovanni, 93
Cingolani, Mario, 60, 162*n*
Civiltà Cattolica, 77
Clam-Martinitz, Heinrich, 38
Clemenceau, Georges, 53
Clerici, Edoardo, 116
Clerico-Fascists, 70
Clerico-Moderates, 48, 73
Coccia, Ivo, 85
Colombo, Luigi, 96
Colonnetti, Gustavo, 56
Comitato di soccorso per i profughi meridionali, 36
Commer, Ernst, 8-9
Commonweal, 102
Communist Party (Italy), 57, 116, 121, 132, 133, 135, 138. See also Palmiro Togliatti
Communists, Catholic, 177
Conci, Enrico, 12, 18, 26, 43, 52, 57
Confederazione Generale Italiano del Lavoro, 133
Consiglio trentino del lavoro, 9
Constituent Assembly, 140, 142, 144
Consulta (Trent), 52
Consulta Nazionale, 144, 146, 147, 171*n*
Cornaggio, Carlo Ottavio, 48
Il Corriere d'Italia, 71
Costantini, Cardinal Celso, 125
Council of Foreign Ministers, 145
Credaro, Luigi, 52
Crispolti, Marquis Filippo, 48
Cristiano-sociali: see Christian Democracy (Trentino, Austria-Hungary)
Croce, Benedetto, 101, 108, 126

Dalla Torre, Count Giuseppe, 101, 102, 113
De Carli, Edoardo, 10, 26
De Courten, Raffaele, 137, 172*n*

Index

De Gasperi, Alcide: and Acerbo project, 71-72; ancestry, 2; and Ardeatine Caves murders, 126; arrest and imprisonment, 86-94; and *AUCI*, 5, 6, 8, 9, 11, 20, 71; and autonomy of Christian Democratic Party, 130; and autonomy of Trentino, 17, 52, 53, 54, 61; and Aventine Secession, 76, 78, 79; and Balkan Wars, 26-27; and Battisti, 18, 155n; birth, 2; at Bologna Congress (1919), 53-54; at Castel Gandolfo, 121-122; and Catholic Action crisis of 1931, 111-112; Catholicism, nature of, 7, 149; and *CLN*, 121, 122, 123, 126; children and family life, 110-111; and Church in 1930's, 112-113; and "clericalism" charge, 16; and collaboration with Communists, 131-132, 135, 138; and collaboration with Socialists, 13, 73, 76-78; and Committees of National Liberation, 141; as communal councilor of Trent, 24; composition of first government, 172n; and democratization of imperial government, 16; in Diet at Innsbruck, 29; as director of *Il Nuovo Trentino*, 50-51; as director of *La Voce Cattolica*, 15-16; education, 2-3, 6, 15; election to Italian Parliament, 57, 74; election to *Reichsrat*, 25; and Endrici, see Endrici; and events of 1930's, commentary on, 101-108; and Fascist corporativism, 106; and *FUCI-movimento laureati*, 115-116; and formation of Christian Democratic Party, 115-119; and French Catholicism, 104-105; and Henry George, 24-25; and German Catholicism, 19-20; Germany, visit to (1921), 59-60; and Giolitti, 57, 150; at Innsbruck (1904), 12-13; and institutional question, 121, 124, 134; and Italian Catholicism before First World War, 25; and Italian intervention, First World War, 31-34; and Italian intervention, Second World War, 114; in Italian Parliament, 57-58, 62, 68, 72, 74, 75; and Lateran Pacts, 95-97; in Lateran Seminary, 122-125; and Libyan War (1911-1912), 25; marriage, 63-64; as minister of foreign affairs, 139-140, 142-143, 144-146; and Murri, 7, 9; and Mussolini, 22-23, 67-71, 73, 87-88, 111-

De Gasperi, Alcide—*Cont.*
112; at Naples Congress (1920), 56; and Nazism, 103-104; and Nenni, 123, 124, 141, 142, 172n; and Nitti, 54, 56; organization of workers, 8, 10, 11, 21; and Paris Peace Conference (1919), 53; and Parri resignation, 146-147; and partisans, 136; and *Pascendi*, 20; and platform of Christian Democratic Party, 127-130; political philosophy of, 127-130, 148-151; political secretary of *Partito Popolare Italiano*, election as, 74; as premier, 148; pro-Austrian accusation, 58, 78-79, 83; at *Propaganda Fide*, 125-126; and purge, 52, 137; and racial nationalism, 18, 107-108; in *Reichsrat*, 26-27, 29, 38-40, 42-43; and Republic of Austria, 104; Rome, visits during First World War, 31, 32, 33, 34, 157n; at Rome Congress (1925), 80-82; secretary general of Christian Democratic Party, election as, 134; and Soviet Union, 59, 105, 131, 145; and Spanish Civil War, 105-106; spelling of name, 153n; temperament as youth, 3, 6-7; and Togliatti, 109, 132, 135, 138, 171n, 172n; and Toniolo, 7, 130, 170n; and Triple Alliance, 25; at Turin Congress (1923), 70; and *Unione accademica cattolica italiana*, 10, 11; and Italian university issue, 12, 13, 20; as Vatican Library employee, 99-101; at Venice Congress (1921), 60-61; and Vicenza incident, 83-84; last will and testament, 109; and women in public life, 24; and relief activities, First World War, 36-37; writings, 92-93, 94, 101-109

De Gasperi, Amedeo, 2, 3, 7
De Gasperi, Augusto, 2, 83, 87, 88, 164n
De Gasperi, Francesca, 63, 87, 88, 89, 110, 125
De Gasperi, Marcella, 2, 24
De Gasperi, Maria Romana, 95, 123, 125
De Gasperi, Mario, 2
De Gaulle, General Charles, 146
De Gentili, Monsignor Guido, 4, 15, 18, 31, 52
Della Torretta, Tommaso, 119
Delugan, Baldasarre, 18, 26
Delugan, Don Giulio, 95, 99, 112, 114, 117, 163n

De Nicola, Enrico, 123, 147
De Vecchi di Val Cismon, Cesare Maria, 111
Diaz, General Armando, 41
Di Cavallerleone, Ferrero, 123
Di Cesarò, Duca, 73
Di Valdegamas, Corteo, 108
Dollfuss, Engelbert, 104
Donati, Giuseppe, 48, 73, 76
Dumini, Amerigo, 75

Einaudi, Mario, 65
Endrici, Bishop Celestino, 4-5, 11, 15, 40, 52, 83, 94, 95, 114, 157*n*
Erzberger, Matthias, 32
Ethiopian War, 107, 113

Facta, Luigi, 62, 64, 65
Falck, Enrico, 116
Farinacci, Roberto, 113
Fascio, National Italian, 43
Fascist Party: elections of 1919, 55; elections of 1921, 57; elections of 1924, 72-74; events of October 1922, 65; in Trentino, 74-75
Fascist Regime: and Catholic Church, see Catholic Action, Lateran Pacts, Pius XI; and corporativism, 92; "Exceptional Decrees," 84; Special Tribunal for Defense of the State, 84-85
Fede e Lavoro, 4
Federazione universitaria cattolica italiana (FUCI), 112, 115-116
Fenoaltea, Sergio, 121, 123
Il Fermo proposito, 48
Ferrari, Francesco Luigi, 61, 69
Finzi, Aldo, 75
First World War: and Italian Catholics, 33, 34, 49; and Trentino, see Austria-Hungary
Flor, Silvio, 58
Fogazzaro, Antonio, 9
Fourteen Points, 42, 53
Francis Joseph, Emperor, 9, 26, 38
Fülop Miller, René, 99
Fünder, Friedrich, 9, 32

Gallarati Scotti, Tommaso, 101
Gasparri, Cardinal Pietro, 49, 78
Gemelli, Father Agostino, 50
Gentiloni, Count Vincenzo, 48
Gentiloni, Pact, 48, 55
George, Henry, 24-25
Gesswein, Monsignor Alexander, 28

Giolitti, Giovanni, 48, 55, 56, 57, 62, 76, 150
Giordani, Igino, 79, 100
Gobetti, Piero, 79, 81
Goetz, Baron, 40
Gonella, Guido, 123, 127, 134
Governatorato di Trento, 51-52
Grandi, Achille, 50, 116, 127, 161*n*
Grandi, Dino, 118
Grandi, Rodolfo, 26
Graziolo, Don Giuseppe, 4
Gronchi, Giovanni, 48, 61, 67, 71, 74, 116, 119, 122, 123, 126, 127, 144, 162*n*, 172*n*
Grosoli, Count Giovanni, 50
Guadagnini, Giuseppe, 75, 79, 83
Guardini, Romano, 99
Guelf movement, 113, 116
Guidone, Luigi, 89

Henlein, Conrad, 107
High Commission for Sanctions Against Fascism, 137
Hitler, Adolf, 19, 103, 104, 113
Hitze, Franz, 20
Hopkins, Harry, 139
Hussarek, Max von, 42

L'Illustrazione Vaticana, 102
Innsbruck incident, 12-13
Institutional question, Chaps. VII and VIII, *passim*
Italian Confederation of Laborers, 50, 133
Italy: armistice, Second World War, 119-120; intervention in First World War, 31-34; intervention in Second World War, 113-114; peace proposals after Second World War, 144-145

Jacini, Stefano, 71, 116, 143, 162*n*
John XXIII (Pope, 1958-1963), 149

Karl I, Emperor, 38, 41, 43
Ketteler, William von, 4, 101
Kufstein, Franz, 9

Labor Democratic Party, 116, 119, 144
La Malfa, Ugo, 116, 121, 122
Lanzerotti, Emanuele, 18
La Pira, Giorgio, 116, 129
Lateran Pacts, 95-97
Lateran Seminary, 122-123
La Tour du Pin, René de, 105

Index

Leo XIII (Pope, 1878-1903), 46, 47, 89, 108
Liberal Party (Italy), 48, 72, 116, 144, 147, 148
Liberal Party (Trentino, Austria-Hungary), 3, 16, 18, 26
Lloyd George, David, 53
London, Treaty of, 34
Longinotti, Giovan Maria, 73, 123, 161-162n
Longo, Luigi, 136
Lorenzoni, Giovanni, 12
Luccetti, Gino, 83
Lueger, Karl, 7
Lussu, Emilio, 144, 172n

Macchio, Baron, 31-32
Macmillan, Harold, 139
Macmillan Memorandum, 139
Malavasi, Gioachino, 113
Malfatti, Valeriano, 18, 26, 43
Malvestiti, Piero, 113, 116
Mancini, Ferdinando, 86
Manning, Cardinal Henry, 101
Marazza, Achille, 140
Maria Josepha, Archduchess, 36
Marini, Amedeo, 89
Maritain, Jacques, 105
Martire, Egilberto, 70
Marzotti, Luciano, 84
Mason Macfarlane, Noel, 126
Mattei, Enrico, 144, 171n
Matteotti, Giacomo, 64, 75, 76
Mauri, Angelo, 85, 161n
Maurras, Charles, 105
Maximalist Socialist Party, 64, 73
Meda, Filippo, 46, 49, 56, 62, 64, 72, 73, 89
Meda, Gerolamo and Luigi, 69, 116
Menestrina, Giuseppe, 35
Mercati, Monsignor, 97
Merler, Vittorio, 2
Merlin, Umberto, 67, 162n
Mermillod, Cardinal Gaspard, 9, 101
Micheli, Giuseppe, 56, 162n
Miglioli, Guido, 34, 48, 53, 54, 61, 64, 69
Milani, Fulvio, 67, 162n
Mingrino, Giuseppe, 58
Modigliani, Giuseppe, 64
Mole, Enrico, 144
Molotov, Vyacheslav, 145
Montalembert, Count Charles de, 108
Monti, Monsignor, 100
Montini, Giorgio, 73, 74, 162n

Montini, Giovanni Battista, 115
Morandi, Rodolfo, 140
Morelli, Renato, 138
Movimento laureati, 115-116
Mun, Albert de, 92
Murri, Don Romolo, 4, 7, 9, 46, 49
Mussolini, Arnaldo, 78
Mussolini, Benito, 64, 83, 84, 92, 96, 119, 121; and Acerbo project, 72; and De Gasperi, 22-23, 67-70, 71, 73, 87, 88, 111, 112, 117; fall of, 118; formation of first government, 65, 67; and Lateran Pacts, 95-97; in Trent, 22-23

Negarville, Celeste, 116, 138
Nenni, Pietro, 121, 122, 123, 124, 138, 140, 141, 143, 172n
New York Times, 132
Nitti, Francesco, 52, 54, 55, 56, 147
Non Abbiamo bisogno, 112
Il Nuovo Trentino, 50, 53, 68, 75

Olgiati, Father Francesco, 50
Opera dei Congressi, 45-47
Orlando, Vittorio Emanuele, 44, 64, 147
Ortodossi, Olviero, 113
L'Osservatore Romano, 101, 111, 112
Ossicini, Adriano, 117
Ozanam, Frederick, 4, 108

Pacem in terris, 149
Palazzini, Don, 122
Pan-Germans: see *Tiroler Volksbund*
Panizza, G. B., 18
Paolazzi, Bonfiglio, 18, 34
Parri, Ferruccio, 116, 136, 143, 144, 146, 147
Partisans, 136, 171n
Partito Popolare Italiano: Bologna Congress (1919), 50, 53-54; and Catholic Church, 71; collaboration with Mussolini, 67-70, 161n; collaboration with Socialists, 56, 64, 65, 76-77; composition, 55; dissolution, 84; divisions within, 50, 69-70; elections of 1919, 55; elections of 1921, 57; elections of 1924, 73-74; formation, 49; Naples Congress (1920), 56; program in Parliament (1921), 59; Rome Congress (1925), 80-82; in Trentino, 54; Turin Congress (1923), 70; Venice Congress (1921), 60-62
Partito Popolare Trentino, 16, 17, 18, 25, 38, 43, 51, 53, 54

Party of Action, 116, 119, 138
Pastor, Ludwig von, 99
Pecori-Giraldi, Lt. Gen., 52
Pelloux, Luigi, 5
Pennati, Alessandro, 56
Pertini, Sandro, 140
Piccardi, Leopoldo, 119
Pius IX (Pope, 1846-1878), 45
Pius X (Pope, 1903-1914), 11, 47
Pius XI (Pope, 1922-1939): and De Gasperi, 95, 101, 110, 111; and *Partito Popolare Italiano*, 71, 77-78
Pius XII (Pope, 1939-1958), 133
Il Popolo (Rome), 76, 82, 127
Il Popolo (Trent), 4, 35
Il Popolo d'Italia (Milan), 78-79
Porta, Father Alfonso, 122
Pucci, Monsignor Enrico, 71

Quadragesimo Anno, 106, 112

Rampolla, Cardinal Mariano, 9
Reale, Eugenio, 138
Regina Coeli prison, 87, 90, 94, 164n
Reichspost, 9, 32, 107
Reichsrat, 12, 16, 20, 26, 29; allotment of seats (1906-1907), 155, 165n; elections of 1907, 17-18; elections of 1911, 25-26; session of 1911, 26; during First World War, 35-43, *passim*
Rerum Novarum, 4, 45, 47, 101
Righetti, Igino, 115, 116
Risveglio Trentino, 35
Rodanò, Franco, 117
Rodinò, Giulio, 71, 125, 138, 162n
Rodolfi, Armando, 113
Roman Question, 49, 50. See also Lateran Pacts
Romani, Carlo, 164n
Romani, Ida, 88
Romani, Pietro, 63, 71, 85, 87, 88
Romita, Giuseppe, 116, 117, 121
Roosevelt, Franklin D., 106
Ruffo della Scaletta, Prince Rufo, 59, 67, 85, 86
Ruini, Meuccio, 101, 119, 121, 122, 126, 138
Russia, 38, 40. *See also* Soviet Union

St. Germain, Treaty of, 56, 57
Salandra, Antonio, 76
Salvatorelli, Luigi, 116, 119
San Francisco Conference (1945), 140
Saragat, Giuseppe, 122, 138

Sardagna, 2
Scelba, Mario, 134, 141, 144, 169n, 170n, 172n
Sciurba, Vincenzo, 85
Scoccimarro, Mauro, 117, 122, 123, 137, 138, 172n
Scotoni, Mario, 4
Segni, Antonio, 134
Seipel, Ignaz, 7
Sella Valsugana, 88, 110, 168n
Severi, Leonardo, 119
Sforza, Carlo, 126, 137, 138
Sindacato Agricolo Industriale, 21
Socialist Party (Germany), 59-60
Socialist Party (Italy), 158n; elections of 1919, 55; elections of 1921, 57; during and immediately after Second World War, 116, 121, 124, 140. *See also* Nenni
Socialist Party (Trentino, Austria-Hungary), 3, 18, 22
Società operaia cattolica di Trento, 4
Società studenti trentini, 5
Soleri, Marcello, 116, 122, 137
Sonnino, Sidney, 32, 33, 89, 157n
Sopramonte attack, 75
South Tirol, 1
Soviet Union, 59, 105, 132, 133, 145. *See also* Russia
Spataro, Giuseppe, 71, 74, 116, 119, 127, 134
Special Tribunal for Defense of the State, 85
Sterzing, Congress at, 40-41
Strazzuso, Achille, 86
Stresemann, Gustav, 85
Studium, 108
Sturzo, Don Luigi, 55, 56, 59, 74, 85, 96, 113, 132; at Bologna Congress, 53-54; and collaboration with Communists, 132; and collaboration with Mussolini, 67, 69; exile from Italy, 78; and fall of Facta, 64; and formation of *Partito Popolare Italiano*, 49, 50; as head of Catholic Action, 33, 49; relations with Socialists, 64-65; resignation as political secretary of *Partito Popolare Italiano*, 71; at Venice Congress, 61; veto of Giolitti, 160n
Suarez, Francisco, 28

Tangorra, Vincenzo, 67
I Tempi e gli uomini che prepararono la "Rerum Novarum," 94, 101

Tino, Adolfo, 116
Tiroler Volksbund, 13, 18-19, 40-41
Tisserant, Cardinal Eugene, 101, 110
Tito, Marshal, 142
Toggenburg, Count, 35
Togliatti, Palmiro, 109, 125, 126, 132, 135, 138, 143, 172*n*
Tonelli, Albino, 18
Toniolo, Giuseppe, 4, 7, 47, 102, 105. See also De Gasperi and Toniolo
Tornaquinci, Medici, 138
Tovini, Livio, 70
Trent: Communal Council, 24, 156*n*; Fascist activity, 83; industrial activity before First World War, 2; secondary schools, 3
Trentini, and attitude toward Italy, First World War, 32, 42-43
Trentino: autonomy issue under Hapsburgs, Chap. II, *passim*; cooperative movement before First World War, 21-22; economic conditions, 2; Italian clergy, 4; parties before First World War, 3-4; population in 1910, 1
Il Trentino, 16-17, 19, 24, 31, 35, 50
Treves, Claudio, 64
Trieste, 142-143
"Trust" (*Società Editrice Romana*), 48, 73
Tupini, Umberto, 126, 127, 162*n*
Turati-Starace-Farinacci resolution, 84
Turati, Filippo, 64, 76

Uberti, Giovanni, 56
Umberto, Crown Prince, 125, 126, 137, 138, 140, 148

Union of Soviet Socialist Republics: *see* Russia, Soviet Union
Unione accademica cattolica italiana, 10
Unione economico-sociale, 47, 50
Unione elettorale, 47, 48, 50
Unione politica popolare, 11
Unione popolare, 47
Unitary Socialist Party, 73, 75

Valiani, Leo, 140
Valussi, Bishop Eugenio, 5, 11
Vassallo, Ernesto, 67
Vicenza incident, 83-84
Victor Emmanuel III, King, 45, 80, 94, 118, 120, 124
Vienna, city of, 5-6; University of, 6, 8, 15
Viola, Giovanni, 56
Violanti, Carlo, 89
Vitoria, Francisco de, 28
La Voce Cattolica, 4, 10, 15-16
Vogelsang, Karl, 4
Volunteers of Liberty Corps, 136

Wagna incident, 39-40
Wang, Shih-Chieh, 145
Weimar Constitution, 92
"White" organizations, 56, 133
Wilson, Woodrow, 43, 53, 106
Windthorst, Ludwig, 92
Wirth, Karl, 59-60
Würzburg congress (1907), 19-20

Zamboni, Anteo, 83